POLITICAL IDEOLOGIES
OF ORGANIZED
LABOR

POLITICAL IDEOLOGIES OF ORGANIZED LABOR

RUTH L. HOROWITZ

Transaction Books
New Brunswick, New Jersey

Library of Congress Catalog Number: 76-58229
ISBN: 0-87855-208-1
Printed in the United States of America.

Basil Blackwell are agents for the
publications of **Transaction Books** in Great Britain

Library of Congress Cataloging in Publication Data

Horowitz, Ruth L   1932-
    Political ideologies of organized labor.

    Bibliography: p.
    Includes index.
    1. American Federation of Labor—History. 2. Labor policy—United States—History. 3. Trade-unions—United States — Political activity — History. 4. Congress of Industrial Organizations — History. I. Title.
HD8055.A5H67   322'.2   76-58229
ISBN 0-87855-208-1

Contents

List of Tables

Preface

The story of labor's struggle for a measure of power and public respect is long and complex. It is also full of violent and intense drama. Moreover, its impact on the shape of America's industrial order and the direction of American public policy cannot be underestimated. Because labor's "coming of age" was stormy and its influence over the terms of American life so crucial, its history continuously attracts new generations of American students and scholars.

The life of America's labor movement during the New Deal administration of Franklin D. Roosevelt is proving particularly fascinating. For one thing, these were especially "turbulent years," as one scholar put it, a time when strong and willful personalities committed themselves to the full mobilization of America's working men and women in order to achieve their full citizenship in American life. For another thing, it was at this time that organized labor secured terms and standards for its participation in American industry which prevail in large measure to this very day. Thus, out of our attraction to times of challenge, even upheaval (for at such times the premises upon which our social worlds stand are most visible to us), and out of a need to trace again and again the trails that led most directly to the present contexts in which we live and work, the American labor movement of the thirties is proving a particularly compelling object of attention.

This might be reason enough to add yet another book to those which already exist on the subject of the American labor movement of the Great Depression decade. There is, however, another, and it is one that I find more important. The idea has grown popular that the more or less "enlightened" protective legislation passed during Franklin Roosevelt's administration on labor's behalf was a response to consistent and emphatic demands for it from the great union organizations of America's working class. That is, New Deal labor legislation is typically thought of as a "reflection" of labor's essential interests. But the historical record shows that such conclusions cannot be drawn so tidily or generally. First, important voices among labor's leadership (mainly of the AFL) continuously registered unease about administration proposals for protective legislation out of the fear that they would, if enacted, diminish worker and union self-reliance. For the moral fiber of individual workers could not but be weakened, it was supposed, by dependence upon government benefits, and unions might have little appeal to the unorganized worker if he could be assured of government protection independently of union membership. Moreover, such legislation would provide for arbitration or regulatory boards which many feared would be staffed by opponents of organized labor. Thus, to protect the integrity of individual workers, to promote incentives for unionization among the unorganized, to reduce the influence of labor's opponents in industrial disputes, many union leaders frequently expressed skepticism toward protective and welfare legislation, very much as a matter of "labor's interest."

Second, although these doubts and suspicions did in fact finally fade from labor's outlook and New Deal labor legislation was ultimately embraced, acceptance resulted largely from the changing composition of America's work force, the popularization of new ideas by the CIO about how the life of organized labor ought to be conducted under twentieth century industrial conditions, and effective government efforts to promote support for some protective measures to offset the greater devastation the Great Depression was wreaking in the United States of the thirties. It is not at all clear that some constant, ahistorical labor interest surfaced finally during the 1930s to receive satisfaction at last from government sources. To correct the overly simple idea, then, that organized labor uniformly and insistently clamored for the labor legislation passed during the New Deal and that it did so to satisfy interests resident in its midst since the first appearance of workers on the historical scene, a close review of organized labor's life and struggles during the New Deal period in the United States is worth undertaking.

This in fact is the nature and purpose of the chapters to follow. I do not expect, however, that in completing them I will have strongly challenged or drastically revised understandings of organized labor during the New Deal period which have been made available by a number of able labor historians and analysts. I think I will have done well to tell an old story as clearly and as thoroughly as possible and, in the process, caused the reader to reflect upon the nature and problems of working people in the United States in the light of an important phase of their total struggle.

At this point I should like to acknowledge the value of comments offered by Professors Henry Berger, Walter Dean Burnham, Richard E. Dawson, John Kautsky, and John G. A. Pocock, when this manuscript was being written. I am quite grateful to them (as I am for much stimulating and excellent conversation in general). And I should add, of course, that the shortcomings of the present book are my responsibility entirely.

Introduction

Labor movements in various industrialized nations have followed a number of divergent political paths. Some of their organizations rebelled against the prevailing capitalist system and sought a radical reconstruction of economic relationships by revolutionary means. Others accepted the prevailing economic framework but actively sought to promote labor's influence in political life by forming a distinct labor party or by establishing an alliance between the labor movement and a political party with a broad constituency. Still others sought to minimize political involvements of any type and focus labor's attention on strike action and collective bargaining for the purpose of improving the economic situation of workingmen. Perhaps this latter course did not completely exclude political activity, but it did limit it to only the most occasional lobbying for specific goals and to evaluating the labor records of candidates for public office put forward by existing political parties.

Even a casual review of American history would show that in the United States, leaders of labor organizations have at one time or another committed themselves and their followers to each of these paths. Revolutionary syndicalism was promoted by the Industrial Workers of the World and managed a certain influence in the early part of this century. Communists attempted the mobilization of workers for revolutionary ends and sought to expand the influence of their revolutionary party in labor circles. Socialists of various types sought to construct labor parties with the idea that these could acquire the power of government by competing in elections and could consequently acquire an opportunity to revise industrial conditions and relationships. In the early nineteenth century, workingmen's parties were formed, although such efforts were merely sporadic and the organizations did not endure for long. Nevertheless, they pressed for legislative prohibition of monopoly growth, reduced working hours for hired labor, and better public education, among other things, in order to restore the independent workman as a politically alert and contributing citizen of his community. Later in the nineteenth century, existing unionization movements, like the Knights of Labor, sought alliances with the Greenback-Labor party and, later still (in 1892), with the People's party. In contrast to all of these, the American Federation of Labor (AFL) emerged by 1886 and influenced American labor to eschew political radicalism and reformism, indeed, political involvements of any kind. It urged instead that workers organize for concerted economic action, concentrating on strike activity and bargaining with employers through union representatives. Finally, in 1936, the Congress of Industrial Organizations (CIO) arose and actively worked for the politicalization of organized labor until new alliances were forged with the Democratic party. The CIO's influence was to prove enduring, and since 1955, when the AFL and CIO merged, organized labor in America has considered maintaining its ties with the Democratic party vital to its interests.

Until the emergence of the CIO, the AFL prevailed as the most dominant influence on American labor, and those following other paths strayed off into obscurity despite their brief and even dramatic moments of success. Thus, despite the diverse and divergent tendencies of the American labor movement, it came in the last decade of the nineteenth century to prepare itself for economic battle in order to gain immediate improvements in the wages of workmen and the length of their working day, and came also to avoid political entanglements stemming from efforts to reform or repudiate industrial capitalism by means of pressure for legislative enactment or revolutionary mobilization. In essence, Samuel Gompers, the Federation's first chief executive, and a majority of AFL members urged upon the American labor movement a modest twofold strategy: first, to pursue with single-minded dedication the buildup of union strength so that employer resistance to worker demands might be worn down, serious negotiations to improve industrial conditions might occur, and firm contracts to guarantee the improvements might be secured; and second, so that unionists would not be divided from each other on account of political loyalties, and so that the union movement might become self-reliant and stay independent, workers were to avoid dependency on government or legislative enactments for support or favors. This modest strategy was supported by an overwhelming majority of unions by 1886, and so, even though the American labor movement had harbored every kind of political orientation, it came to work for limited economic goals and to cast a suspicious eye on law, government, public officials, and political parties of all kinds.

Given that independent political action was gaining in popularity among the workers of Europe at a time when the more or less apolitical AFL came to dominate the American labor movement, it is worth noting that much in American life in the nineteenth and early twentieth centuries created predisposing conditions for the Federation's triumph.

First, America's workers were divided by race, religion, ethnic origin, and even language to a greater degree than workers elsewhere. This invited much discord among them and became a factor in the political disunity of the labor movement. For example, the National Labor Union (NLU) was formed in 1866 in an attempt to give national scope and cohesion to local labor associations then scattered across the country. The NLU promoted a program seeking legislative reform of industrial conditions. In the 1870s, however, a number of German immigrants among the membership raised a demand for socialism and angrily left the NLU when they gave up hope of converting its leadership (in addition, that period also saw fights within the NLU over admission of black members, for black workers were in this period acquiring a reputation as strike breakers.) Moreover, Welsh and Irish immigrants laboring in Pennsylvania's coal fields during this period were enemies, with the Irish acquiring a public reputation for radicalism, violence, and generally brutish behavior, and the Welsh for political moderation. And Jewish and German workers, in the garment and brewery trades respectively, were interested in socialism, especially during the 1870s and 1880s, and were unenthusiastic about other matters of concern to native American workers. Finally, during all of its last years, the Knights of Labor was torn by dissention over the legitimate role of political action in a labor movement, alienating socialists and "pure and simple" trade unionists alike, numbers of them being Jews and Germans suspicious of the many native American middle-class professionals who were attracted to the Knights. It is also well known that the Slavic Catholic immigrants in the steel industry and coal regions were resented for a long time by native American workers in the later nineteenth century. Gompers and the AFL leadership feared the disarray in the American labor movement and persuaded organized labor to disavow political partisanship and political action in the interest of promoting a semblance of labor unity. A discouraging history of interracial labor strife, always aggravated by periodic waves of immigration, finally made labor susceptible to the AFL's prescription for political behavior.[1]

Second, unlike workers elsewhere, American workers could easily gain a free public education for themselves, or at any rate, for their children (even, although to a much more limited extent, a free or inexpensive one at the college level, as state and municipally supported colleges and universities slowly became widespread). This promised them some escape, even if only ambiguously, from permanent working-class status, and thus relieved some of the frustrations of striving for self-improvement in an industrializing society which was closing down options to small land or business ownership. Educational opportunity made it less urgent for American workers to attach themselves to or form political organizations, dissident or otherwise, in a unified and stable way in order to achieve a measure of recognition and improved status.[2] The compatibility between educational opportunity as an escape valve and the AFL's political attitudes should be obvious (although it contained some potential threats to union building which eventually came to be recognized in the 1950s).

Third, many workers in the United States showed the influence of a prevailing national belief that America was classless, or at least that all who exerted themselves and "worked hard" could expect to improve their lot in life irrespective of their social backgrounds or origins. They often strained to give some reality to this rhetoric, certainly to the extent of focusing on the acquisition of economic goods rather than on increases in political power to improve their standing in American society. It can easily be imagined how the AFL, with its emphasis on securing economic benefits, could appeal to workers under this influence. Few of the speeches of the AFL leadership in the early days of the Federation's birth failed to contain some reference to the idea that hard work and long workdays entitled workmen to the same immediate economic fulfillment and social standing that others enjoyed from their labors in the fabled land of opportunity.[3]

Finally, the pace of industrial and technological change was more rapid in late nineteenth- and early twentieth-century America than it was in many European countries. While this factor had an initially radicalizing effect on the working-class population and its leadership in the United States, it also generated so great a wealth of goods and money that worker claims for a modicum of economic security and income redistribution could be met before radical political associations could become deeply rooted.[4] This point, raised in recent years by John Laslett, is a valuable corrective to the idea that the ideological character of American labor leadership is alone responsible for the level of political interest and kind of political ideas popular with American workers. It is also worth noting in this connection that Val R. Lorwin's thoughtful study of the French labor movement contains the observation that the slow rate of French economic growth and technological development was conducive to the stabilization of radical labor leadership in France in the late nineteenth and early twentieth centuries.[5] In the United States, however, the rapidity of industrial development encouraged trade union incrementalism and the AFL's policies found a base of support in the structure of American industry and the level of its output.

All of these factors mitigated against the likelihood of a highly politicized labor force in the United States (much less a class-conscious one with revolutionary ambitions). And they provided favorable conditions for the growth and dominance of the AFL, an organization which tried to focus on the achievement of labor unity by reducing the value and need for political association and action on the part of workingmen and maximizing the value of union association for economic ends. While certain fashions in historical explanation used to have it that Americans possessed a native practical genius which came to be reflected in the economic incrementalism of its trade union movement by 1886, in contrast to Europeans, including European workers, who were said to be "ideological" and even "utopian" with a certain disrespect for "realities," it appears to have been the cleavages among American workers and the presence of educational "safety valves," the extreme individualistic ethos of American society and the dispersal of the population after rapid industrialization, which discouraged sustained labor interest in political alliances and political organization. Besides, the American labor movement had always contained too many immigrants for the argument from indigenous practicality to be very convincing. In view of these considerations, it is not so difficult to understand the failures of the

AFL's predecessors and the successful appeal of its "modest strategy," even at a time when labor movements in Europe were exhibiting different tendencies.

Yet modest as the AFL strategy was, it was not so simple as may appear on first consideration. Indeed, Gompers elaborated upon it until it was a "creed," a set of beliefs about how people ought to behave under industrial capitalism, about how the parts of an industrial capitalist society functioned and ought to function in relation to each other. To this creed, he gave the name "voluntarism." In view of this, it is not quite accurate to say only that the AFL promoted a narrow set of goals which decisively reduced the value of politics and the interest in legislation for labor. It also generated an ideology in terms of which American labor came to live for many years (the occasional claims about the nonideological state of organized labor in the United States notwithstanding). This is not to say that voluntarism involved meanings which were vastly different from those contained in the strategy the AFL proposed for the build-up of trade unionism in the nation. It did not. But it was an expansion on AFL policy which managed to provide unionists with a larger framework for viewing American society as a whole than could be provided by a mere strategy, and as such it could exert an influence on men's thinking even when the basis for the AFL's strategy would one day erode and fade away.

As is widely known, voluntarism emphasized that industrial capitalism was powerful and nearly infinite in its capacities for survival. Such a system could be counted on to set the conditions of existence into the indefinite future. Moreover, it was held, capitalism preserved certain conditions which were valuable for the survival of liberty despite its evident flaws and injustices. Revolutionary political action aimed at destroying it was, therefore, worse than a waste of time. It was absurd and it risked the possibility of instituting a still more imperfect order. Workers, it proposed, ought to turn instead to the correction of the injustices which had grown up under industrial capitalism, especially those which affected them most directly and negatively. But despite the voluntaristic counsel that industrial capitalism should be reformed rather than repudiated, "voluntarists" did not believe that legislation, even "prolabor" legislation, government, public officials, or political parties could effectively institute the needed reform. Each in its way was regarded as an extension in the political sphere of the interests of the men who formulated the laws and ran the government and party organizations. And none of them had a stake in protecting labor or representing its real interests. Only workingmen could understand and protect their interests, and only labor organizations built by workers could voice their grievances and secure good industrial conditions and labor-employer contracts to perpetuate them. Thus, union building was the only appropriate form of social action workers could take under capitalist conditions to relieve the pressures and injustices capitalism brought into being.

Despite the fact, however, that AFL voluntarists were quite adamant about their point of view, they were ultimately to be confronted by conditions in the early 1930s which raised serious doubts about the validity of voluntarism. First, the Great Depression was so profound in the economic ruination it wrought in America that many people outside the AFL sought and even demanded reform legislation and positive government initiatives to deal with it. Second, union organization drives during the depression years were met with so much employer resistance and hostility that organized labor needed aid from government to expand, or even merely retain, its influence with unorganized workers. Third, by 1936, a challenger to AFL dominance of the labor scene, the CIO, arose, and it was willing to deny and abandon voluntarist assumptions, influencing a huge portion of the American labor force to do likewise. Shaken by popular attitudes, by government measures in response to them, by its need to find external support in order to survive, and by the CIO's new political interests and policies, the AFL began a halting and confused effort at ideological reconsideration.

Describing and evaluating this process of ideological change in the tradition-bound minds of the leaders of the AFL during the "depression decade" and in the bolder spirits leading the CIO at that time will constitute the object of this study. In particular, I shall be concerned with an account of how the AFL related to an environment which favored legislative reform and positive government, and also with the elements of the CIO ideology which provided new prescriptions for labor's political behavior in the United States.

It is true that a number of scholarly studies of the American labor movement during the Great Depression years have already touched upon these concerns.[6] Indeed, one of them has been explicitly focused upon the ideological predispositions of organized labor during the thirties.[7] Yet the nuances, complexities, and varied details involved in these highly important ideological developments have not been brought to the fore fully and clearly. Moreover, their specific implications for organized labor's conception of its role in America's political and economic life have not been fully probed and assessed.[8] Thus, despite the fact that the political ideologies of organized labor during America's New Deal period have received intelligent attention by students of American labor history, there is something to be gained from further and more complete consideration of this subject.

It needs to be said at the outset that the American labor movement was not shaped by contemplative men given to philosophic reflection. The movement was founded and perpetuated by individuals living in the throes of crisis and in a state of continual absorption with problems of union survival. Therefore, if one wishes to study ideological change on the labor scene, especially during the 1930s, a time of action and turmoil, one cannot do so by studying lengthy and rigorous treatises authored by workmen or their leaders. There are none. There are, instead, a variety of scattered statements about public issues current at the time which convey, often in a diffuse and indefinite way, ideological sentiments. More specifically, several legislative measures passed under the Roosevelt administration during the 1930s became especially salient for the labor movement at that time, and its participants conveyed the state of their ideological commitments largely in response to them. These were the National Industrial Recovery Act (NIRA, 1933), the National Labor Relations Act (Wagner Act, 1935), the Social Security Act (1935), and the Fair Labor Standards Act (FLSA, 1938). Study of the changing ideological pattern of the American labor movement during the New Deal years is largely a process of plotting labor's reaction to these measures. In the pages to follow, then, I will proceed by describing labor's attitudes toward the above-stated enactments in a series of chapters which analyzes them one by one. I will try to establish the bases upon which differing AFL and CIO reactions occurred and evaluate the impact of this on labor's political understanding.

To carry out the purpose of this effort, I will need to do several things. I will need to carefully review the contents of statements defining and explaining voluntarism made by its leading spokesman, Samuel Gompers. This is in addition to analyzing the historical experiences and sociological foundations which supported voluntarism. The two chapters following this one will be concerned with these tasks. In this way, I will have provided a basis for making clear and explicit the transitions of a later time. I will then consider the impact of the depression of AFL thinking during 1929-32 to see in what ways voluntarism was affected by the dramatic event and how this helped to influence the future thinking of organized labor. Next, I will examine and review the terms of the important labor-related legislation passed by the New Deal government of Franklin D. Roosevelt between 1933 and 1938: the NIRA, the NLRA, the Social Security Act, and the FLSA (Chapters V, VI, VII, and VIII, respectively). In this way, the terms of organized labor's reaction to the enactments can be determined with precision. Finally, I will consider the statements made by CIO representatives (especially John L. Lewis, Sidney Hillman, and Philip Murray) which elaborate a new antivoluntarism. A concluding chapter will explain and assess relevant findings.

It should be made completely clear that I am not actually examining ideological attitudes of the whole of American labor but only of that portion organized into the two mainstream organizations, the AFL and the CIO. Moreover, it should also be indicated that I cannot even fully characterize the ideological orientations of the whole membership of both federations, for very little evidence is available which would allow for extensive generalization about responses of their rank and file. To pursue my purpose, then, it will be necessary to recognize the limits of the data and correspondingly limit generalizations about the ideological attitudes of organized labor to such workmen as could have left a clear record of their ideological sentiments through conventions held by their trade unions, and even more specifically, to the union leadership level—local and national—whose speeches and comments are readily available in recorded convention proceedings. Thus, this ideological study will be held to apply mainly to *union leadership and not to union membership as a whole*. There is some evidence of both congruity and incongruity between these two strata, but there is presently little data available from which one might fully or even adequately assess ideological differences or similarities between union leaders and union members during the New Deal period. The possibility thus remains that this study will be partial and open to question with the introduction by other commentators of material demonstrating sharp or important cleavages between leaders and members of trade unions in the period under consideration here.

Notes

[1]Gerald Grob, *Workers and Utopia*, pp. 11-33. An account of the formation and policies of the NLU and the extent to which racial problems played a role in the decline of the organization. Wayne Broehl has illus-

trated some of the Welsh and Irish antagonisms in the Pennsylvania coal regions in the late nineteenth century. See his *The Molly Maguires*, pp. 82-85, 161. Also see Lewis Lorwin, *The American Federation of Labor.* Lorwin frequently stresses the role played by language and ethnic differences in dividing socialist-minded Jewish and German workers from indigenous American labor. He also cites from *AFL Convention Proceedings* to show that by 1890, Gompers and the AFL Executive Council were hard at work erasing these differences. That the Knights of Labor were wracked by disputes in its last year until its demise in 1892, is one of the commonest observations available in any history of American labor. A particularly good account may be found in Grob, *Workers and Utopia*, pp. 34-137. By contrast, Val R. Lorwin's *The French Labor Movement* makes the point that French labor was sufficiently homogeneous to identify as a class.

[2]Reinhard Bendix, *Nation-Building and Citizenship* (Garden City, N.Y.: Anchor Books, 1969), pp. 105-12. Bendix argues that the right to an elementary education was sought by European labor as a part of a drive to secure meaningful (in addition to formal) citizenship in industrializing society. The American workman of the 1820s also sought this and raised a demand for general free public education. This has been documented by Helen Sumner in her chapter "Causes of the Awakening," in *History of Labor in the United States*, John R. Commons et al., 1:169-84. Bendix also points out that national governments in Europe *slowly* developed an interest in public education as part of their need to secure the cohesion of the national community and socialization of the citizenry by means which enhanced governmental control over the distribution of education. In the United States this interest developed rapidly and early on the part of the American government and the institution of free public education did not have to be an object of prolonged political struggle for labor. See also Derek C. Bok and John T. Dunlop, *Labor and the American Community*, p. 388. It is noted that free and widespread education in the United States served to reduce labor's political intensity.

[3]See the speeches of Samuel Gompers in *Labor and the Common Welfare*, 2 vols. ed. H. Robbins. Also, that American workers responded to such appeals is one of the standard points made in American labor history texts.

[4]John Laslett, *Labor and the Left.*

[5]Lorwin, *French Labor Movement*, pp. 15-18.

[6]See Walter Galenson, *The CIO Challenge to the AFL*; Irving Bernstein, *The Turbulent Years*, James O. Morris, *Conflict within the AFL*; and J. David Greenstone, *Labor in American Politics.*

[7]George G. Higgins, *Voluntarism in Organized Labor in the United States, 1930-1940.*

[8]Irving Bernstein's *Turbulent Years* does investigate some political consequences stemming from ideological shifts in organized labor movement during the thirties. However, the images of the industrial universe and political authority which underlay AFL and CIO policy and ideology

remain merely implicit and thus implications for organized labor's concept of its role in U.S. society remain merely implicit. We are left only with a labor tendency toward embrace of the Roosevelt administration for economic or power advantages and a government tendency to seek a base of support in labor's ranks. J. David Greenstone's *Labor in American Politics* also focuses upon elements of American labor ideology and is concerned to relate changes in it to changes in the relation of America's organized workers to American politics. The volume, however, only skims the ideological predisposition of organized labor during the New Deal years.

POLITICAL IDEOLOGIES OF ORGANIZED LABOR

Chapter 1
Voluntarism Defined

In what follows, I will be concerned mainly with developing a picture of what voluntarism meant from the reflections of Samuel Gompers, its clearest and most self-conscious representative. Historical experiences and sociological dimensions of the labor movement which supported voluntarism as Gompers understood it will be treated in the next chapter.

"Voluntarism" was never developed by Gompers, a founder and for many years chief executive of the American Federation of Labor, into a profound or even necessarily consistent philosophic statement about the nature of things and persons. Rather, it was patched together hurriedly by him under the heavy pressure of union building and under difficult circumstances. As a result, it exhibited the limits (and some of the virtues) of any expediently devised viewpoint. Nevertheless, voluntarism emerged as a coherent and encompassing perspective on the world capable of substantial influence over the course and structure of the American labor movement.

Gompers's elementary starting point was his hostility to "classical economists" who, he felt, had popularized the notion that society's economic order was governed by impersonal "natural laws" and that rational social behavior consisted of conforming to them.[1] Considering that Gompers's views are so often likened to assumptions held by the laissez faire "classicists" or, equally often, regarded only as a reply to various socialist or "utopian" radicalisms, this may come as something of a surprise. But let us not forget that many industrialists, economists, and government leaders in the nineteenth century justified social action which promoted efficiency in production and exchange as rational, in appropriate conformity with the "nature" or "laws" of a market economy. This implied that action which obstructed efficiency out of consideration for expressive human needs was "irrational." A labor leader, especially of Gompers's type, with great ambitions for the labor movement as well as for his own career in leading it, could not take kindly to the idea that "laws" pervade the economic realm which resist control, limitation, or direction by the will of people subjected to their functioning, especially by the will of laboring people who had been so ground down in the course of economic development. How could it be "irrational" to obstruct such alleged laws by limiting their capacity to wreck the lives of the toiling majority of a population? They must be controlled if they exist at all, and since no evidence could satisfy Gompers that they did exist, advice to conform to them must be regarded as a pernicious design to suppress labor or as benign nonsense. He never tired of repeating:

> Wages are ... paid on the trial and balance principle, fixing them as low as the workman will stand and not according to any rational, well-formulated theory. That is to say, the distributive share allotted to the wage-earners is the result of human activity ... and *not* the normal or inevitable result of any law.[2]

It became axiomatic for Gompers that social groups had a perfect right to affirm their will over the economic sphere and force it to serve their human needs.[3] It followed easily enough from this that such a right belonged at least as much to laboring groups as to others. Indeed, Gompers held, labor could and did serve to remind the public of this principle when it appeared to have been generally forgotten, and in this labor even acquired a responsibility for the moral enlightenment of society.[4] Thus, voluntarism was based on an initial assumption that human will must make economic activity submit to human needs, a task labor must take the initiative in carrying out. Yet voluntarism connoted much more than an elementary humanism in the economic sphere, and this "more" made of it the antisocialist and antiradical ideology so familiar to every student of American labor history.

The labor movement for Gompers involved the worker in a process of self-definition and self-organization. Workers needed to combat the idea that their labor power was a commodity to be sold at cheap prices advantageous to employers, and had instead to affirm themselves as a community of human individuals entitled to such a portion of the industrial wealth as would help them improve themselves materially, morally, and culturally. Only through strong and well-knit trade union organization could such self-definition proceed.[5]

But the nature of capitalist society would have to be well understood in order to make such efforts effective. Workers had to learn that they possessed specific interests as a class, which no one but themselves could or would press forward for them and to which employers would not easily reconcile themselves. These interests derived precisely from their "employed" status and the needs of employers to decrease labor's portion of the general wealth in order to expand both business and profits. The very fact that labor was regarded as an exchangeable commodity by the men who owned and ran industry showed Gompers that employers constituted a "class" of persons who, by the very nature of their relationship to economic enterprises, could not recognize or accept the labor force as a collection of human beings with human appetites for "improvement," "culture," and free participation in the larger society. That is to say, because they had a heavy stake in viewing labor as a usable resource, employers could not view the work force from a perspective other than economic efficiency. Labor, Gompers repeatedly stressed, had an opposite stake in affirming the human worth of the individuals who comprised the work force and thereby a stake in claiming all the social goods to which as human beings they were entitled. It followed from this that the interests of workers and employers were in fundamental opposition and that industrial relations were marked by "class struggle."

> Because employers as a class are interested in maintaining or increasing their share of the general product, and because workers are determined to demand a greater and ever greater share of the same general product, the economic interests between these two are not harmonious. . . . That has been my position . . . never changed in the slightest. There are times when for temporary purposes, interests are reconcilable, but they are temporary only.[6]

The fact that capitalist industrial relations divided men into opposing classes should not lead anyone to suppose that a revolution promising classless equality for all was necessary, desirable, or a cure for the difficult conflict they engendered. All that it implied was that labor would have to recognize that its need to exert trade union pressure would last as long as the capitalist system did. Beyond such a point, Gompers insisted, it was not possible to foresee what new conditions would demand of workers. Moreover, Gompers stressed that employers performed very valuable investment and managerial services which sustained and rationalized economic activity for the whole society. And in an environment where public liberty has such a long tradition as in the United States, and where political institutions are structured so as to sustain it, both employers and workers needed to cooperate against external enemies toward preserving it.[7]

It is also important to understand that Gompers had additional, if not always fully developed, reasons for considering the development of "issue areas" in which cooperation could be achieved. He identified the private property tradition with political liberty and he felt that employers could uphold the latter by virtue of their support for the former. He despised "trusts" for their bigness and because their concentration of wealth enabled them to exert undue pressure on government and the courts. But he revered the institution of private property. Therefore, he felt that employers were entitled to a portion of the general wealth in view of their services, and also to enable them to preserve private property, a necessary condition of liberty, with enough resources to make the necessary investments to sustain it and smooth its operation.[8] Thus, while workers must make it expensive, unprofitable, and impossible to ignore labor's human wants and demands, they must leave to Caesar what was Caesar's, that is, they must never intrude on the functions that belonged to managers and owners.[9] This would lead to negative consequences, politically and economically, for everyone. And since there was a social plane, that of protecting from external threat the libertarian heritage and the institutions which fostered it, on which workers and employers could meet as "citizens," the mutual value of such association must not be totally destroyed or disregarded (it must be admitted, however, that Gompers gave this point extraspecial importance on the eve of World War I).

The outcome of this reasoning was that trade unions needed to become strong but not revolutionary in their goals. Labor had to focus upon structuring effective unions through the development of collective-bargaining principles,[10] and techniques as well as craft principles of unionism, both of which were conceived as powerful instruments toward that end. But there were other conditions yet for the build-up of a strong trade union force, not so easily relegated to the instrumental level, and more revealing about what voluntarism meant beyond the few initial assumptions stated so far. Gompers's definition of these other conditions finally made him affirm the value of "voluntary organizations" as the real carriers of a society's important values and as the real agents of constructive social reform. It is this affirmation which comes to be the essence of voluntarism. Still, it would remain unintelligible apart from Gompers's conception of the nature of a political apparatus and its role in governing the social groups that make up a society.

Perhaps our best approach to this aspect of the matter would lie in first noting Gompers's attitude toward legislation, for by assessing the capacity of law to order public association, Gompers felt that men could make judgments on the efficacy and value of government in general. In this regard we ought to consider Gompers's attitude towards the kinds of legislation which would bear most directly on labor's needs. His regard for two kinds of law is especially important here. The first sort bears upon the freedom of men to form unions and to pursue such tactics as the strike, boycott, and picketing by means of which workers may secure better terms for their labor. The second bears upon the use of the government's taxing and regulatory powers as a medium by which workers may secure a distribution of economic benefits and working conditions more favorable to themselves.

Gompers had sympathy for the first type of legislation, if only because legal recognition of union rights would help to overcome the fears that unorganized workers might harbor about associating themselves with unions. Then too, such laws sanction the right of unions to engage in collective bargaining and set terms in private contract for peaceful coexistence between themselves and employers. Indeed, government, in passing such laws, fulfills its function of recognizing the right of all social groups to legitimately pursue their own interests without having to rely on debilitating government benefits to compensate for such deprivation as they may have suffered. This was the basis on which Gompers could give such strong support to the Clayton Act when it was passed in 1914. Whatever the advantage to be gained from this, however, it would not finally be any law which protected such recognition. To the second type of legislation, "social legislation," which involved regulating the conditions of work and distribution of economic security, Gompers was altogether and unalterably opposed. He rejected with much resentment any kind of government role in regulating the work day or wage minima and in instituting health or welfare insurance, and, though to a lesser degree, even old-age insurance.[11]

It is true that Gompers had substantial sympathy for the legal institution of a system of employer's liability and workmen's compensation. For it was, according to him, entirely unjust for injured workmen, or their widows and orphans, to bear the heartbreaking strain which could be placed upon them by industrial accidents or deaths. But his general skepticism about or resentment of "social legislation" which would permit government a hand in the distribution of benefits to labor was so great that he ended up entertaining only the most modest proposals on this score.[12] Gompers had essentially two reasons for his stance. First, government regulation of compensation for work and conditions of work would tend to set a minimum necessary standard from which no employer could be made to depart, thus making a struggle for maximum compensation and better conditions more difficult, if not impossible. Second, any amount of government regulation, however minimal or designed for specific situations only, could set a precedent to extend government power over the whole society, something which could result in a more severe repression of labor than already existed and generate the spread of a more general tyranny.[13]

These reasons were strenuously underscored by labor's experiences with legislation passed ostensibly for its protection, but which after passage was used agaunt labor unions. The cases of the Sherman Anti-Trust Act, passed in 1892, and the Clayton Act, passed in 1914, provide examples for why Gompers's mistrust of most legislation became deep and unequivocal. Prior to the Sherman Act, injunctions in labor disputes had been issued by the government through state or federal courts under the equity power to protect property against imminent or irreparable injury. Now an employer could seek an injunction against a union by presenting a bill of complaint alleging the latter's conspiracy to injure his property, and in this gain protection against "imminent" damage to himself. In addition, the Interstate Commerce Act could also be used to bring complaints against labor unions and courts could issue injunctions based on its provisions.

After the Sherman Act was passed, however, it proved surprisingly capable of offering additional weapons against labor, and Gompers's hopes that it would be applied properly against the trusts themselves were dashed. For under the Sherman Act, private parties could still bring suit by charging a conspiracy to interfere with interstate commerce, despite the fact that the right to issue an injunction remained in government hands.[14] While this could be used in the interests of "trust busting," it could also be used by employers to continue to seek antiunion injunctions. This, in fact, is what employers did. Moreover, employers found other uses for the act. For example, persons sustaining injuries as a result of actions declared unlawful now might sue those committing the acts for triple damages. If a union could be proved guilty of a "contract, combination, or conspiracy in restraint of trade or commerce," an "injured" employer could deplete the union's treasury by a suit, and even collect from individual union members.

Labor launched a vigorous campaign to secure immunity from the antitrust laws and to secure changes in equity procedures. Hope for relief appeared to be in sight with the passage of the Clayton Act, which Gompers hailed as labor's Magna Carta. Section 6 of that law read:

> The labor of a human being is not a commodity or article of commerce. Nothing contained in the anti-trust laws shall be construed to forbid the existence and operation of labor, agricultural, or horticultural organizations instituted for the purposes of mutual help and not having capital stock or conducted for profit, or to forbid or restrain individual members thereof, be held or construed to be illegal combinations or conspiracies in restraint of trade under the anti-trust laws.

In addition, Section 20 forbade injunctions between employer and employee, between employees themselves, and between employees and those seeking employment. Moreover, if a court felt an injunction against workers possible or justified on some ground, reference had to be made first to a listing of some ten labor activities Congress regarded as "peaceful" or "lawful" so that no union or workman could be implicated on illegitimate grounds. How much of the existing statute was in the end altered by the act remained an open question, for there was no mention in the Clayton Act of cases between an employer and *his own* employee. Moreover, a series of cases occurred in which the Supreme Court rulings reflected ambiguity and division of opinion on this matter. Finally, by 1921 the Supreme Court, in a decision on *Duplex Printing Press Co. v. Deering*, ruled that union use of a secondary boycott was illegal, not covered by the Clayton Act, and did not grant labor immunity from injunction.[15]

Many experiences like these convinced Gompers that the courts would make even the most benign piece of legislation a weapon against labor. It is true that Gompers went so far as to support laws limiting child labor, the use of prison labor, and the influx of immigrants into the country. While humane considerations certainly entered into the issue of child labor, Gompers mainly sought to limit the number of competitors for available jobs so as to make it possible for the existing labor force to demand better payment for services, and he felt that such limitation could not be secured by extralegal means. In all other essentials, legislation not specifically designed to make unionism legitimate was regarded as having little or nothing to offer workers. Not only would the courts pervert its letter and spirit, but laws would be framed so as to permit such perversions. Also, laws themselves would not change men, their morals, their commitments, their acts. Men unreconciled to labor's coming of age would continue to find ways to employ existing laws to justify antiunion actions.

The upshot of all this was that Gompers and the leadership of the AFL considered that activity on behalf of alleged prolabor legislation merely engendered the idea, or rather the illusion, that a social problem was solved with the passage of a law. It could, therefore, even lead men to a demoralizing dependence upon government to do what people should do by and for themselves if their citizen vigor, strength, and liberty are to continue to have any meaning at all. He said acidly:

> Whither are we drifting? .... The ... people are hugging the delusion that law is a panacea. Whatever the ill or the wrong or the ideal, immediately follows the suggestion — enact a law. If there is no market for cotten, those interested demand a law. If there is a financial crisis, a law is demanded to protect special interests. If the desire for physical strength and beauty is aroused, laws for eugenic marriages are demanded. If men and women speak ill-considered or unwise words, laws that forbid their speaking in that manner are proposed. If morals are bad, a law is demanded. If wages are low, a law or commission is the remedy proposed. Whether as a result of laziness or incompetency there is a steadily growing disposition to shift responsibility for personal progress and welfare to ouside agencies. What can be the result of this tendency but the softening of the moral fiber of the people? When there is unwillingness to accept responsibility for

one's life and for making the most of it, there is also a loss of strong, red-blooded, rugged independence and willpower to grapple with the wrong of the world and to establish justice through the volition of those concerned. Many of the things for which many are now deludedly demanding legislative regulation should and must be worked out by those concerned.[16]

Thus, legislation is impotent as a moral force and excessive reliance upon it can only render a population bereft of initiative and vigor. Even the passage of acceptable legislation, such as that sanctioning trade unionism, would not relieve unions of the responsibility of self-assertion and self-protection. Then, too, and perhaps even more important, law is not "impartial," springing from the brow of men with a superior capacity for disinterestedness.

What is legislation but class legislation or the formulation by one group ... what they deem ... in their interests? Few laws are passed by unanimous consent. It follows, then, that tariff legislation is "class legislation" in the interests of consumers; that our laws protecting property are class legislation handed down from the middle ages when the property holding classes controlled the government, made the laws, and directed their administration.[17]

And not only is legislation an extension of class interest or power, but government itself is rarely something other than an aggregate of merely powerful and organized men capable of imbuing it with their own perspective so that it cannot impartially serve the public:

Some say that the state is an agency through which the people obtain results—that it exists for their service. But the state is not some impersonal thing. It has no existence outside the people that compose it.[18]

All in all, according to Gompers, little was to be gained from political efforts to secure legislation.

This, however, has so often been misinterpreted to mean that Gompers considered political pressure valueless that a word is necessary at this point to explain that Gompers's skepticism about the value of legal statute did *not* imply that workingmen would do well to steer clear of politics altogether. He explicitly said more than once:

> No one having any conception of the labor problems . . . would for a moment entertain the notion, much less advise the workers, to abstain from the exercise of their political rights and their political powers.[19]

Moreover, while Gompers considered most legislation to be of little value, he recognized, as I have noted, that some legislation for labor was acceptable, such as the type which would recognize the legitimacy of unions, restrict the job market, and reduce competitive pressures on workingmen. Not only this, but in order to guarantee to whatever extent possible that legislation promising even minimal benefit to labor is not hopelessly warped by governmental institutions, it will also be necessary for friends and even members of organized labor to seek public office.

> We want legislation executed by labor men; we want trade unionists in Congress and more . . . in the State legislatures, in our municipal courts and . . . executive offices . . . on the magisterial benches . . .[20]

The AFL not infrequently supported candidates for public office, brought pressure to bear on politicians,[21] and even displayed a weak but discernible tendency on the part of its members to vote for Democratic party candidates before the New Deal.[22] What Gompers and others in the AFL did counsel, however, was that given the minimal worth of laws, and given the likelihood of their misuse against labor organizations, workers should not give political action the highest priority, certainly never turn their attention to it at the expense of union building and union action in the economic struggle against employers, and, above all, never permit either of the major parties to take the labor vote for granted as its own. For then the "favored" party would surely compete less earnestly for the labor vote, or, even worse, simply instrumentalize labor for uses of its own. Also, because a union policy of favoring one party over another might promote divisive infighting among the membership, political *partisanship* (as distinct from a tolerable leve of *participation*) must not become any part of regular union policy. It was vital to Gompers that "in the exercise of the political power of workers" labor never "cast to the winds the experience and tangible results of ages" and carelessly "hazard the interests of labor in a new era of political partisanship."[23]

That Gompers and the AFL leadership opposed partisanship more than politics is further supported by considering the role of voluntarism in sustaining labor alliances in local politics. While craft unions were not much interested in either national legislation or party politics, they were closely concerned with work codes, licensing and apprenticeship laws, appointments to inspectors' jobs, influence in obtaining contracts, local help in strikes, and, as Michael Rogin has pointed out, even their "share of political graft."[24] Local politicians, moreover, did not resent AFL interest in local political affairs because voluntarism "required no commitment on political issues that might upset a local alliance."[25] Because the voluntaristic outlook and union leaders at all levels of the AFL opposed independent political organization (since this would reverse labor's appropriate priorities, placing union building second to party building, an activity which could only distract labor from developing its inner strength), workers at local levels could be Democrats in Democratic cities or Republican in Republican cities, and thus remain open to support for local party machines.

While it was clearly not AFL practice to stay out of the political field entirely, it had additional reasons for wanting to restrict its political activities, especially at the national level, to the strictly necessary. For since government was supposed to be inherently preoccupied with rule and coercion, it could never become a major agent for change in a society. This fact would make a heavy political emphasis on labor's part a waste of time and energy.

For Gompers, government existed for the purpose of guaranteeing individuals in a society against attack, for the purpose of smoothing conflict between social groups by persuasion, and to generate supportive responses to the social norms upon which a society's cohesiveness depends. Unfortunately, it was invested with police powers for the maintenance of these ends. These it would use to sustain order and stability so that it could carry on its business with little interference and at maximum efficiency. It thus had an inherent stake in order and police powers to enforce it. Moreover, the individuals who comprise "government" develop an interest in perpetuating themselves in power and in aligning themselves with groups in the society (like employers) which will help them toward this end. This gives government an added reason to support a status quo because the empowered individuals within it derive their power from a given balance between social groups and are strongly motivated to preserve this balance. The tendency, then, of government to maintain a status quo, plus its police power to coerce citizens into obedience, can and does make it a coercive enemy of change.

Gompers taught that labor can never support a status quo in which it is a weak and vulnerable force. Since government can have no stake in changing labor's condition, labor must take matters into its own hands. A period of extended conflict between employers and employees will be necessary before a change in the status of labor can occur and such a period will do more to change employer attitudes toward dealing with labor than can ever be accomplished by legislation. Government can adjust to the new balance between workers and employers established by conflict, and it may even act to protect such new relations since its power will come to depend on the new status quo. Gompers stressed, however, that government be kept out of the conflict so that acceptable formulas for coexistence between workers and employers may be found. After all, even if government intervention would do no harm, it could do no good either. Government representatives neither manage industry nor are employed in it. They have no experiential base in industry, at least not of the kind built up by daily involvement with it. They cannot even understand industrial experience. Thus, only employee and employer voluntary interaction can discover and set the terms of industrial equity and justice. At most, government may indicate its understanding of the need for this process by laws or public statements which promote voluntary interaction and bargaining in the industrial sphere.

None of this was a plea for the promotion of industrial conflict. On the contrary, the AFL was always cautious in its policies and moderate in its actions. In fact, the idea that government ought to let industrial conflict "happen" freely was intended as a formula for the creation of maximum industrial harmony. After all, what will really happen in the course of unfettered industrial conflict? Labor will build its strength and power simply because employer class actions and industrial conditions will force workers to take such steps. This will impress employers with the need to come to reasonable terms. Besides, building unions will sophisticate and educate workers. It will teach them the art of organization as a part of self-governance. They will as a result learn how to deal with conflict by nonviolent bargaining through organizational representatives. Employers and employees will thus develop motive and sophistication enough to deal with each other by bargaining methods.

This principle was universally applicable for Gompers. The industrial case was but a particular illustration of what was more generally true. Social conflict is simply the result of the fact that some parties have fewer advantages than others. If the disparity is great enough, the disadvantaged party will seek to improve its status. It can do so only by engaging the advantaged party in conflict. Only these parties will have the kind of experience which can generate true understanding of the elements of the conflict. They must thus be left absolutely free to establish acceptable terms of peace between themselves. These terms will always involve a new balance of power between the contending parties. Government intervention in their dispute can only prevent the new balance from emerging, and thus results in the perpetuation of the advantages of the stronger party at the continual expense of the weaker. It is, therefore, absolutely essential that the field of social interaction upon which government may exercise its power be kept small and narrow. The contenders in a given conflict will find some formula by which they will agree to live on a durable basis through their chosen organizations and representatives. These are the *voluntary associations* that grow up in the course of social conflict to represent the interests of the contending parties and to which the participants in the contention belong. In the course of "battle" they acquire and perpetuate sophisticated understanding of the nature of the conflict and of how to negotiate the terms of peace and cooperation. Government must be made to let them create social harmony. In this way, the society will be both stable and free. The absence of "compulsion" at the government level will let citizens find the terms by which they will live, and having found them, they will live peacefully according to them. The voluntary association is the agent of this resolution.[26]

So absolute a value was "noncompulsion" that it was considered a necessary condition for the conduct of internal union affairs. Constituents of the AFL, at local and state levels, were seen to require complete freedom to govern themselves and determine the demands to be made upon employers in their respective trades. By meeting their own problems their own way, each small unit would educate itself and others in the unions about aspects of the labor struggle and problems of conducting it under different conditions and with various types of persons, and ultimately would be capable of taking strong initiatives with sound information which would prevent the crippling burdens that extreme dependency upon a central leadership could cause. In fact, the federation organization model was preferred because it was so amenable to "intraunion" voluntarism. In 1924, Gompers went so far as to boast eloquently, even sentimentally, of the fact that the affiliates and constituents of the AFL did follow a policy of severely limited intervention in their affairs by the national union leadership.[27] He even went so far as to suggest that this fact enabled the AFL to attain more than mere economic progress. The principle of "noncompulsion" in union affairs engendered the habits of independence and democratic living among workers. The "voluntary principle" as an organizational style thus involved the moral improvement of the workingmen.

However much voluntarism as a mode of internal Federation association might uplift the character or organizational intelligence of workmen, it was too much to ask of them, Gompers considered, that they stay loyal to their unions simply on this basis. A democratic worker morality needed space for exercise, it is true, but also something akin to a "material base" of support. Organizing the unorganized was a vital element in building that base, but increasing union power by sheer numbers would not be enough. Strategies for securing tangible material benefits, in a sense "pay-offs," were fundamental. Unions needed to sustain insurance plans and large strike funds for times of need, even if this meant charging high membership fees to establish them. Expertness in negotiating contracts with employers was a vital element in sustaining that base. Rash and injudicious militancy must never be permitted to endanger securing or maintaining material benefits. Strikes and boycotts must be employed cautiously for that reason. Pressing unions in one trade into meddling in the affairs of unions in another trade would prove unacceptable for this reason as well. Gompers stressed strict "trade automony" on the supposition that men would only reduce the possibilities of winning maximum benefits if they intruded in areas, by sympathy strikes or other actions, where they had little knowledge or immediate self-interest.[28] To galvanize the whole "working class," to ignore the virtues of "trade automony," was merely to invite protracted battles in which all might be lost.

Thus, securing short-term economic ends became a means to support and deepen the democratic education of workingmen. Yet despite the importance attached to economic increments, these were subordinate to an end, not ends in themselves. Maintaining the automony of AFL units remained the key to any and all goods desired by labor, short-term economic benefits as well as worker democracy. The unions were left free to adopt such benefits as they saw fit, to provide for their own strike funds, and to consider what initiatives they were to take in strikes and boycotts. No Federation unit was to interfere with another's autonomy to determine these things, for such interference would undermine the material basis as well as the morality of labor democracy. The primary units of the AFL were the national craft unions separated into locals, and after these the city centrals and the state federations. The latter two could not interfere with the jurisdictions of functions of the former. In fact, their voting power at Federation conventions was to be limited to one regardless of membership, whereas the proportional principle applied to the craft union locals. The national-level "Executive Council" of nine (a president, six vice-presidents, a secretary, and a treasurer) could provide advice and help to all affiliates, but could issue no orders or directives. As an internal organizational ideology, then, voluntarism invited an identification between economic benefit and democratic practices, but not substitution of the former for the latter.

Still more, however, was promised to labor by adherence to the voluntary principle, although such promise emerged chiefly as the result of competition with socialists for the leadership of the AFL between 1890 and 1914. The strategy of securing short-term benefits as a support for democratic labor practices came to be seen as capable of limitless application. Unlike socialism, which posited worker control of industry as the proper "end" of labor, voluntarism, Gompers declared, posed no "ends" at all. Gompers translated "ends" to mean "limits," and thus by a verbal trick, he was able to give voluntarism a nearly millenial tone, so that workers could embrace it as something more than a strategy for pursuing economic benefit, even more than a moral guide to democratic action, but also as a binding faith promising them a future as open as the world's possibilities. This is clear in Gompers's repartee with socialist Morris Hillquit before the Commission on Industrial Relations in 1914:

> GOMPERS; *Just a moment. I have not stipulated $4 a day or $8 a day or any number of dollars a day or eight hours a day or seven hours a day or any number of hours a day, but the best possible conditions for the workers is the aim.*
> HILLQUIT: *Yes; and when these conditions are obtained—*
> GOMPERS (interrupting): *Why, then we want better.*
> HILLQUIT (continuing): *You will strive for better?*

GOMPERS: Yes.

HILLQUIT: *Now, my question is, will the effort on the part of organized labor ever stop until it has full reward for its labor?*

GOMPERS: *It won't stop at all.*

HILLQUIT: *That is a question—*

GOMPERS *(interrupting): Not when any particular point is reached, whether it be that which you have just declared or anything else. The working people will never stop.*

HILLQUIT: *Exactly.*

GOMPERS *(continuing): In their effort to obtain a better life for themselves and for their children and for humanity.*

HILLQUIT: *Then, the object of the labor union is to obtain social justice for themselves and for their wives and for their children.*

GOMPERS: *It is the effort to obtain a better life every day.*

HILLQUIT: *Every day and always.*

GOMPERS: *Every day. That does not limit it.*

HILLQUIT: *Until such time—*

GOMPERS: *Not until any time.*

HILLQUIT: *In other words—*

GOMPERS *(interrupting): In other words, we go further than you. (Laughter and applause in the audience.) You have an end; we have not.*[29]

The momentarily millenial glow which Gompers cast upon the voluntarist idea was superficial. In essence, it remained for him and his followers a set of notions which justified the absolute autonomy of labor organization from external influences and the virtues of obtaining economic gains to sustain labor's strength. Finally, he linked these ideas to a negative attitude toward government and legislation on the premise that these constituted obstructions to the achievement of a healthy "balance of power" in the industrial sphere. This association of ideas remained at the heart of the voluntaristic outlook.

Notes

[1]Gompers never did specify which "classical economists" he was attacking nor did be bother to weigh their assumptions in detail or with any care at all. Nevertheless, he left no doubt about the fact that their premises provoked his hostility at an early age and that all of what he consequently came to stand for followed from this reaction. See his *Seventy Years of Life and Labor*, vol. 2, chap. 1. It should be kept in mind, however, that despite the firmness of Gompers's claims about his ideological

ancestry and sources, the autobiographical volumes are highly impressionistic and veer off now and then into self-justifying improvisations.

[2]Florence C. Thorne, *Samuel Gompers: American Statesman*, p. 44.

[3]Gompers, *Seventy Years*, pp. 1-3. It might also be added that Gompers was skeptical about *all* "impersonal forces" which transcended social life and resisted human control, including God. And he rejected all views, including those of Judaism and Christianity, which counseled submission to them. His strong "secularism," exhibited even in his youthful days, contributed much to his suspicions about market "forces" or "laws." See Bernard Mandel, *Samuel Gompers: A Biography*, pp. 9-12.

[4]Samuel Gompers, *Labor and the Common Welfare*, pp. 23-44.

[5]That Gompers had the moral and cultural improvement of workers in mind, as well as their material improvement through the strengthening of labor unions is also noted by Fred Greenbaum, "The Social Ideas of Samuel Gompers," *Labor History*, no. 1 (Winter 1966): 37-38. See also Gompers's own comment on AFL aimed at the general betterment of workers in Morris Hilquit, Samuel Gompers, and Max J. Hayes, *The Double Edge of Labor's Sword* (New York: Arno and The New York Times, 1971), pp. 94 and 96. This is a reprint of testimony on the part of Hillquit, Gompers and Hayes before the U.S. Commission on Industrial Relations of 1912.

[6]Samuel Gompers, *The American Labor Movement*, p. 23; see also United States Industrial Commission of 1899, *Report on the Relations of Capital and Labor*, Vol. VII (Washington, D.C.: Government Printing Office) p. 644, for similar statement by Gompers on the "class divided" character of capitalist industrialism. Also, Gompers' belief in the inherently opposed interests of labor and employers and the necessity of class struggle is widely considered to reflect the early and strong impact on him of socialist literature and politics. In fact, Gompers identified himself as a socialist in the early stages of his career—although he never actually joined socialist organizations and expressed reservations about socialist policy (Mandel, *Samuel Gompers*, pp. 17-19).

[7]This view was held by Gompers even before it was a convenient stance, during World War I, from the point of view of coaxing government, through glowing promises of full labor cooperation and patriotism, into making concessions to labor demands. See President's Report, *AFL Convention Proceedings, 1910*. Also, Gompers was an officer in the National Civic Federation, an organization dedicated to a program of social reform and which sought (and played) a major role in the conciliation of labor and employers in industrial disputes. Gompers's contact with varied "enlightened" employers in the NCF, as well as its more general views, significantly influenced him on this point. For a full discussion of Gompers and the NCF see Marguerite Green, *The National Civic Federation and the American Labor Movement, 1900-1925*.

[8]This meant, however, that the portion of the general wealth not invested for "honest" industrial needs must be given back to the workers. See Gompers, *American Labor Movement*, p. 20; also, for Gompers's

stand on "honest investment" see United States Commission on Industrial Relations of 1912, *Final Report and Testimony Vol. II* (Washington, D.C.) pp. 1531-32.

[9]See the extensive extract from Gompers's public address in Chicago 1 May 1908, in Thorne, *Samuel Gompers*, p. 50.

[10]Collective bargaining was conceived as a mode of fixing the terms of employment by means of bargaining between an organized body of employees and an employer or association of employers acting through duly authorized agents. For workers it is intended to weight their side of the bargaining situation with more power over the terms of the worker-employer contract than they could exert as individuals, and it is a method of securing the equality which is inherent in the free contract assumption in American law. While this bargaining method was strongly promoted by Gompers, and was considered by him to be labor's most useful instrument for the attainment of its aims, it is not, however, in itself inseparable from the voluntaristic framework. Various socialists, while fiercely critical of voluntarism, have been able to accommodate collective bargaining practices as a short-term labor strategy, useful to workers if only as training and preparation to enlarge their demands upon the employer class.

[11]See Gompers, *American Labor Movement*, pp. 14-16; editorial, *American Federationist* (January 1917):47; and "Testimony Before Congressional Commission on Resolution for a Committee on Social Insurance, April 1916," *American Federationist* (May 1916): 347.

[12]See Mandel, *Samuel Gompers*, pp. 182-83. It might be added, as Mandel points out, on the workmen's compensation issue Gompers was ignored by organized labor which insisted upon stronger measures.

[13]See Gompers's editorial, *American Federationist* 24 (January 1917): 47-48; idem, *American Labor Movement*, pp. 15-16.

[14]The act also provided the government itself with more firm and extensive ground on which to sue for injunction against a party "obstructing interstate commerce." In 1894, Attorney-General Richard Olney secured an injunction against Eugene V. Debs and the American Railway Union for violating the Sherman Anti-Trust Act on grounds of obstructing commerce in the strike against the Pullman Company.

[15]For a full discussion of the legal uses of the Clayton Act against labor, see Stanley I. Kutler, "Labor, the Clayton Act, and the Supreme Court," *Labor History* 3, no. 1 (Winter 1962): 19-38. The passage previously cited from the Clayton Act may also be found in this article on page 19.

[16]Gompers, *Labor and the Common Welfare*, p. 53.

[17]Ibid., pp. 52-53.

[18]Ibid., p. 45.

[19]Ibid., p. 8.

[20]Ibid.

[21]J. David Greenstone, *Labor in American Politics*, pp. 30-38.

[22]Ibid., pp. 30-31. Greenstone discerns a Democratic party preference since 1906, partially because of the influence of Irish Catholics in the

AFL, but more especially because of the "Republicans' increasingly antiunion posture, which made the AFL's protestations to strict nonpartisanship increasingly untenable."

[23]Gompers, *Labor and the Common Welfare*, p. 8.

[24]Michael Rogin, "Voluntarism: The Political Functions of an Antipolitical Doctrine," in *Labor and American Politics*, ed. C. M. Rehmus and D. B. McLaughlin (Ann Arbor: University of Michigan Press, 1967), pp. 108-28. Rogin overstates the antipoliticism of voluntarism considerably and thus "exposes" the local political involvements of the AFL as instances of hypocrisy or naivete about "doctrinal" implications. Nothing in Gompers's writing or speeches justifies so extreme a characterization. Nevertheless, Rogin's study, by emphasizing the political activities of the AFL at local city levels, is a corrective to the frequently held and mistaken view, generally traceable to Selig Perlman and Philip Taft, that voluntarism lacked any tolerance or assigned any worth to political activity. In support of his contention, Rogin cites some valuable local voting and other studies (see p. 126n). Another, more bitter "exposure" of some AFL political involvements, may be found in John Hutchinson's *The Imperfect Union*. Here it is shown that the presence of individuals relatively free of union discipline (the AFL business agent or walking delegate are examples) could be found drifting off into politics to extend or protect themselves in practices of bribery and coercion. Also professional criminals with links to local public officials sometimes made unions a field of criminal activity. It sould be made clear, however, that the emphasis of this work is not on AFL political activities but on the corrupt elements within unions who, on occasion, drifted into the political sphere for protection or profit.

[25]Rogin, p. 127.

[26]Louis Reed, *The Labor Philosophy of Samuel Gompers*. Reed's study is a highly competent elaboration of Gompers's thought, and though done over forty years ago, remains the best extensive treatment of the subject to date.

[27]See Thorne, *Samuel Gompers*, pp. 59-62, for complete text of Gompers's message to the 1924 AFL Convention. It focused upon the virtues of voluntarism in internal union affairs. Gompers was, however, inclined to "bossism" and personal machine building within the AFL despite his ardent defenses of the voluntary principle. He was not above working around it to promote his own power and standing (see Mandel, *Samuel Gompers*, pp. 100-106).

[28]This stress was also made emphatic by Gompers's close associate, a founder of the AFL and president of the Cigar Makers' International Union of America, Adolph Strasser. See his statement before the Senate, Committee upon the relations between Capital and Labor in 1883, 49th Cong. 1st sess. as given in *Report of the Committee of the Senate upon the Relations between Labor and Capital*, 1885, vol. 1, p. 460.

[29]Hillquit, Gompers, Hayes, *Double Edge*, p. 124. Also, it should not be thought from this that Gompers bested Hillquit throughout their ex-

change. The encounter was between equals and Hillquit even showed himself more agile than Gompers at various points.

Chapter 2
Voluntarism: Bases of Support and Survival

Voluntarism was never developed very elaborately by its leading spokesmen, even by Gompers, beyond scattered observations about the value of voluntary associations and noncompulsion in all affairs involving the exercise of authority. It was meant essentially to justify and guide immediate courses of action and to mobilize particular kinds of persons to carry them out. An important question to ask about it, then, is: to whom voluntarism actually appealed and what kinds of organizational and policy consequences followed from its capacity to mobilize that particular group of people. That voluntarism assumed universalistic poses is beside the point. The point is that its often improvisational and thematically limited character, its appearance in writings geared to deal with urgent and immediate social business, shows that it was a mobilizing ideology intended to appeal to a specific and identifiable audience and not the whole of mankind. Thus, we shall want to know, in order to understand it better, whom it mobilized, why it could mobilize them, and what they managed to gain from an adherence to voluntarism. To make the characteristics of voluntarist followers distinct, it is necessary to consider first how they became differentiated from the rest of the labor movement and came together in the AFL.

The first major attempt to organize labor on a unified national basis occurred with the formation of the National Labor Union in

August 1866. The NLU held a series of congresses until 1872 in attempts to integrate the various labor organizations then in existence. These were scattered about the country and had been formed largely before the Civil War. They were, essentially, a congeries of skilled mechanics and all-around journeyman-craftsmen puzzled by, and resentful of, the onset of massive industrialization, its increasing subdivision of labor, and the loss of economic independence and public status it was causing them. The NLU reflected the outlook of these men which was fixed on restoring earlier conditions which favored their autonomy. It was thus bent on arresting the spread of industrial mechanization, restoring smaller production units, and protecting cooperative stores and workshops formed by workmen. It espoused monetary reform and advocated cheap credit to enable workmen to build up their own store of capital to sustain their own enterprises. It also called for the eight-hour day in order that workmen would have leisure enough to be informed participants in public affairs. Because it could not see how better economic compensation for labor, such as higher wages, could address labor's fundamental dilemma, it gave its attention wholly over to pressure for reform legislation, to the advocacy of legal redefinition of the industrial environment so that it could be restructured to restore and protect the workingman's autonomy and public status. In sum, the NLU dedicated itself to a reversal of corporate growth and mass industrialization and sought laws which would oppose, offset, or offer alternatives to this. Strikes or other forms of collective action aimed specifically at employers or designed to secure mainly wage or hour improvements for workmen employed in industry were essentially irrelevant (after all, corporate and industrial growth was relatively recent and could be seen as transitory, something which would survive only as long as government would permit).

But within the ranks of the NLU substantial discontent emerged among the unions of skilled workers—printers, machinists, molders, blacksmiths, coopers, and others. Impatient with legislative reform aimed at restoring prior conditions, they began to demand ways to achieve tangible economic improvement in their immediate situation as "wage labor." Moreover, the NLU had attracted some unions of immigrant workers (mainly German) imbued with the ideas of the First International, and they began to agitate for the establishment of a national labor socialist alliance. The NLU leadership, on the other hand, remained preoccupied with a "restorationist" mode of thought, despite the fact that a clear "trade unionism" (organization for collective bargaining purposes) and a militant socialism were taking shape in the minds of the membership. The severe rifts this produced, as well as the decimation of the NLU financial resources from the effects of business cycles, led to the disintegration of the NLU by 1872.[1]

Yet between 1873 and 1881 these three orientations were to find new organizational expression. For in December 1877, the socialist groups, aroused to a peak of militance by the great railroad strikes of that year, formed the Socialist Labor party, with a platform advocating class struggle toward the end of establishing a socialist commonwealth in the United States. And in January 1878, the Noble Order of the Knights of Labor, which had been organized in 1869 by Uriah Stephens as a secret society, became established as an open organization advocating a program very much like that of the National Labor Union. It added further emphasis on reorganizing productive and distributive activity in the economic phere along cooperative lines as the means to do away with humiliating industrial conditions. Finally, a third organization emerged as a loose federation of craft unions sponsored by skilled mechanics of various types (many of whom had come out of the old NLU). They shared a class struggle emphasis with the socialists, but geared it toward nonrevolutionary ends, such as wage increases and the shorter workday. That is, they saw employers as possessing interests diametrically opposed to those of labor and the need for the latter to carry on a vigilant and constant struggle against the former. But the purpose of such a struggle was not the achievement of massive human transformation of even labor's ultimate command over the industrial order. Rather, it was undertaken solely for the purpose of securing the best possible material compensation for labor which could be attained under given circumstances.

Of this trio of organizational and ideological possibilities, it would be the "economistically" oriented craft unions which would emerge as the dominant force in the labor movement between 1886 and 1895. This happened for many reasons. Certainly chief among them were the organizational zeal and skills of men like Samuel Gompers and Adolph Strasser (both of the Cigar Workers) and P.J. McGuire (of the Carpenters), among some others, who played vital leadership roles in them. But the fact that their competitors were weakened by internal disorders and suffered from insensitivity to the temper of American workers cannot be underestimated as factors which favored the increased influence of the pragmatic craft unions.

The craft unions solidified themselves organizationally and ideologically by 1881. Steps were taken in this direction because people like Gompers, Strasser, and McGuire, who had all been more or less involved with socialist groups during the 1870s, had become convinced by this experience that political partisanship was tearing the labor movement apart. Moreover, it was offensive to the indigenous American population because it was so often carried on in alien terms. They urged a less political trade unionism upon the skilled workers who had been disappointed with the old NLU, the current Knights of Labor, or any other labor organizations favoring political involvement of the workers. As a result, a number of people from the craft unions promoted plans for a new labor federation which would reflect this outlook (the Typographical Union played a leading role in this).

A conference to found such a federation was finally held in Pittsburgh on 15 November 1881, attended by 107 delegates (including some from the Knights and scattered other labor organizations). The Committee on Plan of Organization was headed by Samuel Gompers who recommended that the new organization be known as the Federation of Organized Trades Unions of the United States and Canada (Canadian union locals were called to the conference). Since the Knights at the conference identified the designation "trades union" with craft workers only and felt that the new organization's title would offend and alienate unskilled workers, a change was accepted and the Federation of Organized Trades and Labor Unions of the United States and Canada (FOTLU) was founded. Various efforts were made at the conference by the Knights and socialists in attendance to commit the new organization to sweeping or militant political action, but these were successfully thwarted. There was willingness to accept the idea that some political pressure for legislation favorable to labor should be systematically exerted and the new federation did set up a legislative committee to secure such laws as might promote better conditions for workmen. But this move resulted less from some compromise gesture toward the Knights or socialists than from the respect of Gompers and his colleagues for the example set by British trade unionism which had been strengthened by integrating a similar committee for limited political action into its structure. In fact, a constitution was adopted at the conference which was modeled after that of the British Trade Union Congress.[2]

This period of "solidification" by the pragmatic skilled workmen was quickly followed, however, by the severe weakening of the Knights of Labor. For the latter would prove itself far out of step with American workers (and, eventually, incapable of surmounting its internal conflicts). When the FOTLU was founded, economic conditions in the country were deteriorating and the deterioration was accompanied by a wave of labor unrest culminating in a series of major strikes between 1884 and 1885. Increasing numbers of workers went in search of union leadership. Because the Knights of Labor included, even sought, unskilled and black as well as white members, a wide variety of workers turned to them, despite the Knights' opposition to strike methods (though the Knights played down this opposition under the pressure of the circumstances). By contrast, the FOTLU was dwindling into insignificance. The Knights looked as if they would emerge as the leaders of American labor (most accounts of the Knights in this period indicate that membership was rising rapidly and that it reached a peak at roughly 750,000). But in 1886, a movement to support the eight-hour day stirred the whole country to a virtual general strike. The FOTLU joined in and strongly supported the strike and in this found itself very much in tune with labor's real feelings. It began, as a result, to gain in membership. The Knights, on the other hand, steadily reaffirmed its old nonstrike attitude and began to lose members in large numbers.

The craft unions underwent another period of solidification during these events. Foreseeing their opportunity, officials of the FOTLU issued a circular against the Knights calling for a conference of trade unions to convene in Philadelphia on 18 May 1886 to consider further possibilities for strike and other actions. At that meeting a drastic proposal was put forward which demanded that the Knights cease to organize in trades where the FOTLU craft unions already existed, at least not to organize these without explicit permission from the FOTLU. Many members of the Knights favored finding some basis for reconciliation with the FOTLU. But the Knights' General Assembly ignored the proposal and inflamed matters by admitting the independent Progressive Cigarmakers' Union at the same time that it expelled from its ranks cigarmakers who belonged to the International Cigarmakers' Union associated with the FOTLU. This angered the craft unions of the FOTLU and they issued a further call to all trade unions in the country to attend a convention scheduled for 8 December 1886 to be held in Columbus, Ohio. Over forty delegates attended, representing some twenty-five labor organizations. At the convention they decided to form, for purposes of mutual assistance, a national federation of labor. The FOTLU, with Gompers's urging, agreed to merge with them. An expanded American Federation of

Labor was thus born and Gompers selected to be its first president.[3]

During this period of craft unionist strengthening, however, the Knights of Labor was tearing itself apart in internal dispute. At least since 1878, the Knights had a policy of admitting elements from all social groups of society to membership (barring, however, lawyers, bankers, and saloonkeepers). The inclusion of farmers, shopkeepers, small employers, and a variety of self-employed professionals like doctors, on the grounds that they were engaged in types of labor and had a stake in social reform, managed to drastically reduce the proportion and influence of workers in the Knights. Factious squabbling broke out regularly between the different elements in the Order and not infrequently between its labor elements and the others. But now, under the impact of further craft unionist gains, the infighting became intolerable as many members began to urge abandonment of the Knights' traditional policies, especially as regarded strikes and concerted action for wage and hour improvements in concrete trades. The fierce and divisive disputing weakened the Order irretrievably.

It might also be mentioned that cooperatives initiated by the Knights (many of these between 1884 and 1886) were failing, and this too was taking its toll on the organization. Also, because of the gains among workers made by the Knights during the strike wave of 1884-85, employers and even local churches were enlivened to screeching attacks upon them, and many members were convicted on criminal conspiracy and rioting charges. This could not fail to sap the Order of much of its strength. But the Knights had so rent themselves internally, especially in the 1886 period, that it is likely that they still would have been left in tatters without the influence of these factors. By 1890 they were reduced to shreds. Members even began straggling into the AFL. The field was cleared for the young federation. Though it had been strengthened by its own efforts, the new AFL could never have gone so far as to dominate the labor scene without the convenient suicidal inclinations of the Noble Order of the Knights of Labor.

The AFL, however, not only profited from the inner dissolution of the Knights of Labor; it also gained by virtue of the fact that the dominant contemporary socialist organization, the Socialist Labor party, embarked on a course of inner conflict which would finally reduce it to impotence, thus further clearing the ground for the new Federation.

The Socialist Labor party had come into being between 1876 and 1877 as a result of efforts by scattered socialist groups at unification around a single-minded revolutionary program. Soon after its establishment, it became the major, if not only, voice of organized socialism in America, a position it would hold until the later 1890s. The SLP had been open to internal factionalism from the time it was founded. For it included, then, "Lassalleans," the party's "right wing," committed to a purely political plan of action (such as competing in elections, allying with, or supporting varied populist movements), and Marxists, the party's "left wing," committed to fostering the growth of militant industrial workers' organizations (especially trade unions) and subordinating political action, at least as the Lassalleans understood it, to this end. This produced numerous faction fights. Indeed, by 1878, a number of the party's "left wingers" even withdrew to form an "International Labor Union" and later, by 1881, to join in the founding of the FOTLU which eventually became the AFL. Moreover, between 1881 and 1883 additional syndical and anarchist factions had formed within the party (although these withdrew to affiliate with the anarchist Black International). But these internal divisions notwithstanding, the party was the dominant socialist force in 1877 and would remain so for some two decades. It was, as a matter of fact, effectively making gains in membership,[4] and making an impact through a well-developed publication apparatus which, among other things, sponsored a number of socialist newspapers in several languages. Finally, whatever the dispute over political action within the SLP, it was making relatively good showings in elections.[5] In the light of all this, the socialists, organized chiefly around the SLP, were posing a competitive challenge for the emerging AFL.

The Socialist Labor party, however, would lose all this ground by virtue of decimating internecine strife, and by the late 1890s it was well on the way to becoming an irrelevant sect hardly capable of resisting the increasing growth of the AFL. In the 1890s, under Daniel DeLeon (who had joined the party in 1886), the SLP attempted to transform itself into an American Marxist movement from the immigrant radical organization it had mainly been until then. This involved not only increasing English-speaking emphasis in its publications, but also adopting a policy of securing influence within the prevailing workers' organizations at the time, specifically the Knights of Labor and the AFL. Indeed, this was referred to as the party's "boring from within" policy. The effort to "bore from within" the Knights of Labor failed dismally, not the least reason being the disarray prevailing within the Order itself. And the effort with respect to the AFL ended similarly (though here the reason had more to do with the fact that Gompers and others successfully out-maneuvered an SLP attempt to secure an AFL charter for its Central Labor Federation and thus to virtually establish itself within the AFL).[6]

After the failure to "bore from within" both the Knights and the AFL, the party, in 1895, organized a Socialist Trade and Labor Alliance intended to be a militant and competitive trade union organization. In other words, DeLeon and his associates embarked on a dual unionist course. This formation of the STLA was to be the turning point which would undo the SLP, for many members of the SLP opposed dual unionism. DeLeon, however, by way of response to this opposition was vituperative, dictatorial, and generally denied in virulent terms the right of any party member to oppose the policy undertaken. For, DeLeon held, if the opportunism and "fakery" of the Knights, and particularly of the AFL, were not utterly exposed and totally replaced by a principled revolutionary trade union organization, the American working class would be forever led astray from its proper historical destiny. The opposition held, on the other hand, that a separatist trade union movement colliding head on with other major (and growing) union organizations could not end otherwise but by isolating itself and destroying its influence and resources. De Leon and his party allies denounced such concern as fakery worse than that which even the AFL practiced and determined to wipe it out as a force in the SLP.

Waves of expulsions and fierce personal denunciations of those who disputed the wisdom of De Leon's course followed. The membership was vastly diminished in this campaign for revolutionary purity while hatreds, fights, humiliations, and insults ran rampant on all sides. An "anti-De Leon" rebellion occurred finally (in 1899) which led to the formation of a new Socialist party in 1900 (which would not undertake to compete with the AFL as a labor organization). The Socialist Labor party lay in ruins, a shadow of its former self. There was nothing for it to do but abandon attempts to become the major instrument of socialism in America and confine itself to "education" of the masses through several of its remaining publications (a task it carries on to this day). The business of gathering and orgnaizing labor would be left to others.

And so every step forward taken by the "antipolitical" skilled workmen was paralleled by rifts within the ranks of their major competitors which doomed the latter to insignificance and cleared the way for the former. It is true that the craft unionists could hardly have gained in strength without deliberately and skillfully seizing opportunities for organizational solidification and expansion. Still, it is unlikely that they could have gone so far as to dominate the labor movement as they did by the end of the nineteenth century without the internal disorders and insensitivities of their rivals to aid them.

Now, all of this tells us how the craft unionists became differentiated from other sectors of the labor movement and organized around an increasingly dominant AFL. It does not, however, address the matter of why voluntarism appealed to them. That is, we have yet to consider why the AFL unionists felt that the logic of their experiences as workers could be expressed by the voluntarist outlook. In their discouragement with the National Labor Union, the Knights of Labor, and the socialists who came together in the Socialist Labor party, they did not turn, as they might have (and as other unionists would one day), to some other course of political action of their own. What was it about the skilled craftsmen who joined and built the AFL that made them translate their industrial experiences into the politically skeptical terms of voluntarism?

An important characteristic of the workers attracted to the AFL, at least in its earlier days, was that they often had previous backgrounds in management, or at least supervisory positions, and in owning small business enterprises before they were driven into the labor market. Thus, they brought to their experiences as "hired labor" laissez faire biases once shared with employers. Moreover, in their former status they acquired the habit of exercising a high degree of independent judgment in work and business decisions, and this gave them a degree of expertise relatively equal to any employer for whom they would work in the future. In fact, it was even called upon to resolve difficulties in a variety of work situations they underwent. They would, as a result, have particular reason to think that all problems encountered in the industrial sphere were manageable by the participants in the industrial process themselves, apart from the machinery of government and the application of political legislation. Indeed, even where they had been only immigrant workers, with little opportunity to acquire laissez faire notions directly from varied business circles, their work skills nevertheless placed them in positions involving a high degree of initiative and independent judgment such that collaboration with employers on more or less equal ground was possible and notions about the regulation of the industrial sphere solely by employer-employee consultation or negotiation could take root.

It might be pointed out that much in the structure of industrial technology, business enterprise, and general labor attitudes in the late nineteenth century added to the craft worker's's suspicion that those evils of the industrial system oppressive to labor were in fact open to regulative influences outside government. For example, mechanization had not yet progressed far enough to eliminate the need for him in large numbers. Thus, he was in high demand with employers and saw himself as crucial to industrial functioning. In addition, most markets for particular goods were not yet extraregional or national in scope, and firms did not often see the need to hire special personnel to oversee, plan for, or generally attend to them. Insofar as such a task was undertaken, it was often given over to the more skilled workman. Finally, professional production managers with specialized technological or business education were not easily available, with the result that skilled craftsmen were called upon from time to time for technological or business managerial advice. In the light of all this, what government act or measure could possibly compare with the craft worker's own power to bring about reform in the industrial sphere by means of his strikes or other forceful actions? Besides, many firms employed little supervision and operated on a piece-work basis (as in the garment trades). Skilled workers, therefore, had a strong voice in directly determining conditions, such as prices, for their output. This added much to their confidence in the notion that they had rights to determine their own wages through direct negotiations with employers apart from any external agencies. Also, because all these factors (and other things besides, such as his higher wages) enhanced the skilled craftsman's prestige among his fellow workers, he would often be given leadership rights and responsibilities to make decisions about working conditions on their behalf.[7] And this gave him the feeling that his general approach to industrial life and its problems was trusted by and suitable to the working masses. This gave, indeed, a certain validation to his faith that something other than government would bring needed reform and regulation of industrial life.

At any rate, by virtue of their economic background, the kind of labor they performed and the industrial setting in which they performed it, a laissez faire understanding of society and its relation to political agencies, became well developed among skilled craftsmen. And this predisposed them to the voluntarist appeal of the AFL (and, of course, inclined the Federation to sustain this mode of appeal). Below, Table 1 schematizes the factors influencing and sustaining autonomy in the work process, at least in a number of instances, and illustrates the connection between "autonomous" craftsmen in given industries and their unionization in the AFL.[8]

Table 1

SOME EXAMPLES OF UNIONIZED
AUTONOMOUS WORKMEN (PRE-1914)

KEY OCCUPA-TIONAL GROUP AND WORK GROUP STATUS	CAUSES OF AUTOMONY	KNOWN UNION STATUS
Coal Industry Contract Mining: In anthracite mining the piece master, a petty contractor, employed helpers. In bituminous mining, pick miners were unsupervised.	1. Supervision difficult 2. Piecework 3. British mining traditions 4. Knowledge and rough skills of pick miners	Initiated predecessors of Mine Workers Union, major part of membership.
Potteries: Jiggermen, kilnmen, and other contract workers were the key group: jiggermen employed 3 helpers.	1. Piecework 2. Manual skills 3. British traditions	Dominant group in Operative Potters Union.
Iron: Puddlers and rollers were employing subcontractors; they hired helpers and were responsible for operation of parts of a mill.	1. Technical knowledge of iron metallurgy 2. British tradition 3. Manual skills, strength 4. "Sliding scale" of piece rates	Founders of predecessors of Amalgamated Ass'n of Iron, Steel and Tin Workers; later, powerful groups within the union.
Stove Moulding: Journeymen hired,	1. Piecework 2. Tradition of self-	Founded and controlled the Molders'

		Union.
trained and directed "bunks," learners and helpers.	employment as a side enterprise to a blast furnace.	
Newspaper Printing: Compositorforemen supervised less skilled crafts in small shops and managed composing room.	1. Piecework (prelinotype) 2. Publishers' disinterest in production management 3. British traditions.	Dominated typographical unions by secret society and alliance with conservative union leaders.
Clothing: Cutters scheduled and directed work; skilled tailors (custom) or machine operators in readymade clothing were often subcontractors, hiring and training less skilled labor.	1. Extreme lack of management and fragmentation of business units, homework and sweating system. 2. Piecework. 3. Labor contracting possible because of immigrant labor.	Journeyman Tailors, initiators of the unions that became the United Garment Workers and the ILGWU.

It must be emphasized, however, that the men who joined the AFL would not support unmodified laissez faire notions of the sort which favored total business autonomy from government regulation or rampant individualism. On the contrary, they were receptive only to such laissez faire images of the world which had been "adjusted" or formulated for particular use in labor struggles and to support labor's own power. That is, they were attracted to laissez faire doctrines which transferred principles once applicable to individuals and businesses operating in a capitalist order to *all* groups operating under these conditions. More particularly, they were attracted to the idea that a noninterventionist government policy with respect to the liberties of individuals or those of business enterprises was appropriate for all groups, especially those made up of disadvantaged persons, seeking to establish themselves or make reasonable gains in a society.

Although the value to them of such an altered "laissez fairism" consisted primarily in merely legitimizing the struggles the skilled workers wished to undertake on labor's behalf, it is necessary to point out that it also served them in other important respects. For one thing, they experienced through it a certain continuity in their understanding of the world so that they were not thrown into utter confusion by the change in status many of them had undergone with a "fall" into the labor market. For another thing, their new notions could also seem to be in keeping with American traditions of long standing and thus make their acts of labor organizing, considered "un-American" by many in the nineteenth century, publicly proper if not, indeed, actually patriotic. Finally, anxious to protect the measure of "status" they enjoyed with respect to unskilled workers, they were especially well served by notions which permitted this. For they were threatened by leveling socialist or other ideologies which stressed the similarity of all workers, without regard to the differences in interests, skills, and entitlements to reward among them. They needed some vague doctrine which proclaimed labor's rights without explicating theories about the essential sameness of the whole working class. Indeed, this was so strong a need that the AFL's presentation of just such a doctrine helped it to keep increasing its craft worker population well into the twentieth century.[9]

There were important policy consequences for the AFL which followed from the craft worker's embrace of the "laissez faire-like" doctrine of voluntarism. As was noted before, craftsmen perceived the industrial order to be entirely dependent upon their skills and services to function efficiently. That is, they understood themselves to be indispensable to the production process. This implied to them that craft workers, rather than unskilled workers, were in the best position to pressure employers into meeting labor's demands, since (a) they could not be replaced if they went on strike or otherwise withdrew their skills from production, and (b) they were better paid than other workers and so could sustain long strike periods for better conditions of work. They could, and assumed that they should, serve as a sort of labor "vanguard" which, through their union organizations, fought for and fixed the best conditions of work possible in different trades. Their efforts, it was assumed, would result in better conditions for all workers. The result of such reasoning was that voluntarism became associated with craft unionism as a matter of principle. Unskilled workers in general, as well as those placed in special AFL bodies, like the Federal Labor Unions, were advised to enhance their own best interests, not by pressing inclusive industrial unionist notions upon the AFL, but by accepting the leadership of their skilled "big brothers" since the latter alone were in a position to protect them both. Because the craft worker would need unfettered freedom to protect the whole of labor, the unskilled worker was advised not to reduce the effectiveness of his craft brother by promoting his own separate claims too far, and still less should he demand leadership rights in the AFL to an excessive extent, creating in this a conflict of interests within the organization.

Socialists and others agitated at the turn of the century for industrial unionism.[10] They stressed that the craft principle would become, if it was not already, structurally obsolete. It divided the labor movement into hundreds of autonomous craft organizations incapable of accepting an appropriate degree of discipline from a central leadership, thus producing ill-coordinated and confused labor campaigns. Moreover, they argued, the logic of modern industry will increasingly lead to employment of unskilled labor and thus lead to the continuous enlargement of the unskilled labor force. For mechanization, the trend of the future, would continue to break down the complex skills united in an individual craft worker and divide the components among several unskilled laborers. More complex machinery would thus simplify work tasks and demand of the worker less knowledge of "craft." And as factories filled up with the unskilled, labor tactics would have to shift to mobilizing maximum numbers and amalgamating existing unions into a few large industrial unions. Then, too, the unskilled would identify less and less with a craft or with craft leadership and more and more with the varied workers in a plant or even a whole industry. Finally, the massing of numbers and a centralized leadership to coordinate action would become the only way to be effective against businesses enlarging daily into powerful corporate giants themselves increasingly governed by a centralized leadership.

Gompers and the AFL drifted halfheartedly along with this idea. By 1901 the AFL adopted its policy of putting unskilled workers into affiliates called Federal Trade Unions (although it did previously accept a few unskilled workers and relegated them to Central Labor Unions, the equivalent of Federal Trade Unions).[11] But under Gompers's direction it still kept strongly to the short-sighted idea that collective bargaining methods would be most effective when pressed by craft workers who could not be coerced by employers because of their valuable skills.[12] He, and the AFL, remained convinced that craft workers, better paid then others, could best support and promote union organization which could survive bad times and deal powerfully and confidently with employers. By contrast, the unskilled worker was badly paid, more readily laid off, and easily replaced with strikebreakers during strikes. He necessarily lacked qualities and resources with which to build strong organizations, despite the development of industrial conditions which favored increases in his number.

Further challenges to this idea would emerge continuously. For example, the Industrial Workers of the World (IWW) argued effectively for a unionism along industrial lines, and it innovated "sit down" and mass picketing techniques for the conduct of union organizing on an industrial basis. But the IWW (formed in 1905) developed its strength chiefly among workers in rough and isolated areas, attracting some coal miners, lumberjacks, migratory workers, workers on construction gangs, and the like. As a result, its members, probably never exceeding some 120,000, were dispersed or wiped out fairly easily. Certainly the AFL never came to its aid when brutal employer suppression and lack of financial resources threatened it with total decline. This may even be considered a factor in its final demise. But "industrial unionists" would stay, in the main, within the AFL in the belief that any strong action of theirs which would result in "dual unionism" would greatly cripple the unity and strength of the labor movement as a whole. It would not be until 1936 that a leadership would emerge, both politically acceptable and sufficiently prestigious to masses of workers, which could promote industrial unionism on an enduring basis.

We might remember in all this that the unskilled worker in the late nineteenth and early twentieth centuries was often a newcomer to industry from a farming area, or an immigrant with weak or even nonexistent ties to a native American ideological idiom into which he could translate his claims. Thus, he had little chance to challenge the craft unionism associated with voluntarism and reshape it in his own image. The result was that a craft unionist voluntarism could be decisively (even if only temporarily, as it turned out) strengthened by the absence of enduring and articulate pressure from unskilled workers themselves to reconsider the potentialities of industrial union principles.

The AFL's voluntarism, once habitual with the Federation's craft workers would prove capable of surviving until the Great Depression brought the special difficulties which it would not surmount. This was helped along in part by periodic union-busting drives sponsored by employers and antilabor court rulings, both of which served to confirm voluntaristic explanations for the behavior of employers, government leaders, and the judiciary. Also, the enlightened and liberal "welfare capitalist" strategy, gaining popularity with some employers in the decade of the 1920s, would deepen AFL mistrust of any and all social welfare, insurance, or regulatory schemes not devised by itself and secured by private negotiation and contract. While many employers of this period, inflamed by the patriotic passions stirred by World War I, and living in paranoid fear that the Soviet Revolution would be repeated on American soil if labor agitation kept up, went in for brutal union busting, others among them attempted to respond to labor pressure by instituting labor "representation" plans, for the purpose of humanizing and easing employee-employer relations. These were meant to incorporate union demands that labor have a voice in the determination of industrial policy. They turned into plans for tightening employer control over employees. Employers set up shop committee systems which included several workers to satisfy representation demands. They encouraged employee purchase of stock shares in their respective companies. They set up company unions and purchased group insurance plans for their workers. At the same time, bona fide trade unionists were driven out of plants. Moreover, other workingmen became so firmly tied to these "benefits" that they easily submitted to subordination and employer threats. Despite the fact that after 1924 AFL unions suffered very significant losses in membership and strength, and despite the fact that a greatly weakened AFL sought to survive by reducing and benevolently wording its demands upon employers, the AFL still attempted to organize its own insurance benefit plans to counter employer power. Edward J. Evans, one of the trustees of the Union Cooperative Insurance Association, founded in 1924 by the International Brotherhood of Electrical Workers, said:

> Our organizers went to shops throughout the country and everywhere we found that the cheap group insurance offered by the boss had the effect of tying the men to their jobs and making them afraid to join the union that would protect their interests. For two cents per worker per day the employer could get certain kinds of group insurance and then save fifty cents to one dollar per worker per day in wage increases that the union would have obtained for the men. If the man quit or was fired his insurance quit. So we formed our own company and offered better group insurance at cheaper rates to hold good not merely while the worker is with a particular employer but just as long as his union card was paid up.

> Union membership grew, wage increases followed, and so
> we beat the boss at that particular game.[13]

Thus, even as welfare capitalism weakened the trade union
movement, voluntarism came even more to represent the virtues
of worker and union automony from all external authority.

Still, it might be thought that the willingness of the AFL to cooperate with the federal government during the period of World
War I would have weakened the tenacity of voluntaristic assumptions. After all, the AFL had reserved its policy of neutrality during wartime and adopted a prowar attitude. Why could it not go
further in modifying its traditonal stance? In 1907 Gompers was
firm and clear that the spilling of workingmen's blood on foreign
soil in the interests of a national policy would merely waste and
reduce the labor force and yield it no advantages. Worker attention should not be distracted, he insisted, from the chief goal of
building worker organizations by a call to arms. Unionization
must go on, war or no war. Indeed, nothing could be more heroic
than the patient struggle for the affirmation of labor's rights. Even
the world as a whole would be uplifted, ultimately, more by the
latter than the former.

> It requires more heroism in men and women to bear the
> brunt of great sacrifice, of quiet, silent suffering for the bet-
> terment of the human family than is manifested upon the
> gory field of battle. To endeavor to ... uplift ... our fellows
> ... in the work of this century, which you, the toilers ... are
> effecting with a heroism ... that may not be understood or
> appreciated in our time. ... Those who follow us will realize
> ... that as we perform our duties to our fellows, we shall
> have performed the great work for the social uplift and uni-
> versal peace.[14]

By 1914 Gompers was already in the process of a slow turn when
he noted that "patriotism lifts men above the level of expediency"
and that the "man or the woman who gives ungrudgingly" in war
"brings us close to the beauty and purpose of life."[15] By 1916, so
that the American entry into the war would not create a condition
in which laboring men would be suppressed in an imminent mobilizing effort, Gompers assured the National Civic Federation:

> There are no citizens of our country who are more truly pa-
> triotic than the organized wage-earners. ... We have done

our share to protect the nation. . . . No one can question the value of the ideals that direct the labor movement.[16]

From this, Gompers and other AFL leaders would go on to express shock and horror at the "German atrocities" reported in the press and to speechmaking which encouraged the workers to believe that nationalist sentiments were morally elevated and virtuous.

This about-face was completed by 1916 as the United States appeared to be headed for involvement in World War I, and AFL leadership began to see in a wartime alliance with the government a means to secure some protection for labor.[17] This was because government leaders looked nervously to organized labor for cooperation in the coming mobilization effort and also because the war industries, spurred on by lucrative government contracts, staged a wild competition for labor as their needs for manpower increased dramatically. In 1916 Samuel Gompers accepted a place on the Council of National Defense, and as the AFL perceived all of the advantages of the new situation, a conference met on 12 March 1917, attended by 148 representatives of 79 AFL affiliates, the AFL Executive Council, and representatives from several unaffiliated unions (but which had been working within five AFL departments), and voted to give the government unqualified support in the event of war.[18] In all of this it was expected that government power would be used to intervene in such labor disputes as arose in the course of the war on behalf of organized labor,[19] and that representatives of organized labor would be rewarded with positions in government agencies where they could better assure that such intervention as occurred would benefit, or at least not damage, labor organizations. When the United States entered the war, Gompers could exchange a loyal and patriotic labor force mobilized for wartime cooperation for the outlawing of the use of the militia for strike duty, for more favorable government decisions in labor disputes, and for representation of organized labor on all government agencies formulating and administering national defense policy.[20] AFL representatives served on the War Labor Board, the War Industrial Board, the Fuel Administration Board, and the Women's Board. In addition, union membership was virtually doubled between 1915 and 1920.[21] The growth was especially phenomenal in industries directly active in war production.[22] It should also be noted that in addition to labor's improved situation during the war, labor leaders in posts of administrative or policymaking responsibility associated with government leaders regularly and on friendly terms. In view of all this, the reversal of AFL war attitudes and the relative advantages enjoyed by labor in its alliance with government during the war, we might have thought, as mentioned before, that voluntarism would have shown signs of erosion.

But there is evidence which shows that the government-labor friendship was regarded as a wartime measure, temporary, not meant to last, and finally no challenge to voluntarism at all. In the first place, the governmental machinery devised during the 1917-18 period for purposes of war planning and mobilization, and resulting in increased government regulatory powers, could have been at least partially maintained and given a civilian character. It was not, however, and almost certainly with labor's urgings, it was dismantled. In the second place, after President Wilson appointed Gompers to be chairman and one of two American representatives on a Commission on International Labor Legislation which was set up to establish an international labor organization (as part of the Peace Treaty of 1919),[23] Gompers participated while making many statements indicating that the glow of voluntarism had not faded in the least. Indeed, he tried to convert labor participants from all over the world to its leading assumptions. The result was his own confusion and frustration with the reaction of the European representatives. Samuel M. Lindsay, a close student of the International Labor Organization and the International Office it established, writes of this experience:

> Is it any wonder that Mr. Gompers as chairman, and the American delegates as members, of the Commission on International Labor Legislation, appointed by the Peace Conference in Paris, January 25, 1919, found themselves in strange company when they met with their European colleagues? ... Small wonder that their colleagues so often failed to understand them. ... They spoke a different language. The apostle of voluntarism ... was unable to make even his English-speaking colleagues understand his point of view. ... The difficulties growing out of this situation were largely due to the divergence of attitude toward labor legislation on the part of Americans dominated by the theory of voluntarism and of the European delegates, who accepted a positive theory of labor legislation. ...[24]

But despite the side issue of the frustration generated by voluntarist commitments at the international meeting in 1919, it was clear that the American labor leaders were unwilling to abandon or even modify them.[25]

It might still be argued, however, that surely the many AFL

statements made between 1919 and 1924 which gave support to the kind of "social legislation" formerly and consistently opposed by the AFL, and which on one occasion even supported the Plumb Plan for government control of railroads, indicated the mellowing of voluntarism and the onset of major transitions in the AFL point of view. This could be explained as the result of a developing radical insurgency within the AFL itself, pressing for reform and probably activated by a combination of factors like the expanded union growth of the wartime period and a series of bitter strikes which had occurred in coal and steel by 1920. Expansion created heightened expectations during the war, while these were frustrated by obstacles increasingly posed by government officials, employers, and economic recession after the war, factors which could certainly have activated the radical elements (meaning here mainly industrial unionists) within the AFL.[26] The fact is, however, that these statements turn out upon a bit of close examination to have been surface concessions to the insurgent element and a shrewd series of improvisations designed to preserve ideological and policy traditions intact.

After the war, reconstruction plans, it seems, were offered by government leaders, business leaders, labor leaders, and everyone interested in advertising some notion for the conversion of a wartime society to peacetime. Advocates of a full return to laissez faire vied for public attention, together with advocates of increasing government regulatory power over industry. The AFL joined in this general activity and promoted a "Reconstruction Program" of its own.[27] It stressed mainly the right to organize for labor; an "American" standard of living for all; reasonable hours of work; equal pay for women; the abolition of child labor; heavy limits on immigration; the right of union organization for public employees; the development of water power and transportation by government; a graduated tax on usable land over and above the acreage actually cultivated by the proprietor; free speech; improved workmen's compensation laws; a progressive income tax; a progressive inheritance tax; development of state universities; inclusion of labor as well as employers in administering employment agencies under municipal, state, or federal control as well as the further institution of such agencies under tripartite control; housing improvement; opposition to militarism; and generous rehabilitation and compensation programs for returning war veterans. But—and this is the crucial element which seemed to signal departures from voluntarism—it also advocated government ownership of public and semipublic utilities. Yet, a keen observer of the AFL, Lewis Lorwin, shrewdly pointed out that this statement was vague and "not specific about railroads, the only industry in which the issue was at all prominent."[28] Its vagueness, its placement behind more traditional priorities, made it clear that it was, in fact, little more than a sop thrown to the restless radicals within the AFL.

Later however, in 1920, the AFL went so far as to specifically approve the Plumb Plan for the control of railroads by the government (together with labor and employer representatives). But, significantly, this approval was given only after the strenuous protests of Gompers, Matthew Woll, and John Frey (the unflinchingly traditional voluntarists who had formulated the reconstruction plan which included the advocacy of government ownership of utilities) had been worn down and finally withdrawn. The furor of dispute made it necessary for them to make further concessions to secure support for the organization.[29]

Now, while the railroad controversy declined in fervor after 1920 and with the election of Harding to the presidency, unrest within the AFL continued to be stimulated by mounting government and employer opposition to unionization. It grew worrisome enough to the AFL Executive Council to force from it a series of concessions until 1924.

> Disregarding for the moment the tenets of voluntarism, the AFL committed itself to the nationalization of railroads, mines and public utilities. In 1921 and again in 1923 the Federation approved of old-age pensions. It also supported the Sheppard-Towner Maternity and Infancy Act of 1921, which provided for mothers' pensions and the care of infancy.[30]

In 1923 the report of the Executive Council to the Portland convention, entitled *Industry's Manifest Destiny*, alternatively known as the *Portland Manifesto*, sounded a call for worker representation in the destiny of industrial society on the basis of a partnership between workers and employers, wherein each, while not usurping the other's functions, would form one-half of a national economic or industrial council to plan for and direct industry.[31] Given the departures in attitudes toward some legislation between 1921 and 1922, and the prior concessions to a regulatory role for government in industry, the *Portland Manifesto* of 1923 appeared to be another radical step toward the abandonment of voluntarism and the adoption of national planning. Several of the more sensitive students of this situation agree, however, that the "Industrial

Council Plan" in the *Portland Manifesto* was left utterly unrelated to government ownership or regulation of industry. Not a word was uttered which even hinted at government participation in the scheme. In fact, it could be seen as a plan to decisively exclude government intervention in industry. It was, therefore, another bone thrown to the radicals while bolstering the voluntarist tradition.[32] As one scholar has it:

> The *Portland Manifesto* was, before all else, a desperate eleventh-hour improvisation to maintain the primacy of voluntarism.[33]

In 1922 the railroad unions had called a conference on political action which was held in Chicago. Representatives arrived from over twenty AFL international unions, eight state federations, and the Chicago Federation of Labor, in addition to representatives from the Socialist party, the Farmer-Labor party and some farmer organizations and religious groups. There the Conference for Progressive Political Action was established for the purpose of electing candidates who would promote labor's interests while in state and federal offices. This event was produced by a felt need to defend labor against the hostile atmosphere of the twenties. By 1924 the AFL went along with the decision of the conference (meeting in Cleveland that year) to nominate a third-party candidate for the presidency of the United States. This acquiescence came from the desire of the AFL not to become too isolated and to maintain at least loose connections with other groups. Senator Robert LaFollette of Wisconsin accepted the presidential nomination, and Burton K. Wheeler of Montana accepted the vice-presidential nomination. The AFL even went along with the platform of the conference which included, among other things, proposals calling for increased government regulation of the economic sphere. All this would tend to show that the AFL was abandoning traditional voluntarism. But appearances were as deceptive in this case as they had been in the case of the *Portland Manifesto*. This venture into party politics was accompanied by a public AFL statement indicating that its activity was not to be regarded as any shift in traditional policy whatsoever.

> Cooperation hereby urged is not a pledge of identification with an independent party or a third party, nor can it be construed as support for such a party, group, or movement, except as such action accords with our non-partisan political

policy. We do not accept government as the solution to the problems of life. . . . Neither can this cooperation imply our support, acceptance or endorsement of policies or principles advocated by any minority groups or organizations, that may see fit to support these candidates.[34]

The old-time voluntarists had upheld the "faith" and continued to hold sway over the AFL, especially strengthened in their conviction by the fact that the presidential campaign carried on by the conference in 1924 ended in failure.[35] This was accomplished by pursuing a strategy of concession to insurgent challenges and was greatly aided by the weaknesses and defeats of the challengers. In the prosperous industrial growth of the "New Era" between 1925 and 1929, despite the fact that an economic boom proved only a mixed blessing to organized labor, the AFL clung to its voluntarist convictions. The years after 1929, however, where to bring on the most severe challenges of all.

Notes

[1]For a particularly good and extensive summary of the history of the NLU, its demise, and the developments which immediately followed, see Gerald Grob, *Workers and Utopia.*

[2]While similar trends toward labor federation, especially among *craft* worker units, existed in England, France and Germany at this time, Gompers, who emigrated to America from England, was especially familiar with union trends in Great Britain and promoted familiarity with them among American workers with the results noted. Jt must be mentioned, however, that while the Parliamentary Committee of the British Trade Union Congress served the function assigned by the FOTLU to its legislative committee, the BTUC was more political than its rough American counterpart. For it would go on to organize the British Labor Party, a move which could never have been made or even accepted by the FOTLU or the later AFL which it brought into being.

[3]The AFL still regards 1881, however, to be its founding year. The masthead the *American Federationist* dates the AFL founding from 1881, suggesting that the events of 1886 were a mere development from 1881.

[4]Estimates about SLP membership vary, but most accounts agree that by 1879 the SLP had some 10,000 members and was still growing. See Carl Reeve, *The Life and Times of Daniel DeLeon*, p. 35.

[5]Ibid., pp. 40-41.

[6]Accounts of this event have become virtually standard in American labor histories. But for an especially clear and brief presentation of the facts see Nathan Fine, *Labor and Farmer Parties in the United States, 1828-1928*, pp. 138-39.

[7]See Benson Soffer, "Theory of Trade Union Development: The Role of the Automonous Workman," Labor History 1, no. 2 (Winter 1960): 141-63. This very useful study shows that craft workers strongly affected by the above mentioned factors steadily streamed into the AFL. In fact, Soffer points out further, that they often even acquired the power to supply employers with skilled labor, thus generating a certain employer dependence upon them. This study however was essentially meant as a critique of the idea that petit-bourgeois orientations or backgrounds among workers led them to resist or avoid unionization.

[8]This table is taken from ibid. In fact, because data on background of AFL members in the formative years is well nigh impossible to acquire, a good deal of the generalizing on this matter provided in the study is based on the research of Soffer. Sources of information and data for this table and for generalizations are available in a valuable appendix Soffer has added at the end of this study. It should be pointed out that under the heading "Causes of Autonomy" in the table, there is a category called "British traditions." While this refers to a manner of apportioning work and responsibility in given industries, even extends to include technological method, it remains unexplained in the Soffer study. The connections between autonomy and the AFL unionization are, however, drawn strongly enough so that this ambiguity does not detract from the main point.

[9]For statistical confirmation of the fact that the AFL was overwhelmingly an organization of skilled workers, and that craft worker predominance increased as the AFL matured (to the point where it became less and less representative of American labor) see James O. Morris, Conflict within the A.F.L, pp. 10-13. It might be added that this fact both reflected and encouraged a certain racism on the part of the AFL. See Bernard Mandel, Samuel Gompers: A Biography, pp. 140-42.

[10]Almost from its founding, the AFL confronted opposition to many of its policies from its socialist members. DeLeonites bolted the AFL by 1895 but others remained and were instrumental in pressuring the AFL into compromises with industrial unionism. In the course of fifteen AFL conventions after 1901, some twenty or more industrial union resolutions were introduced by city central bodies, state federations, single individuals like Victor Berger of the Socialist Party, by national union delegations, and by the federal or central labor unions.

[11]In 1901, with Gompers's "Scranton Declaration," a place was made in the Federation for the United Mine Workers' industrial union and the way was paved for further compromises with industrial unionism as pressures to make them arose. The declaration appeared in the AFL Convention Proceedings of 1901, see especially p. 240.

[12]Nothing in the foregoing, however, should be construed to mean that a craft worker-dominated labor organization, such as the AFL, is inherently incompatible with industrial unionism. For example, the Parisian Bourses du Travail, were sporadically at first, but firmly by 1886, organized on a basis and by workers similar to those of the AFL. The

Bourses were also composed along federation lines, with a strong emphasis on the strength and autonomy of union locals, and had a predilection for individualistic and voluntaristic ideologies together with a primarily craft worker membership. It too dominated the French labor scene at the time of its birth. The *Bourses* exhibited a much greater susceptibility to militant class consciousness and industrial unionism than the AFL ever did. This was so (not because of the "French character" often referred to in order to explain this phenomenon) because the *Bourses* had merged, by 1902, with the *Confederation General du Travail* (CGT) which had been founded in 1895. The CGT was committed to anarcho-syndicalism. It was moderate in its tone at first, in order to disengage the French labor movement from the well-meaning reformers and intellectuals it regarded as irrelevant, and to do so without seriously offending them. Also, it sought alliance with the more conservative *Bourses*. After the merger, however, much of the CGT became more openly revolutionary and advocated militant "direct action," though it retained in common with the *Bourses* a strong and unyielding hostility to socialist and other political parties and political organizations. Both the *Bourses* and the CGT were united on the idea that no outside force or group be permitted to use the labor movement for its own ends. But the attainment of leadership positions by militant CGT members in the merged organization gave the French federation a radical character unlike the AFL's. This accounted for the fact that the French craft workers favored building of labor unity on industrial union lines.

[13]Extracted from Robert W. Dunn, *The Americanization of Labor*, pp. 22-23.

[14]Samuel Gompers, *Labor and the Common Welfare*, p. 213.

[15]Ibid., pp. 213-14.

[16]Ibid., p. 217.

[17]In one book it is argued that Gompers, initially a pacifist in some sense, became nationalistic over time. This together with his dislike of German authoritarionism, his desire to use patriotic rhetoric to crush opponents and his scheme to acquire a voice in policymaking circles on foreign affairs, accounts even more than seeking gains for labor for AFL cooperation with government at this time. See Simeon Larson, *Labor and Foreign Policy*.

[18]*AFL Convention Proceedings*, 1917, pp. 73-78; also mentioned in John R. Commons et al., *History of Labor in the United States*, vol. 4, *History of Labor in the United States, 1896-1932*, Selig Perlman and Philip Taft, p. 403.

[19]Perlman and Taft, *History of Labor*, pp. 403-9, for an account of the government's War Labor Board in labor disputes which arose during the war. The net outcome was uneven but far from hostile to organized labor.

[20]Lewis Lorwin, *The American Federation of Labor*, pp. 142-45.

[21]Leo Wolman, *Ebb and Flow in Trade Unionism*, pp. 110-16.

[22]*See AFL Convention Proceedings*, 1919, p. 62; also Perlman and Taft, *History of Labor*, p. 410.

[23]Wilson had in mind when he took this action stemming a tide of labor unrest. By 1919 labor was actively discontent. The "Great Strike" in the steel industry was underway. See David Brody, *Steelworkers in America*, pp. 231-62. Such unrest was heightened by the depression of 1920. On the strikes of the immediate postwar period see Perlman and Taft, *History of Labor*, pp. 435-88. That Wilson acted in response to a postwar labor insurgency is stressed by George Higgins, *Voluntarism in Organized Labor in the United States, 1930-1940*, p. 41.

[24]James T. Shotwell, ed., *The Origins of the International Labor Organization*, pp. 338-39. This citation was first called to my attention by Higgins, *Voluntarism in Organized Labor*, p. 42.

[25]See Higgins, *Voluntarism in Organized Labor*, pp. 42-44 for an account of the issues over which Gompers clashed with the European delegates. Higgins concludes that "Gompers was sufficiently intransigent in his demands of the Commission to suit the fancy of even the most adamant of voluntarists."

[26]The "labor progressives" who had actively sought to promote industrial unionism, independent political party building, and worker education centers like the Brookwood College experiment had agitated since 1918 for change in AFL policies and an end to AFL obsequiousness in the face of attacks on unionism in the 1920s. Moreover, as compromises with the industrial unionism continued, starting in 1901 an industrial union element developed within the AFL and began to contend for power within the organization. Even Andrew Furuseth, president of the Seaman's Union, and O'Connell of the Metal Trades Department, who were not "anti-voluntarists" by any stretch of the imagination, were pressing for more militance on the part of the AFL and organizing, if need be, on industrial union lines. Much of the conflict was expressed around the AFL struggle with its Workers' Education Bureau and the figures centered around the WEB. See Morris, *Conflict within the A.F.L.*, especially chapter four.

[27]*AFL Convention Proceedings, 1919*, pp. 70-80; also the *American Federationist* 26 (February 1919): pp. 129-41.

[28]Lorwin, *American Federation of Labor*, p. 175.

[29]Higgins, *Voluntarism in Organized Labor*, p. 45. In general, Higgins follows a line of argument about voluntarism between 1918 and 1924 with which I agree.

[30]Ibid., p. 46.

[31]*AFL Convention Proceedings*, 1923, pp. 31-35.

[32]Higgins, *Voluntarism in Organized Labor*, pp. 47-51; Louis Reed, *The Labor Philosophy of Samuel Gompers*, p. 38.

[33]Higgins, *Voluntarism in Organized Labor*, p. 51.

[34]As cited in Lorwin, *American Federation of Labor*, p. 225.

[35]"Failure" in this context is relative. Data on how well the LaFollette-Wheeler ticket fared, considering the obstacles, has not been dealt with here. It is possible, that the failure of LaFollette-Wheeler to actually win office gave the AFL an opportunity to reaffirm its voluntaristic stance.

Chapter 3
A Year of Dilemmas: 1932

Challenges to the voluntarist outlook arising out of the crash of 1929 presented themselves with surprising slowness considering the fact that economic conditions deteriorated so rapidly and drastically. In fact, it was not until 1932 that some AFL leaders began to imply that Gompersian voluntarism did not provide a sufficiently full range of prescriptions for adapting to the new economic circumstances of the country. Even then, despite some discomforting suspicions, they sought formulas for the preservation of Federation traditions in the face of uncongenial conditions. The outcome of this effort, however, produced ideological dilemmas which would persist and haunt AFL policymaking for years to come.

It will be recalled that the voluntarist orientations of the American Federation of Labor had survived throughout the decade of the 1920s despite a series of temporary compromises which the Federation leadership effected with government agencies and with dissidents from within the ranks of the AFL itself. Moreover, the fact that the atmosphere of the 1920s proved so hostile to unionism seemed to validate voluntarist assumptions about the need to preserve a union movement free of dependence upon any external agent or authority whatever. This of course did not mean that the AFL formulated militant policies or carried out militant actions in the interests of protecting trade union autonomy. In-

deed, the very opposite was the case. The AFL became ob-
sequious in the face of so much public antipathy to "labor combinations." In addition, union-busting drives, which were not
uncommon and were carried out with relish, had weakened AFL
resolve. And "welfare capitalism," which impeded worker freedom of action and significantly inhibited the spread of unionization, also slowed down and alarmed AFL leaders with its effective
institution of employee representation on company grievance
committees, group insurance plans, recreational activities to at-
tract workers in their free time, and even low-cost housing units
near factories. Moreover, industrial mechanization was progress-
ing rapidly, especially after 1924, and the dread of "technological
unemployment" hovered over the AFL, as indeed over all of
labor. Even while the Federation urged a shorter workday and redistribution of work to accommodate everyone, it also felt pressed
to capitulate and urge worker conformity with the new demands
of mechanizing industry for high worker productivity, this as a
mode of securing the jobs of workingmen.

The AFL did not consider a policy of building new strength by
carrying unionism to the millions of unskilled and semiskilled
workers in the burgeoning mass production industries. Its own
craft unionist preferences as well as public hostility to unionism
kept the Federation skeptical about such a course of action. One
could go so far as to say that despite its pronouncements upon the
absolute need to maintain an autonomous, independent labor
movement, the AFL exhibited a marked timidity in adapting to the
hostile atmosphere; it was fearful for its survival and willing to
endure the state of paralysis into which the trade union movement had fallen in the "New Era" of prosperity during the latter
1920s.[1] Even though once-powerful organizations like the United
Mine Workers and the International Ladies' Garment Workers
were approaching disintegration, the Federation's national executive stoically endured. In fact, AFL leaders went so far as to actively ameliorate a hostile public with assurances that the Federation was made up of "decent" and "respectable" citizens who
would never behave in ways offensive to the great American public. Indeed, William Green, president of the AFL after Gompers's'
death in 1924, indicated in a speech he delivered before the Federation's 1928 convention that while the AFL was quite resentful
of the unjust and ill-informed attacks against unions leveled regularly and vehemently by the National Association of Manufacturers (NAM), it could not condone extremist actions and would
never associate itself with those who sought to destroy the public

liberties and civic traditions Americans cherished so highly. The AFL, he claimed, was composed of people who were much like other Americans in their detestation and disavowal of extremists of the communist variety as well as of the type the NAM exhibited with its fierce language.[2]

But AFL timidity through the decade of the 1920s aside, the fact that it also clung to its traditional voluntarism during this time robbed it of any capacities to logically conceptualize courses of action which could respond immediately to the disaster of 1929, either in the way of offering useful proposals for national action in the face of the emergency, or of devising ideas it might itself implement to survive as an organization in the distressful situation. For though the AFL was impressed by the vastness and profundity of the disaster, and it made some utterances about the need to increase government-sponsored public works in order to create jobs, even the need to dispense more relief to the country's most economically crippled citizens (going so far as to call for congressional measures to increase relief funds), for the AFL action could only be conceptualized in "classic" terms: workers were to unionize when possible and then protect the integrity of their unions against external interference.

But the relevance of this stance to immediate circumstances was surely tenuous. For one thing, with unemployment rising rapidly and by the millions, there were few "organizable" workmen and little in the way of union structures for them to protect. Then too, under the impact of voluntarism, AFL leaders saw society basically as a field of conflict between advantaged groups (essentially employers) and disadvantaged groups (essentially workers). Social stability and industrial justice issued from the negotiating activity undertaken by their "voluntary associations." But as it happens, *so too did economic prosperity.* Trade unions could compel the more advantaged employers to agree to an equitable redistribution of the economic resources they monopolized. In securing wages better suited to worker needs, labor would be enabled to purchase the products of industry. This kind of purchasing activity—periodically rejuvenated by union demands for redistribution—sustained business profits and expansion and was a veritable source for such wealth. Such stimulating business activity could only make jobs more numerous and improve the purchasing ability of the working mass still further with even more positive effects on the economic order. Should mechanization reduce the number of jobs at any given time with ill effects upon public spending, unions could negotiate the shortening of the workday and see to it that work was reapportioned to accommodate the whole work force and the redistribution-purchasing cycle might go on uninterrupted. Government had no role in all of this apart from sanctioning the procedures.[3]

Since voluntarism posited unionization as the key to all that was socially positive in industrial society, *including the key to recovery from business cycles*, the AFL hardly knew how to implement a major imperative of its outlook when, after 1929, workers, including union men, lost jobs in seemingly infinite numbers and were unavailable for union membership, whether on craft or industrial lines (besides, increased union drives were so very difficult to finance since AFL funds went mainly to relieve the distress of unemployed union members). For if unions were weakened to the point of ineffectiveness, what then could rejuvenate the economy? Could the government undertake far-reaching recovery initiatives? Yet if unionization was essential to recovery, what initiatives *could* government take apart from encouraging unions to do their socially beneficial work of redistribution? Apart from granting unions relief from crippling court injunctions and perhaps increasing public works to further job distribution, what else could be done that would not threaten citizen liberty? If the government legislated substitutes for union recognition in the interests of redistribution—such as welfare, social insurance, or other income-supplementing legislation—it would only distract or weaken labor, reducing its will to organize and permanently injuring its capacity to deal properly with employer opponents already monopolizing more advantages than they had a moral or perhaps even legal right to command.

Not only was it virtually immoral for government to incapacitate unions in this manner, it was not even an economically practical course of action. For even if employers were taxed to provide revenues for such incoming-supplementing government measures, they would remain free to pass on such costs to a consumer public, of which labor was a part. Workers would wind up paying these costs and the value of the supplement would be diminished. The point of such action will have been defeated. Consequently, nothing other than firmly negotiated contracts between unions and employers for higher wages among other benefits could be trusted as a practical form of redistribution. When this could not be implemented, the society seemed doomed to economic disaster. With unionization frustrated, a condition of economic recovery was destroyed. The AFL, then, could conceive of no positive recovery action that was dramatic, broad, or varied enough to

meet the severity of the circumstances of 1929; and it drifted leth-
argically along for several years with whatever was deemed acceptable by the Hoover administration, especially since little
would be done by Hoover to extend government's authority over
the industrial sphere.

In 1932, however, two dramatic events occurred which rendered voluntarism, already somewhat muddled, subject to outright confusion. On the one hand, Congress passed the Norris-
LaGuardia Act and President Hoover signed it on 23 March. On
the other hand, an antivoluntarist minority within the AFL momentarily achieved enough influence to force the Federation to
accept, at least as a temporary measure, the formerly unaccpeta-
ble idea of unemployment insurance. The first of these events led
to an affirmation of voluntarism, and yet to a certain relaxation of
its antistatist tenets. The latter led to some ambiguities and alter-
nation in its terms. The result was an ideological ambivalence
which compromised old traditions without actually destroying
them.

The Norris-LaGuardia Act was the most far-reaching antiinjunction legislation ever enacted in the United States. Essentially
it indicated that government, at least Congress, was slowly but
definitely gaining an awareness that citizenship rights in a corporate industrial society involved the practice of group combination for the attainment of self-interest, and that this right belonged
especially to those threatened or disadvantaged by industrial development. For example, previously the labor-employer work
agreement, that is the "work contract," was seen in terms applicable to pre-Civil War America, as a formal expression of consensus
between free, autonomous equals for an exchange of goods and
services on mutually advantageous grounds. Labor combinations
appeared as an unnecessary or intolerable interference with this
freedom of contract. Now, it was finally coming to be accepted
that under the conditions of corporate capitalism, employers monopolized all bargaining advantages, making the voluntarists'
equality assumption applying to contracts a mere formalism and
demonstrating that labor combination was, perhaps, inevitable as
a result of this fact. This awareness is clearly expressed in the
"statement of policy" at the outset of the Norris-LaGuardia Act.

> Whereas, under prevailing economic conditions, developed
> with the aid of governmental authority for owners of proper-
> ty to organize in the corporate and other forms of ownership
> association, the individual unorganized worker is commonly

helpless to exercise actual liberty of contract and to protect his freedom of labor, and thereby to obtain acceptable terms and conditions of employment, wherefore, though he should be free to decline to associate with his fellows, it is necessary that he have full freedom of association, self-organization and designation of representatives of his own choosing to negotiate the terms and conditions of his employment, and that he shall be free from the interference, restraint or coercion of employers of labor... in the designation of such representatives or in self-organization or in other concerted activities for the purpose of collective bargaining or other mutual aid or protection.

The act goes on to outlaw the "yellow dog" contract (where workers sign statements promising never to associate with unions as a condition of employment) and place significant restrictions on the use of injunctions in labor disputes.

Now despite voluntaristic admonitions about law and government action with respect to industrial conflict, some positive role for both had long been identified by the AFL and it was, as we have seen, chiefly that of promoting, or at least allowing, independent and unobstructed bargaining between organized groups in the industrial sphere. Government might best fulfill this role by issuing statements urging unions and employers to come to terms, that is, by harmonizing contending industrial groups by persuasion. It might make such statements effective by promoting the idea that unions were legitimate organizations entitled to represent labor's interests to employers. This it could do best by granting statutory labor recognition or at the very least, granting labor unions relief from court injunctions, thus removing a severe obstruction to union self-assertion. The Norris-LaGuardia Act was in complete accord with such AFL prescriptions, with the result that even the most adamant voluntarists could hail its passage. This they did without reserve. As early as 1928 William Green could state that securing an antiinjunction bill was the first order of AFL business without inviting discord or dispute in Federation ranks.[4] Even longer ago than that, in 1914, the staunch voluntarist John Frey, of the AFL's Metal Trade Department, had said:

We have tried in this country, as workingmen have endeavored to do in others, to secure through legislation a guarantee that our rights to organization and to trade union effort should not be interfered with ... This has been one form of legislation which the trade union movement has most heartily and effectively applied. We have endeavored through legislative enactment to have our rights as free men guaranteed so that we could apply our trade union method to regulate the terms of employment.[5]

Given this long tradition of accepting legislation designed to restrict the use of injunctions against labor in industrial conflicts, it should occasion little surprise that the AFL was so receptive to it. Indeed, it was widely known that Federation personnel expended some effort lobbying in order to secure it. Thus, the enactment was greeted with enthusiasm from Federation leaders. Some caution, however, was expressed about the possibilities of its being improperly implemented. As a federal statute it applied only in federal courts, and it was desirable that supplementary state legislation be passed so that injunction relief would be available for labor in state courts. Then too, the terms of the law would still entail judicial interpretation and labor must remain vigilant in safeguarding its new opportunities for liberty of action:

> Our educational work must be continued until judges and lawyers understand the facts of our economic world which are involved in questions for judicial decision.[6]

The AFL nevertheless recognized the purpose of the act to "give labor a more equal opportunity for justice and industrial progress." It conferred nothing less than a "privilege" to engage in constructive union building.[7]

Yet the fact that the terms of the Norris-LaGuardia Act were consonant with the drift of AFL thinking did not prevent some interesting changes from taking place in the language in which the Federation spoke of government. Its antistatist rhetoric was somewhat dimmed by the successful passage of the act, given that government had actually fulfilled a role the AFL had regarded as proper for it. Having enacted the new legislation, government would serve to harmonize contending industrial groups, especially by legitimizing all of the "voluntary organizations" in the industrial sphere struggling for a resolution to industrial conflict and leaving them free to carry their true weight—unhampered by unjust and crippling burdens—to a negotiation process and there to establish the terms of social peace. Not only would government be fulfilling its appropriate role because it gave a certain legitimacy to trade unionism when the injunction bill passed Congress, it also is the case that the whole "industrial citizenry" would be given an opportunity to act in better accordance with voluntarist prescriptions as a result of such legislation. The natural or proper "end" of participants in industry was self-organization into autonomous groups for the purpose of establishing a just balance of economic power. As long as one of the parties (namely, employers) could instrumentalize outside agents (like government) in their own service, the other party (that is, workers) would be too overpowered to make sure that stabilizing balances were established. Thus the Norris-LaGuardia Act, by reducing the likelihood of this unbalance, would make a voluntarist policy truly workable on a broad social scale. It was greeted enthusiastically by the AFL on voluntarist grounds with the result that AFL emphasis on a negative view of the state was vastly reduced.

The passage of the Norris-LaGuardia Act produced in the AFL nothing less than a campaign to applaud and promote the government's new willingness to advance voluntary intergroup bargaining in the industrial sphere. Within weeks after 23 March, editorial statements authored by William Green appeared in the *American Federationist* which welcomed a "new" coordinating role for government. With unprecedented certainty about the virtues of such coordination, the paper noted:

> This is preeminently a period of associated activity; the corporate form of ownership; the dairy instead of the family cow; the packing company instead of the local slaughter houses; the bakery instead of home bread-making; community play centers instead of the family yard; the municipal clinics instead of home remedies. The individual depends upon a number of industries for the necessaries of life; each industry depends upon other industries; until the very degree of interdependence constitutes a social and economic change. The problems of working and living together involve new elements and develop new needs. To promote the successful working out of these various problems for the promotion of human welfare, government exists. It becomes the agency through which associated and related activities are coordinated.[8]

Indeed, all talk hostile to a broadening of government power in economic affairs was now said to suffer from a certain "confusion." What mattered above all was the *quality* and not the quantity of government actions in the economic sphere. If the outcome of such action is better industrial coordination, then governmental action is vindicated:

> During recent years considerable concern has been expressed over the broadened functions of government. Persons with the "business mind" talk forcefully against government in business; the reformers against business in government. Others are fearful lest the government usurp the responsibility of individuals and weaken individual initiative. These fears are based on confusion of the functions of a democratic government with those of an autocratic government. An autocratic government seeks to impose arbitrary authority usually for the advantage of a limited group while under a democratic system the government is a coordinating agency for collective action.[9]

In all of this praise for the government's "coordinating" role, however, it must be remembered that the AFL referred to government positively because it permitted economic groups the freedom and legitimacy to carry on their bargaining activity without outside interference. At no time did the AFL associate government "coordination" with government "arbitration" or "intervention" in the industrial sphere. That is to say, government freedom to act in relation to industrial affairs was conceived in essentially negative terms. It could merely sanction industrial self-regulation by initiatives designed to promote bargaining between labor and capital toward the achievement of healthy economic balances. It could not take positive regulatory action with respect to setting production, wage, hour, or other standards and it could not arbitrate in industrial disputes. It is true that government could go so far as to expend energies providing jobs for an increasingly desperate work force.[10] But its essential function remained that of harmonization and coordination of the citizenry by promoting their bargaining interaction. No new agencies, arbitration boards, or complicated and dubious enabling legislation needed to be constructed for government to carry out this task. All that was required were persons of "wisdom" and "vision."[11] This point was frequently made. A leader of stature rather than a revision of government structure promised to implement the coordinating activities of the government.

> In times of emergency we turn expectantly for leadership to the one official who is able to coordinate all interests and groups and to take hold of a situation to control and direct

development. We want a man in that office who has not tied his hands by weakness or indiscretion—a man who understands the problem of the wage-earner who can find no way to earn his living, as well as the problem of the bank which must be ready to pay depositors. Maldistribution of the proceeds from work has brought us into dire difficulties. Great sacrifices must be made in order to get us out. We need a leader with the wisdom to see the key logs to the jam that is holding back business and with the courage and organizing ability necessary to break up the obstacles.[12]

It should be noted, however, that the need for persons of political talent was stressed in part because 1932 was a year for presidential election. Federation leaders were actually willing at times to concede that something other than "good men" would be needed to guarantee the smooth functioning of government coordination. The AFL expressed a belief that substantially more money should be made available to government so that it could properly "coordinate" the larger society. At the 1932 AFL convention, the Executive Council's report contained a section entitled "Government" which states that in a modern and complex society, like that in the United States, government will acquire increased functions and require increased funds to carry them out properly. These "increased functions," however, do turn out to be only those of coordinating social groups by promoting their constructive interaction and greater responsibilities for data gathering and information dispensing.[13] And thus it is very difficult, after all, to say precisely how much the AFL wished to add to the requirement that good political leadership implement government coordination by sheer insight. Was its request that more money be placed at the disposal of government a reflection of a subtle drift toward accepting enlarged government power? Was it, perhaps, an indirect plea for large appropriations for the Department of Labor, to strengthen and enlarge its staff, its statistical bureaus, and expand its activities? Perhaps it referred to a need for improving relief-dispensing procedures in view of increasing public demand for alleviation of economic want. It appears only in association with the vague idea that firming and improving government coordinating capacities is necessary and is never made concrete as a specific demand or preference for some given policy or outcome.[14] Still, while the request for more government money's meaning remains unclear, it should be considered a product of the positive and hopeful feeling about government generated by the passage of the

Norris-LaGuardia Act—without being taken too seriously as encouragement for increasing governmental power to intervene in industrial life and affairs. It should also be considered primarily as an AFL effort to make some suggestions about how government coordination might be implemented in terms a little more firm than those which call vaguely for good men to undertake the great tasks of the day.

Thus, voluntarism, which had long been capable of accepting certain kinds of government actions (those which promoted, or at least did not obstruct, the union movement), when actually confronted by them, found an easy peace with them. Yet despite a tendency to suppress its antistatist rhetoric in favor of a stress upon the virtues of government coordination, this stress did not involve the abandonment of long-held assumptions. The Federation did not need to make allowances for new government roles or powers involving arbitration of industrial disputes or regulation of economic affairs. Its nonpartisan political policy and its disdain for political activism remained intact. This was expressly affirmed at the convention in 1932 when the Executive Council stated "and we again recommend that the nonpartisan policy . . . be continued."[15]

It is true that acceptance of government coordination might have proved infinitely flexible, eventually capable of connoting government planning and economic regulation. In fact, talk of industrial planning was ambiguous enough to accommodate the idea. Events which will be discussed at length later prevented this from happening, with the result that the Norris-LaGuardia Act did not initiate an AFL need or trend to revise its traditional attitudes toward law and government. Still, it should not be forgotten that "coordination" did remain an open and flexible notion, full of possibilities for revised attitudes toward government authority and not decisively antistatist. That no Federation leader pursued these possibilities in 1932 is significant, but so is the fact that voluntaristic rhetoric became charged with such possibilities. As the future would show, possibilities for revised attitudes toward government authority would become more difficult to suppress or define out of existence.

The Executive Council's report to the 1932 convention indicated how little the AFL's fundamental conception of the proper function of government authority had changed. Yet it also contained a proposal to accept unemployment insurance legislation, with suggestions for its implementation. The recommendation stood in flagrant violation of all that the AFL traditionally had stood for.

Moreover, the Executive Council's proposal was approved and passed by the convention.

How was it possible to believe that government ought to remain external to industrial affairs, and certainly that it refrain from weakening unions with income supplements, and yet to invite and support the passage of unemployment insurance legislation? Surely this was inconsistent with voluntarist premises and certainly a perverse thing to do while at the same time affirming the validity of such premises. In fact, the record even shows that staunch voluntarists protested against unemployment insurance at the very convention which resolved to accept it. The leathery old delegate of the Seamen, Andrew Furuseth, expressed a widespread feeling when he cried out against the Executive Council at the convention of 1932:

> Your responsibility here is frightful. I will not share the responsibility with you in the recommendation to pass your resolution . . . . If you can see no other way out, all right. . . . I can't stop you, but the road you are travelling is the road that leads to the destruction of humanity and . . . of the nation and of all other nations that can find no other way than to make out of a man a pleading beggar and a man who must go for his goods to others.[16]

To understand how this departure from voluntarist traditions could occur, it is necessary to consider the context in which the Executive Council's proposal was made and in which the convention approved the measure. Unlike the AFL's reactions to the Norris-LaGuardia Act, the AFL decision on unemployment insurance was inexplicable when considered simply in the light of its ideological traditions.

A debate on the issue of unemployment insurance had, in fact, been building up after the 1929 AFL convention in Toronto. In that year the Executive Council referred favorably to hearings held by the Senate Committee on Education and Labor on an unemployment bill introduced by Senator LaFollette. The council accepted the recommendations of this committee, particularly the one which declared that there was no need at that time for federal unemployment insurance plans.[17] Little objection was raised from the floor of the convention. By 1930 at the Boston convention, five resolutions favoring unemployment insurance were submitted by AFL delegates. At that time the Committee on Resolutions indicated its traditional voluntarist sentiments when it presented these resolutions for consideration to the convention:

> The issue presented is one of vital importance. It involves the question of whether the American Federation of Labor shall continue to hew to the line in demanding a greater freedom for the working people of America, or whether liberty shall be sacrificed in a degree sufficient to enable the workers to obtain a small measure of unemployment relief under government supervision and control.[18]

Moreover, the committee, by continued use of the word "dole" in reference to unemployment insurance, indicated that the AFL national leadership would not seriously entertain the abandonment of its voluntarist commitments. This touched off a heated debate as challenges from the floor arose against this attitude. The delegates of the "deviant" Wisconsin Federation, with a history of socialist sentiment unusual in the AFL and along with a number of socialist leaders who supported and lobbied for social legislation in that state, resented the committee's attitude. Also, delegate Slavens from Rhode Island pleaded for a change in the AFL attitude, while delegate Zaritsky of the Cloth Hat and Cap Makers Union urged similar reconsideration. The debate was nevertheless temporarily quashed as the convention adopted the report of the Resolutions Committee recommending nonconcurrence in the resolution.

At the next convention, held in Vancouver in 1931, the controversy became intense. Three resolutions were submitted in favor of unemployment insurance. The Resolutions Committee once again recommended nonconcurrence in the resolutions and stated that acceptance of such insurance would lead America's workers to surrender their liberty. This was too much for the delegates from the state of Washington, one of whom arose to disclose that 90 percent of the miners in his local favored unemployment insurance. Delegates from the Meat Cutters, the American Federation of Teachers, and the Post Office Clerks arose to challenge the committee. Even Daniel Tobin, influential leader of the powerful Teamsters Union, spoke in support of the resolutions. A substantial and increasing number of voices within the AFL were coming to consider unemployment insurance with favor. All had stressed that the "voluntary principle" would become a mere formalism and insupportable rhetoric if it were posed to American workers who could not find in it relief from severe economic suffering. Their strength was not to be underestimated. Louis Stark, a specialist in labor reporting for the *New York Times* present at the Vancouver convention, said:

> When the viva voce vote was taken the opponents of unemployment insurance were unmistakably in the ascendant. What a roll-call would have disclosed is a matter of speculation. There were thirty thousand votes in the convention. Speaking with one who is conversant with the sentiment of the various international unions, supplemented by information gained directly by inquiries after the vote had been taken, I was led to believe that a roll call would have disclosed something like eleven thousand to twelve thousand votes for unemployment insurance, a more than formidable minority.[19]

Finally, at the 1932 convention, the Executive Council took new initiatives and came out in support of unemployment insurance in its report before controversy could break out on this matter on the floor of the convention. Now all of the old-line voluntarists were shaken. They charged the Executive Council with hypocrisy no less than with self-deceit in imagining that voluntary principles were consonant with unemployment insurance. John Frey reminded the convention that this step endangered union building because workers would be placated by government-dispensed benefits and would lack incentive to join and strengthen unions. In this regard, he recalled to the delegates the words of an old unionist who is supposed to have said:

> I want to tell you this, men, that if you feed lions cooked meat they are not going to roar. If you want the lions to roar you have to hold raw meat under their noses. . . . The way to get these wage-earners interested in the trade union movement and make it a driving force is to convince them that, in addition to the self-protection that they should have through trade-union organization in the shop, it is only through the fighting strength of that economic organization that you are going to get higher wages and shorter hours.[20]

AFL president William Green replied that securing legislative measures to relieve the strains of unemployment did not exclude the struggle for a strengthened unionism, better wages, the shorter workday, or anything else. Nevertheless, the convention delegates hotly pursued the question of whether union efforts should be focused on securing wage and hour reform through negotiation with employers or on securing economic reform through legislation. Delegate Donelly of Ohio spoke of his experience on a commission to secure a state unemployment insurance law in Ohio and indicated that he regarded both goals as compatible. Yet Howard, of the Typographical Union, doubted the feasibility of such legislation and could not recall where in the world it had ever been a success. Green maneuvered uncomfortably between supporters and opponents of unemployment insurance, trying to bring about reconciliation. The numerous supporters of tradition were stung and smarting. The convention did approve the measure backed by the Executive Council. It even did so with the strong support of the United Mine Workers, which had presented a full and favorable report on unemployment insurance to the convention.[21]

During the year 1934 systematic and straightforward statements on unemployment insurance, the manner in which it ought to be applied, and the amounts of payments to be made to workers under specified conditions, had become common in the pages of the *American Federationist*.[22] All previous objections to the measure had apparently been laid to rest (although it should be borne in mind that the AFL took little action to actually secure it).

It is obvious that the AFL leadership supported unemployment insurance in order to prevent it from becoming a source of serious disunity in Federation ranks. Its promoters were gaining in number and economic conditions were continuing to provide them with a basis for their claims. It was inevitable that the issue would become a serious threat if permitted to remain open and unresolved. Yet, while support for unemployment insurance was intended to move toward AFL unity rather than away from voluntarism, the traditional assumptions of the AFL could not remain unaffected by the maneuver. It could hardly make this departure from tradition without rationalizing it heavily. In doing so, traditional notions could not remain intact and unchanged.

First and foremost, the very idea of unemployment insurance had to be made compatible with unionism. That is, AFL leaders were pressed to explain why what was formerly regarded as corrupting was now consonant with the integrity of unionism. The Executive Council showed itself quite sensitive to this problem. It said of itself:

> The Executive Council has always endeavored to guard jealously the organization structure of the American Federation

of Labor. For that reason the Council was apprehensive over the effect which compulsory unemployment insurance legislation might have upon the exercise of the right of working men and women not only to join but to maintain membership in trade unions.[23]

One way in which the council sought to relieve apprehension was by devising an unemployment insurance plan which would contain a guarantee that to be eligible for insurance benefits, unionists would not have to accept work at any time "contrary to the rules and regulations of their organizations or employment under conditions such as tend to depress wages or working conditions."[24] Another way was reflected in the lengthy report on unemployment insurance which was presented to the convention by a delegation from the United Mine Workers. There it was argued, first, that unemployment insurance was a limited measure which would not make the worker's struggle for self-improvement through unionism any less important than it had always been. Shorter hours, job security, higher wages, and other benefits remain to be won and much work, therefore, remained before the unions to undertake. Second, unemployment insurance was no novel idea. It had many precedents at state and local levels of government, in foreign countries, and even *union benefit funds might be construed as precedents.*

> An unemployment fund is no new idea in our country, although it is only lately that it has become the subject of serious legislative consideration. The German-American Typographical Union has had an unemployment benefit since 1884. In April, 1931, forty-eight labor unions had in operation various systems of unemployment relief covering about 35,000 workmen.[25]

All of this was in addition to reserve funds set aside by some fifteen industrial corporations for the "benefit of their unemployed." Pointing to union and employer systems as models, to the systems of Belgium, England, Germany, and the Irish Free State, to such state and local reserves in America which may have been applied to unemployment relief, it was concluded that this wide range of experience showed that neither citizens' liberty nor the workingman's appetite for self-improvement were negatively affected.

> It seems foolish to say that unemployment insurance will operate against the organized labor movement. The great

purpose of union labor is to bring all our workers the American standard of wages and working conditions. Attainment of this objective through the organization of labor is frustrated by the preponderating pool of unemployment. The pressure . . . for jobs coupled with the fear of many of those employed that they may lose their jobs, constitute the real barrier to the organization of all industrial workers.[26]

Not the existence of a government hand to relieve economic stress, but the continuing existence of massive unemployment was a menace to free men and to the union movement. In fact, this statement contains the insinuation that job scarcity set workers against each other, made the employed more nervous about securing what gains they had, and reduced the inclination of the unorganized to take any risks at all on behalf of unionism. Thus, a total absence of financial security was more of a menace to the public liberty and worker organization than government-dispensed insurance funds distributed to tide workers over periods of unemployment.

But by this reasoning union membership could be made compatible with *any* kind of social insurance as long as eligibility did not depend on accepting conditions below union standards. Moreover, all types of social insurance, being merely supplementary to a main source of income derived from work, would be too minimal to preclude union pressure for improvement of working conditions. All kinds of private and public charitable distribution could serve as precedents for income supplementation. Finally, it could be argued that if minimal security was in fact a precondition for further unionization, then increases in amounts of such security, if not range and coverage, would add further to the cause of unionization. By what criteria, then, could the AFL rule out acceptance of any other kind of welfare or insurance benefit sponsored or funded by the government, aside from unemployment insurance?

The AFL failed to establish standards by which unemployment insurance, but not other kinds of government-distributed benefits, could be accepted. After all, Federation leaders could not anticipate the fact that the future would bring the Social Security Act into being. They imagined that the door had been closed on this issue and that the most important need of the moment was the offer of assurances to the membership, and especially to the opposition "purists" like Andrew Furuseth and John Frey, that neither the world nor unionism would be thrown into chaos and tyranny by unemployment insurance. The reasoning applied to reduce the threatening appearances of the insurance proposal was so broadly applicable, and no clear criteria had been established by which unemployment insurance but not other types of welfare or insurance legislation would be accepted, that voluntarism was rendered ambiguous and questionable. In fact, the report of the United Mine Workers on unemployment insurance, in an attempts to stir the convention to support of the controversial measure, concluded on a note which clearly bristled with antivoluntarist overtones.

> Neither the arguments nor the power of organized labor have led to the stabilization of industry. Let the power of the state be directed to this end.[27]

Thus, in the process of exhorting the convention on behalf of a controversial measure, with the primary intention of securing Federation unity, the ideological personality of voluntarism became ambiguous, uncertain, and diffuse as the Executive Council, and others cited, grew more partisan in defense of the insurance proposal.

On the one hand, then, support for the Norris-LaGuardia Act had provided occasion for AFL affirmation of voluntarism. On the other, the issue of unemployment insurance pushed the Federation close to negating it. Yet even the voluntaristic basis for supporting the injuction bill led the AFL to perceive government in sympathetic terms. Congress had led government to fulfill the main function allowed to it by voluntarist tradition. The Federation was inclined to praise this kind of government role. It thus deemphasized its antistatist vocabulary and brought to the fore that rhetoric which supported the role of coordination. The result was that the tenor of voluntarist antistatism was reduced to a lower key. If considered together with the dilution, if not subversion, of voluntarist tenets which was the outcome of the unemployment insurance controversy, one could get the impression that the AFL did not have an ideology apart from a confused acceptance of notions becoming popular with a diffuse majority of Americans.

During the 1920s, especially after the death of Gompers in 1924, the AFL raised no militant slogans or brightly colored banners. Compromise was a keynote of the times for the Federation. It is also true that government, and particularly employer policy, was so hostile to unionism that voluntaristic attitudes could survive quietly on mistrust of their acts and intentions. Thus, stubborn antistatist and antilegislation principles could be reasserted despite surface compromises. However, by 1932, when government seemed to play a "new" role, the "proper" one assigned to it by AFL tradition, the affirmation of voluntarist notions no longer involved negation of government behavior. The AFL could adapt to the situation without harboring rancor or reservations. Toleration or acceptance of a given government policy no longer stemmed from a mistrustful and skeptical timidity. Yet this fact diminished the firmness of voluntaristic notions and engendered, or at least opened the door to, possibilities involving a more positive view of the government. Finally, the pressures which forced the Federation to accept unemployment insurance at its 1932 convention reduced the clarity and consistency of AFL thinking.[28]

With clarity diminished and consistency deeply disturbed, was it possible for voluntarism to survive as a distinct view of events capable of informing or guiding Federation policy toward definable ends? Even if it could, would its somewhat lamed condition make the AFL vulnerable to further compromise or confusion as its traditions continued to be strained by contemporary pressures? Some answers to these questions are available in an examination of AFL attitudes toward the National Industrial Recovery Act passed in 1933.

Notes

[1]See Irving Bernstein, *The Lean Years* for an account of the incapacities of unionism in the decade of the 1920s.

[2]*AFL Convention Proceedings*, 1928, p. 608.

[3]For statements illustrating this association of ideas as the key to economic difficulties see editorials which appeared in the following: *American Federationist* 36, no. 12 (December 1929): 1430-31; ibid. 37, no. 7 (July 1930): 789; ibid. 38, no. 1 (January 1931): 21; ibid. 38, no. 7 (July 1931): 802; and *AFL Convention Proceedings*, 1932, pp. 22-30, 34-35. This view persisted and even gained emphasis in 1933. By then the AFL was willing to consider the Depression as a phenomenon to have been caused by a failure to fund workers, through their unions, with a purchasing capacity sufficient to stabilize the economic system. See the *American Federationist* 40, no. 4 (April 1933): 342.

[4]*AFL Convention Proceedings*, 1928, p. 7.

[5]*AFL Convention Proceedings*, 1914, p. 424. It should be mentioned, however, that in 1914 the heralded Clayton Act was passed, a piece of legislation about which the AFL enthused that year. A more skeptical attitude did set in after the disappointing experiences with the Clayton Act.

Still, the hope for favorable legislative treatment of labor's right to organize survived, and even played a role as a motive in the AFL's cooperation with the government during World War I.

[6]*American Federationist* 39, no. 4 (April 1932): 378.

[7]Ibid.

[8]*American Federationist* 39, no. 6 (June 1932): 620.

[9]Ibid.

[10]*American Federationist* 39, no. 7 (July 1932): 730

[11]Ibid.

[12]*American Federationist* 39, no. 8 (August 1932): 857.

[13]Executive Council Report, *AFL Convention Proceedings*, 1932, pp. 74-75.

[14]*American Federationist* 39, no. 10 (October 1932): 1340-41.

[15]*AFL Convention Proceedings*, 1932, p. 374.

[16]Ibid., p. 336

[17]*AFL Convention Proceedings*, 1929, pp. 84-85.

[18]*AFL Convention Proceedings*, 1930, p. 311.

[19]As cited in Higgins, *Voluntarism in Organized Labor*, p. 66.

[20]*AFL Convention Proceedings*, 1932, p. 342. Frey went on to elaborate at length on his belief that the shorter workday rather than any kind of social insurance was the soundest basis for recovery. See pp. 341-344.

[21]This of course, did not mean that approval and support of the measure by the Executive Council left no residue of doubt in the minds of any of its members. In 1933, for example, William Green asked John Frey, who was planning a trip to England, to observe, while there, whether unemployment insurance and "relief measures employed by the State retarded or accelerated the growth of Trade Unionism" (James O. Morris, *Conflict within the AFL*, p. 271.)

[22]See especially William Green's editorial, *American Federationist* 41, no. 12 (December 1934): 1292-93.

[23]Executive Council Report, *AFL Convention Proceedings*, 1932, p. 40.

[24]Ibid. p. 41.

[25]*AFL Convention Proceedings*, 1932, p. 327.

[26]Ibid. p. 334.

[27]Ibid., p. 334.

[28]The 1932 convention even showed that the AFL had little to say about its central value—unionization. Appeals to expand unionism were brief and mechanical in tone. See Executive Council Report, *AFL Convention Proceedings*, 1932, p. 92. This may have been derived, however, from the fact that AFL membership was falling rapidly in 1932. Membership then stood at somewhat over 2.5 million. In 1931 membership was close to 2.9 million. But in 1920, it had reached nearly 4.1 million.

Chapter 4
The AFL Views the NIRA

The National Industrial Recovery Act (NIRA) became a national law on 16 June 1933. It was supposed to create a system of economic planning capable of accomplishing two apparently incompatible objectives: (a) the preservation of a certain traditional competition between business enterprises (considered necessary for high achievement in the industrial sphere) and (b) the promotion of close business cooperation for the purpose of regularizing market and production activity, stabilizing prices, and restoring public confidence in the American economy. Under its provisions the president was empowered to request that business associations, often together with labor representatives, develop codes of fair competition for their respective industries to include price, production, wage, and hour standards. The law also delegated unprecedented peacetime power to the president, for under its terms he could—through duly authorized agents—police and punish violators of established industrial codes. He could even impose codes upon industries which did not hasten to formulate their own in order to cooperate in the alleviation of the national economic emergency. Moreover, all codes were subject to presidential approval and the president was also authorized to set up an appropriate bureaucracy (the National Recovery Administration) to administer the terms of the act.[1]

93

Despite the fact that a great hue and cry was raised against the measure from various congressional quarters, especially against the sweeping powers it delegated to the chief executive, a number of streams of popular thought about economic recovery converged to form a strong current of support and acclaim for it.[2] These drew an initial strength, perhaps, from the climate of opinion brought about by an "overproductionist" understanding of the causes and cures for economic depression which had long circulated among businessmen and professional economists.[3] Nevertheless, they moved large sectors of the public to sympathetic acceptance of the National Industrial Recovery Act.

Generally speaking, overproductionism was a stream of economic thought which stressed the overexpansion of industries producing capital goods (as distinct from consumer goods) as the causal factor in depression. Basic to overproductionist assumptions is the idea that during a prosperous period there is an inevitable growth of industries producing capital goods which exceeds what is warranted by economic circumstances. Because of the excess, reduced investment in the capital goods sector is inevitable. The excess may come to light because of monetary factors, because backward areas of the country have reached, temporarily, a maximum growth limit, because of population changes, or because fluctuations in consumer goods production cause changes in the production of capital goods. In any event, production of capital as compared with consumer goods is "unbalanced" and depression is to be avoided or cured by restoring balance. This is another way of saying that better adjustment of capital goods production to social conditions is a means of gaining control over business cycles.

In many circles this general view implied that there was in the United States an excess of producing capacity so that when markets for given commodities were reduced, by a decrease in demand or other difficulties, many industrialists could find no outlet for a vast quantity of their goods. This led to laying off workers, which in turn reduced the purchasing power of the consuming public with drastic results for the economy. Even before the depression there had been talk of the so-called "sick industries" (mining and textiles), those which had experienced a rapid expansion during and immediately after World War I and which found great difficulty in adjusting to a contracting postwar market. It was considered desirable, therefore, that industrial production be better adjusted to public demand.

How could this be accomplished? By the time the recovery

measure was receiving serious presidential consideration, over-productionist assumptions had stimulated three kinds of solutions popular among businessmen, government administrators, and academic intellectuals; each was seen to provide a principle by which industrial balance might be maintained.[4] All three were foisted upon the president and written into the Recovery Act. The act could represent or appear to embody each of them; thus vigorous mobilization of support for it from business leaders, government figures and professional lawyers, and economists (among others) became possible.

One notion (which harkened back to Brandeis and Wilson, even to the Sherman Act of 1890) suggested that the maintenance of a healthy balance between public needs and industrial production was a matter of reducing the power of the trusts to glut the market in fits of rapacious greed and curbing their will to destroy competitors for a share of market activity. Even more than this, what was required was nothing less than the restoration of smaller businesses as the dominant units in industrial production and distribution, as well as restoration of lively and free competition between them. Here lay the natural and genuine corrective to economic imbalance. Smaller industrial units would be technologically or legally incapable of amassing resources for "overproduction" while, at the same time, they would be well enough equipped to service public demands for useful goods. Indeed, the influence of such restoration would be so salutory that government planning for economic stability, a dangerous practice at best, would be rendered unnecessary. Sections of the NIRA calling for code provisions against "unfair competition" could be seen as a political effort to revive an older competitive ideal; yet all who shared "antitrust" sentiments, like Felix Frankfurter, Thomas Corcoran, Benjamin Cohen, James Landis, to name only a few, could endorse—and later work to implement—the Recovery Act with hopes that the era of big business would fade into the past together with the economic devastation it wrought in the land.

Directly opposed to antitrust "restorationism" was a view which had become highly popular with influential businessmen during the 1920s and which the National Association of Manufacturers devoted itself to developing in books and pamphlets during this period. It held that industrial concentration and the growth of great business corporations was a function of technological progress and enlargement of both markets and populations. To oppose the historically inevitable with irrelevant or outmoded antitrust measures and slogans was worse than useless—it was destructive. It made the efficient servicing of millions of people difficult, if not impossible. Besides, economic balances were attainable without resort to such drastic and ill-founded measures. Let Congress and the courts of the land but permit it, and businessmen could, through their trade associations, cooperate to overcome any overproductive possibilities of modern industrial technology. They could, in fact, set production and price standards conducive to the economic benefit of all. Take away the taint of conspiracy from such cooperation and big business would find formulas for economic vigor and good health in which all might share. Moreover, this too would remove or reduce any need for government planning, an unsavory idea offensive to free people and potentially full of danger. Men like Gerard Swope, vice-president of General Electric, and other prominent business figures like Malcolm Rorty, Henry S. Dennison, Fred Kent, and Albert Deane, professional economists, former members of the War Industries Board with a pro-big business bias like Bernard Baruch and General Hugh Johnson, all espoused the trade association governance of industry. They envisioned America as an emergent cartelized business order in which the industrialists would plan and direct economic affairs. Government would have little to do besides punish and remove incorrigible "chiselers" from the economic field so that they would not obstruct or discredit the beneficent work of the trade associatons.

Gradually the attack on the antitrusters found its way into Congress and into bills that would, for example, prohibit sales below cost, establish resale price maintenance, create economic councils, and give statutory legitimation to the Federal Trade Commission's procedure of encouraging conferences among trade associations on business practices rather than formulating such standards and enforcing them on congressional initiative. President Hoover had feared the presence of "monopoly" in all this and refused to cooperate in the promotion of plans, like those drawn up by Swope, to make "cartelization" possible. But under the Roosevelt administration, exponents of an industrial commonwealth governed by trade associations were able to write some of their ideas into the NIRA. The vital provisions in the Recovery Act which enabled the associations to write their own codes and enforce them through public law, with minimum government intervention in the process, were the result of their handiwork (Gerard Swope and Bernard Baruch, among several others of this school of thought, were key figures in the formulation of the act). Ultimately, then, the business commonwealth "visionaries" and all who shared a positive view of industrial concentration and business self-governance found the Recovery Act entirely acceptable and supported it as the embodiment of their own creed.

Standing between the antitrusters and the trade association cartelists were the "democratic planners" represented chiefly by Rexford Tugwell and to a somewhat lesser extent by Senator Robert Wagner (both harkening back to the years between the turn of the century and 1929 when figures like John Dewey, Father John Ryan, Charles Van Hise, and Herbert Croly sought a compromise between political democracy and industrial concentration). According to them, industrial concentration was both inevitable and, at least potentially, a beneficent way to organize a society's economic life, for it could reduce the uncivilized ferocity of competition characteristic of small enterprise. It could also reduce the waste which resulted from the unplanned economic activity of innumerable small business proprietors. Moreover, it permitted outright industrial cooperation and coordination in the public interest. It did not do this, of course, because it "naturally" brought forth industrial leaders possessed of superior capacities to address the common good. Rather, large-scale industrial operations created a network of interdependency throughout the whole economy so that industrialists could not afford to ignore the well being of the larger population. Their own ruin would follow if they did. Sheer self-interest on the part of big producers in the age of big industry forced public-minded industrial cooperation into being.

But to make the most of the beneficent possibilities of industrial concentration, it was necessary to do several things. In the first place, laws or customs which prevent industrial producers from engaging in healthy cooperation, on the grounds that they are "conspiring" against the public or to suppress "free competition," will have to be modified, or at least applied only in unusual instances of true conspiracy. This, however, will not be adequate in itself (whatever the wishes of the utopian cartelists). For the era of big industry has also permitted a dangerous tendency to develop, which, if unchecked, can provoke economic depression and the incalculable suffering which attends it. It has permitted big industrialists to totally monopolize industrial policymaking. That is, their decisions in this realm have been allowed to reign absolutely, without input or criticism from the rest of the population. As a result, any narrowness, shortsightedness, or miscalculation in their reading of public demand, to which they must be heavily prone for want of involvement in the daily lives of masses of people, strongly influences industrial planning and distribution. As a further result, goods that no one wants or needs may be "overproduced" and may flood the market. People may not buy them and business profits and investments may fall off as a consequence. Jobs may be lost, and so on until full-blown depression may have spread across the land. For this reason, some curtailment of the influence of industrialists over industrial policy is required.

More particularly, all kinds of groups which have developed out of the business civilization of America—small businessmen, labor unions, consumers—need a voice in the decisions of industry so that production and distribution can be closely harmonized with their needs and circumstances. "Big industry" requires the voice of "little people" in its operations so that adjustment of industrial production to public consumption might be properly effected. Thus, while relaxation of antitrust laws is essential in order to give business leaders an opportunity to coordinate production and market activities on behalf of economic stability, it is also necessary that this coordination be done through industrial "councils" which include representatives from labor organizations, consumer groups, from the community of professional economists, engineers, and others, so that industrial policy does not become a mere reflection of the interests, ideas, and even errors of large producers. This might even entail curtailing the ability of large producers to determine their own profits and investments exclusively according to their own desires. But in the end they would be greatly advantaged by the economic stability that would result from more democratic, conciliar industrial decision making. The fact that the NIRA allowed, as we shall see below, for group representation in the code-making process made it possible for advocates of democratic planning to put their faith in it.

Thus, the National Industrial Recovery Act appeared to be a piece of legislation promising sweeping industrial reform along lines which businessmen, government personnel, professionals, and intellectuals could accept despite considerable divergence in their views. All but the most hardened opponents of industrial reform, or those who rejected industrial capitalism per se, felt represented by the recovery measure when the president signed it on 16 June 1933. Would the AFL support a measure which was not only popular with a wide variety of labor's opponents but which also permitted a heavy governmental hand (through the presidential office) in the workings of industry?

The federation greeted the passage of the NIRA with unquali-

fied enthusiasm. In fact, nothing less than soaring romanticism
seems to describe its reaction.

> Now swells the glad voice of the nation,
> Now breaks the bright dawn of a new day;
> Black hopelessness yields to elation,
> Exultant thy cry, NRA!
>
> Lo, labor again rolls its thunder,
> Lifts choral in vast roundelay;
> Lo, powers of greed fall asunder,
> By blue eagle rent, NRA!
>
> Behold o'er the airways of heaven,
> Or deep where men delve in earth's clay,
> Upon the far seas, one to seven,
> Are spread thy broad wings, NRA!
>
> The hosts of mankind now are stirring,
> In freedom from fear's blighting sway;
> Equator to pole sounds the whirring,
> Of azure-hued wings, NRA!
>
> Ride on! To the stars throw thy pinions,
> With light of truth blaze thou the way,
> Thy call reaches all man's dominions,
> Proclaim a new age, NRA![5]

This initial embrace of the administration bill stemmed from several closely related factors. For one thing, if overproductionist assumptions popular in business and other circles fostered a
number of widely held opinions which, at least as of 1933, proved
compatible with the Recovery Act, this also proved to be the case
with "underconsumptionist" assumptions which had been, in a
diffuse way, popular with the AFL for many years. This should be
explained at some length, for it will not only shed light on a source
of Federation enthusiasm for the recovery measure, but it will
also caution against careless association of underconsumptionism
per se with welfare legislation only. Indeed, the AFL's underconsumptionism revealed some strikingly hostile inclinations toward
welfare legislation.

The general outlines of the AFL's underconsumptionist view
are discernible from examining editorials and other public statements made by leaders of the AFL. Briefly, they assert that as popular purchasing of consumers' goods was increased in the course
of industrial development, industrial funds have been used by
those who command them mainly for capital investment or the en-

largement of personal savings. Thus, the cream of industrial wealth has simply been accumulated by the "monied classes," and the laboring or "consuming public" has been left without adequate capacity to purchase what is produced for sale (and, presumably, for its use or need). In sum, the AFL view was that a vast share of national income in industrial society goes to the well-to-do (mainly employer) classes who have either saved large portions of this money or invested it in capital goods. Too small a share goes back into the hands of the masses of laboring consumers. The AFL felt that while the injustice of this situation should be obvious, so too should its destructive, depression-causing consequences.

The union leaders also felt that what was needed to offset or eliminate this condition was a return of funds into the hands of the laboring consumers (the majority of the population)—precisely to the degree that the wealth of an industrial nation was enlarged—so that the consumers may do their necessary and proper share of purchasing in the industrial system. Increasing funds could not be permitted to go primarily into savings or investment by "the rich" (or big employers). Therefore, the AFL favored expanding wages at the expense of industrial or entrepreneurial profits. How was this to be accomplished? The method was quite simple: award regular wage increments to the laboring public and provide those agents instrumental in securing these (like unions) with positive encouragement and legal recognition (quite unlike the Keynesian versions of this view which stressed stiff income taxes upon the wealthy and government expansion of social and welfare services and public works as the means to overcome underpayment of the public rather than simple wage increments and legitimization of unions). For the AFL, government did not need to intrude to directly tax the wealthy, to set up elaborate social insurance or welfare systems in the interests of achieving a proper distribution of wealth.

It should be borne in mind, however, that an underconsumptionist perspective was not elaborated by Federation spokesmen in systematic theoretical form. Rather, it was a loosely related set of broad and general notions, expressed largely in the form of specific demands for specific economic measures to be taken on behalf of economic stabilization and especially on behalf of improving the workman's lot in society. For underconsumptionism did not yet enjoy a real vogue among professional economists in this country upon whom AFL leaders or members, persons untrained in economics, might have drawn to develop it with any real sophistication. Sismondi, Malthus, and Hobson had promoted some nascent form of this view. But it became professionally respectable and influential only after John Maynard Keynes developed and systematized it into a highly coherent body of theory in his *General Theory of Employment, Interest, and Money*, published in London in 1936. And the influence of Keynes upon professional opinion in the United States really set in only as the depression years neared their end (and he was probably more influential toward the close of World War II than at any time during the depression, myths about this notwithstanding).

Now, this crude but definite underconsumptionist view of economic affairs motivated the AFL to support the National Industrial Recovery Act. This was so mainly because the recovery measure encouraged the participation of labor (more specifically, union representatives) in the making of industrial codes which were expected to regularize production, pricing, and other activities (like setting wage and hour standards for labor) in given industries. And as such it could be seen as an invitation to labor to help set standards of recompense for work which would increase the consumer-workman's capacity to purchase needed or desired goods on the market. That the Recovery Act was seen as such an invitation, one awaiting full implementation by the Federation on behalf of sound economic sense, is made evident by statements at the AFL's 1933 convention:

> Labor maintains. . . that if the Recovery Act is to achieve its purposes—jobs for the unemployed and increased buying power—representatives of wage-earners must have a voice in every stage of code-making. Inequitable distribution of income and unemployment were the result of an industrial control from which labor was excluded. We cannot expect to reverse these two causes of economic disaster unless specific provisions are made for wage-earner representation and participation in every stage of control. The American Federation of Labor declare[s]. . . labor representation in every stage of code hearing before the National Recovery Administration. . . .[6]

But the AFL's underconsumptionist attitude was only one (and not the major) factor which led it to embrace the NIRA with enthusiasm. Another was the fact that the new law would relax the terms of the Sherman Anti-Trust Act (for reasons already given or implied), a piece of legislation which had repeatedly been used against labor combinations (in addition to whatever other uses it may have served to curb business combines). For, as was mentioned elsewhere, the Sherman Act provided grounds upon which many injunctions suits could be brought against unions. Indeed, even during the early thirties, the Debs case, the Danbury Hatters case, and others, remained lively memories among AFL members.[7] And yet another factor in the AFL's embrace of the NIRA (and this was undoubtedly the most important factor of all, for reasons that will be obvious) was the fact that the Recovery Act included the famous Section 7(a), granting statutory recognition to trade unionism in an unprecedentedly direct way. This development had been the result of AFL pressure as well as efforts by such "democratic planners" as Senator Robert Wagner and the personnel working with him to help frame the NIRA.[8] Also, President Roosevelt was inclined to accept this in order to maximize a national consensus around the recovery measure, especially since the AFL Executive Council made it absolutely clear and certain that the Recovery Act would be unacceptable to organized labor without such a provision.[9] William Green was even invited to help draft a labor provision which, in terms reminiscent of the Norris-LaGuardia Act, read as follows:

> Sec. 7, (a) Every code of fair competition, agreement, and license approved, prescribed, or issued under this title shall contain the following conditions: (1) That employees shall have the right to organize and bargain collectively through representatives of their own choosing, and shall be free from the interference, restraint, or coercion of employers of labor, or their agents, in the designation of such representatives or in self-organization or in other concerted activities for the purpose of collective bargaining or other mutual aid or protection; (2) that no employee and no one seeking employment shall be required as a condition of employment to join any company union or to refrain from joining, organizing, or assisting a labor organization of his own choosing. . . .

At any rate, the inclusion of a provision which expressly recognized unionism (rather than just primarily reducing injunction burdens upon labor) provided the AFL with a tremendous incentive to support the Recovery Act.

However, crucial as Section 7(a) was in securing AFL support for the NIRA (this point will be explored further), it is important for purposes of this study that we focus more attentively upon yet an additional factor which promoted the Federation's stance. This was the fact that the recovery measure could be grasped by the

AFL as legislation congenial to its own voluntarist predilections about industrial regulation. For codes of industrial standards and behavior were, according to NIRA provisions, to be formulated and written by the major actors in industry *themselves*, industrialists and unionists (though often together with input from a congressional representative of the "public"). In this, the terms of industrial life would be set, the Federation felt, directly by those who would be immediately governed by them. Such codes were, it is true, subject to presidential approval, but they were on no account to be actually formulated or written by the president (unless, of course, industrial participants stiffly refused to compose them independently). As such the AFL could understand the NIRA to be a species of governmental encouragement for employer-employee regulation of the industrial sphere by mutual conference, bargaining, and negotiation.[10] Indeed, the NIRA could even be seen as bringing to a higher fulfillment the "coordinator" role that voluntarism had determined was a proper one for national government. This is not to say that the AFL exhibited *no* qualms over the fact that the president had been empowered by the NIRA to require the creation of codes, punish violators, and establish an elaborate bureaucracy to implement the terms of the act. It was felt that all of this had some potentially dangerous implications. It was necessary to take a calculated risk, however, since the specter of still more dangerous possibilities lurked behind the economic chaos of the time:

> The National Recovery Act was designed to meet the emergency resulting from the banking collapse and business breakdown. It was proposed, discussed and enacted under the shadow of great fear. . . . Two courses of action were possible: either to assume control as a dictator or to secure voluntary cooperation to avert national bankruptcy. The Administration proposed a measure for industrial recovery, following the second course.[11]

But given that the bargaining behavior encouraged by the NIRA was in fundamental accord with traditional AFL preferences, and given too that a provision sanctioning unionism was included in the act, fears about the enlargement of presidential power never loomed very large and were readily soothed by the belief that labor representation in industrial code making was likely to be an adequate counterforce to all possible evils.

The net effect of the AFL's support for the Recovery Act upon its voluntaristic outlook was, at least at the time of the passage of the Act in 1933, very like the effects resulting from its support for the Norris-LaGuardia Act. Its sympathy for the recovery legislation and the legislation's encouragement of trade unionism and bargaining between the groups immediately involved in industry produced in the AFL a tendency to speak of government in positive terms. In fact, it was inclined to see government as an especially prestigious "coordinator" in industrial affairs, that is, as a "chairman" presiding over meetings between industrial "partners," capital and labor.

> This one course is practicable—cooperation for the promotion of mutual purposes. This is the essence of the thing we are trying to do through the National Recovery Act—the establishment of a real partnership in industry under the *chairmanship* of government. . . . Partnership and cooperation is the way to solve our industrial and social problems. It is the practical application of economic intelligence. Such a partnership can function only by interpreting past experience for a guide in future decisions. . . . With such procedure in the spirit of good-will there will emerge a government in industry conforming to human principles of democracy and the ethical standards of Christianity.[12]

And the Executive Council's report to the 1933 AFL convention states more clearly: "We are entering an industrial period of conference with the Government as chairman."[13]

It should be stated, however, that the term "chairmanship" to describe the government role in promoting industrial balance and harmony never appeared to have connoted something especially distinct from "coordination." It seemed to function only to give the Federation an opportunity to confer especially positive approval upon governmental coordination and to place particular emphasis on its value for bringing about voluntary bargaining between labor and employers without threat of government intervention in their disputes or negotiations.

In sum, because traditional notions about government power and legislation held by the Federation were not challenged by the NIRA—indeed appeared to be fulfilled by it—the AFL could approach government in traditionally voluntarist terms. Yet such terms did not take the form of denouncing state intervention in industrial life, but rather were cast in rhetoric which supported a governmental role of coordination, or "chairmanship," in the industrial sphere.

Because of all this it might be concluded that the ambiguities which had begun to make voluntarism diffuse and unclear in 1932 had been resolved or banished, and that the Federation's capacity to formulate policy more or less consistent with its traditions had been restored and strengthened. The appearances of 1933, however, were to prove deceptive. For by 1935, after the Recovery Act had been in operation for two years, the AFL was to find itself as uncertain, ambivalent, and factious about its traditional ideological premises as it had been in 1932. While passage of the NIRA contained elements which encouraged AFL tradition in ideology and policy, its actual implementation by the bureaucracy created to carry out its terms—the National Recovery Administration (NRA)—brought powerful pressures to bear against tradition. Once again the Federation would prove unable to make its ideological commitments decisive, clear, or consistent.

The AFL's Executive Council and the leadership of its most important unions felt that the benefits of the NIRA would be realized only if unionism were invigorated and expanded. Section 7(a) especially made it seem that the Roosevelt administration sanctioned the idea that restoration of economic good health demanded economic redistribution through a growth in labor organization and through an increase in labor representation on councils established to create industrial codes acceptable to labor and employers alike. In fact, the "labor provision" even made it seem that the AFL had a heavy *obligation* to expand the influence of trade unionism among the unorganized on behalf of the economic good of the nation.

> Conscious of the fact that lack of organization among wage earners had been a major factor in the unbalance in distribution of national income which was one of the causes of our economic breakdown, labor regarded the passage of the National Recovery Act as imposing an obligation upon wage-earners to organize into trade unions.[14]

In keeping with this understanding, William Green called a meeting in Washington for all presidents of affiliated AFL unions on 6 June 1933, just ten days before President Roosevelt signed the Recovery Act. At this conference it was decided that labor should strongly participate in the formulation of industrial codes through boards set up by the NRA, indeed, that labor unions should have exactly equal representation with business in this process. Moreover, labor standards the Federation might agree to in collective bargaining should become part of the standards established in industrial codes. And finally, wherever possible labor representatives in code-writing boards should insist on the thirty-hour work week as a necessary standard for industry. Green then issued an appeal to America's unorganized workers to join unions as a matter of public duty, one that was sanctioned by the government. He also sent messages to officials of all AFL-affiliated bodies, urging them to launch intensive organizing campaigns. Despite all of Green's activity, however, John L. Lewis, president of the United Mine Workers, may be correct in seeing himself as the great dynamo behind all of these efforts to realize the promise of Section 7(a).[15] For Green was always cautious and slow to act decisively. Nevertheless, organizing on a great new scale would soon be under way.

While many businessmen around the country had found the NIRA generally acceptable, the inclusion of Section 7(a) (just weeks before the act became law) worried them, and the Federation's clear signal that on the basis of it a great organizing drive would be carried out created a furor among them. The National Association of Manufacturers (NAM) took up the cudgels against the provision and all of its implications. James A. Emery, appearing for the NAM before hearings of the Senate Finance Committee between 22 May and 1 June (shortly before the act was passed), made clear the hostility of business to Section 7(a). The Iron and Steel Institute representatives showed themselves equally virulent. The provision was amended several times in congressional attempts to please all parties. The AFL, however, succeeded in warding off versions which would have seriously diluted the provision. But as the AFL organizing upsurge got under way, the NAM led the attempts to formulate employer policy for dealing with it on employer terms. Unsuccessful in its effort to secure amendment of the labor provision, the NAM now set out to adapt Section 7(a) to its own ends. As Irving Bernstein describes it, the NAM proceeded as follows:

> The Association on August 8, 1933, distributed to its members a notice to employees for posting on plant bulletin boards. The Act, they were told, does not attempt to describe the kind of organization, if any, with which "employees should affiliate." It was not the intent that "employees should pay money into any organization." Constitutions of company unions were printed in large rounds and distributed to employers about the country.

On September 22 the Law Department of the NAM issued a bulletin of interpretation of Section 7(a) as a guide to conduct. The employer remained free to bargain on either an individual or collective basis and, if he chose the latter, might refuse to make an agreement with an employee organization. The employer could ask an applicant for work whether he belonged to a labor union, might deny union officials access to company premises, and was at liberty to advise the employees against joining a trade union. Section 7(a) "has made an important change in the law as to closed shop agreements, and such agreements are now universally void." The company union "form of collective bargaining," the NAM advised, "is legal now, as it was before the passage of the Recovery Act." Further, the employer might legally offer his employees a special inducement, such as group insurance, in order to persuade them to join the company union.[16]

The National Metal Trades Association and the steel industry followed the NAM lead. Company unions were set up all across the country, on the grounds that Section 7(a) did not compel accordance with given types of unionism. Some idea of how this movement developed is given in studies undertaken by the National Industrial Conference Board (NICB). In November 1933 the NICB made a nationwide survey to determine to what extent collective bargaining had progressed under the NIRA.[17] It was found that 45.7 percent of employers were still dealing individually with their employees, 45 percent were dealing through "employee-representation" schemes (a euphemism the NICB used to refer to company unions), 9.3 percent were dealing with labor unions. The percentages of 1933 remained surprisingly stable in 1934 despite increasingly bitter battles waged by the labor unions, a stability accounted for by the fact that company unionism was "holding on." Further NICB study led to the conclusion that "union membership may have grown as rapidly as some have claimed, but such gains are not reflected in the proportion of employees dealing through labor unions."[18] The NICB, in yet another report, further cited a Commerce Department study which noted:

> It is difficult to make an entirely satisfactory estimate, but it is not unlikely that the membership of company unions, which was estimated at 1.3 millions at the end of 1932, was between 2.5 and 3 millions at the end of 1934.[19]

A Brookings Institution study of the NIRA even states that it was

one of the ironies of history that Section 7(a), presumably intended to enlarge the legal opportunities for independent
self-organization, should have thrown the obstacle of company unionism more directly and ominously than ever across
the path of the A.F.L.[20]

None of this is to deny increases in trade union membership
rolls between 1933 and 1934. Between the summer of 1933 and the
winter of 1935, the AFL added nearly one million members to its
ranks. The average paid up membership for 1933 was 2,126,796,
and as of August 1935, membership totaled 2,823,750 and was still
climbing.[21] But it was obvious that company unions, claiming legitimacy under Section 7(a), were also growing rapidly and posed a
severe challenge to the labor movement.

As the company union phenomenon spread, the AFL became
even more determined in its organizing zeal. At the same time
government leaders, particularly General Hugh S. Johnson, the
chief administrator of the National Recovery Administration, and
Donald Richberg, the general counsel of the NRA, refused to clarify the terms of Section 7(a) to indicate whether company unionism was included in it. Both insisted that it was government policy
to stand aside from the labor-employer struggle (an ironic turn of
events) and to secure "fair play" for all the parties. Finally they
issued a number of joint public statements which proved worse
yet.[22] They insisted that employers were obligated equally toward
representatives of all labor groups. Not only were employers to be
impartial toward all labor groups, but both company and labor
unions might even exist in the same plant, each bargaining on its
own behalf with the employer (thereby sanctioning the open
shop). Even further, they stated that neither management nor
labor representatives were obligated to assent to any given proposals from either side. Employers especially did not need to actually conclude a contract with a union to fulfill their obligations
under the law. They merely had to manifest a readiness to confer
and negotiate with all employee representatives.

Other disappointments followed this administrative interpretation of the law. The labor unrest which was surging forward led
the Industrial and Labor Advisory Boards of the NRA to urge
Roosevelt to establish a labor disputes procedure, preferably a
National Labor Board under the aegis of the Recovery Administration (with Senator Robert Wagner at its head). It was launched
on 5 August 1933, primarily to settle labor-management differences by holding hearings in the interests of allowing the board

to reach a decision about the appropriate resolution in a given case of conflict. But the board had no power to actually compel or enforce compliance. Its members could only emphasize the duty to bargain as a dual obligation: of workers to offer terms of com-promise prior to a strike and employers to confer with the workers' freely chosen representatives in good faith.[23] By Oct-ober, several companies had refused to appear at the National Labor Board hearings. In two major cases, that of the Weirton Steel and the Budd Manufacturing companies, the board was openly defied and left paralyzed.[24] The incapacity of the board to compel compliance (other than chiding the disobedient compa-nies and refusing them "blue eagle" emblems, awarded when companies complied with NRA standards) or to take a stand on the open shop (influenced in this by Johnson and Richberg) ren-dered the board inept.

Continuing labor unrest and the imminence of a general strike in the steel industry forced the passage of Public Resolution 44, under which the president established another National Labor Relations Board, and a series of special boards for separate indus-tries outside of the NRA (but under the terms of the NIRA). By 1934 the National Labor Board, functioning under the administra-tive wing of the NRA, surrendered decision-making authority to the National Labor Relations Board established by public resolu-tion to handle collective bargaining aspects of industrial conflict. What followed was a study in bureaucratic chaos.

As if business opposition, company unionism, bureaucratic con-fusion, and the refusal of the NRA to openly sanction unionism were not enough, organized labor found itself increasingly frus-trated in attempts to secure adequate representation in code-mak-ing precedures. As code making increased, it came under the domination of the business trade association. The great consensus which had emerged around the NIRA when it was passed had been steadily eroding, and policymakers representing several lines of thought about its meaning were in a state of perpetual squabbling and dispute over its *ultimate* meaning, changing their minds, redefining its purposes, and making the formulation of a clear government policy impossible. Ellis Hawley put it this way:

> In the background of the National Industrial Recovery Act, then, were three visions of the ideal business structure, three analyses of the depression, three lines of policy recom-mendations, and three sets of policy subscribers, each con-vinced that the other two were basically wrong. The policy of

enforcing competition, said the planners and business ratio-
nalizers, was outmoded, intellectually bankrupt, and a prov-
en failure. The vision of a business commonwealth, said the
antitrusters and national planners, was only a mask for the
proven evils of private monopoly. And the idea of democratic planning, said the antitrusters and business planners, was
a contradiction in terms, a policy that could only result in the
eventual destruction of political democracy, property rights,
individual liberty and the capitalist system.[25]

As early as 1934, it was clear that the writing of codes had deteriorated into a bargaining process with little direction, while the
goal of setting industrial "standards" had been growing more
hazy and distant as a result of the fact that firmness and clarity
had been lost among government representatives.

Essentially, the writing of codes was a bargaining process;
and those that bargained for the government had no set policy to follow. In the early days, as one commentator put it,
policy enunciations were "like the folk lore of the ancients,
. . . transmitted, for the most part, orally and based on the
sometime cryptic recommendations of the Administrator."
Actual policy depended largely upon the judgments and
sympathies of individual deputy administrators; and these
judgments and sympathies naturally varied from man to
man, depending on the deputy's background, the way in
which issues were presented, and the political pressures inherent in the underlying power structure.[26]

With government representatives in the Recovery Administration confused or immobilized, business domination of the code-
writing process became virtually inevitable. Few others could
master the economic and political power of business leaders, and,
most important, General Hugh Johnson had himself long sympathized with the cartelist outlook and encouraged business leadership in the implementation of the law. Moreover, most of Johnson's key subordinates had come from military or industrial
backgrounds and shared cartelist business views and approaches
to recovery problems.[27] The result was little more than a "bargain
between business leaders on the one hand and businessmen in
the guise of government officials on the other."[28] Under the circumstances, the wage and hour provisions in the codes were rid-
dled with loopholes and exceptions while labor representation on
the code authorities was kept to a bare minimum.

Increasingly the Recovery Act became an instrument of cartelization, and it was not long before the AFL leaders and members
expressed their resentment. At the 1934 AFL convention it was
suggested that labor was greatly underrepresented in code making; that the NRA was providing aid and comfort for company
unionism; that the labor boards were either inefficient or hostile
to labor; and, it were not known whether General Johnson was
just a simple fool, at least it was clear that Donald Richberg was a
traitor (he had formerly been a labor attorney). It was reported
that the workers were patient men and would continue to hope for
the best, but that the NRA was straining their patience—and perhaps the AFL should not support the Roosevelt administration
after all, for labor may just be better off organizing a party of its
own. Perhaps the president meant well, but he just did not know
how extensively the NRA had snarled itself up.[30] The range of reactions went from benign puzzlement to outright anger.

At first, disappointment with the NRA's implementation of the
Recovery Act activated the Federation's old ideological "in-
stincts." That is, there was a subtle but sure revival of antistate,
antipolitical insinuations in the AFL's voluntarist rhetoric:

> The experience of the past few months under the National
> Recovery Administration makes plain that political agencies
> are not a substitute for economic organization mobilizing
> and directing economic power.[31]

The one role which voluntarist tradition had allotted to government had failed to prove either durable or workable. The time
had come, then, to recognize that little besides unionization
would avail workingmen.

> It would be a very innocent and naive person who supposed
> that the operation of the existing codes in the coming months
> will serve either to increase money wages or to check the
> increase of prices of goods. In general, the probabilities are
> pointing strongly in the other direction. So much for the
> codes as now existing; and no one supposes that by reopen-
> ing the codes and beginning a new round of dreary public
> hearings we shall be able to cause money wages to rise as
> fast as prices. Our hope lies rather in organization and col-
> lective bargaining.[32]

This point was made both repeatedly and obsessively and often
simply hammered out: "The really effective course of action open

to us is to organize and organize and organize more."[33]

In brief, the side of voluntarism which permitted government and its agencies a role, however minimal and limited to coordination, was slowly turning from plain sight, and the side which insisted that all political agents keep their distance from the industrial sphere was coming into view.

Yet this ideological turn was not to be complete. For even as an antistatist feeling was insinuating itself once again in the statements of AFL leaders, an anger against the power of businessmen was growing so strong and righteous that the AFL was, perhaps for the first time in its history, willing to consider with sympathy government measures which would institute machinery for the *arbitration* of industrial disputes, a consideration which would clearly violate the voluntarist past. While the AFL reaffirmed repeatedly that it trusted mainly itself and that labor's protection, salvation, and fulfillment would come only from its own organizing will and strength, it did not place chief responsibility for the failures of the NIRA at the door of the Roosevelt administration. Businessmen had subverted the Recovery Act by thwarting unionization and undermining labor representation in code making, and something needed to be done to curb their authority to determine all the terms of industrial life. Government had provided an "industrial constitution," as it provided a political constitution, for the guidance of the industrial citizenry.[34] Industrialists and workers committed themselves to this covenant. It had been the heads of industry who broke with it.

Based as it was on good faith, on trust in the good intentions of labor and employers, a betrayal of trust left the NIRA meaningless. Government was important for want of adequate machinery to punish the business violators and compel them to live up to the terms of an act to which they gave promise of obedience. Even the foolish or inefficient labor boards were really broken more by business ill will than anything else. Government wanted for once little else but the voluntary cooperation of labor and employers, and employers thought little of flaunting the government's wish and denying labor its rightful place in the national recovery effort. Perhaps the trouble was, after all, the need for better governmental machinery to compel business compliance with the act, more especially to compel businessmen to recognize unions as legitimate bargaining representatives for millions of workingmen.[35]

Thus, the AFL began to edge toward the idea that government ought to be given some chance to strengthen labor dispute machinery to see if the employers could be brought to their senses, or barring that, to make them pay for their violations. This strong surge of antibusiness sentiment promoted Federation interest in using the instruments of government against the power of employers. The outcome of events connected with passage of the NIRA was, then, to drive the AFL to think in two directions at once. When the policies of the NRA were under consideration, a faith in self-reliant unionism, free of government intervention and free of dependency upon outside agencies, was intensified. When employer behavior was contemplated, the AFL expressed unprecedented willingness to accept government arbitration in the industrial sphere.

At the 1935 AFL convention, the Executive Council demanded that all future efforts at government-promoted industrial cooperation make provision for proper inclusion of labor representatives in setting price, wage, and hour standards (still trying to bring the original intent of the NIRA, as the Federation saw it, to fruition). Not accidentally, heavy emphasis was put also on the virtues of the AFL's traditional nonpartisan policy toward political parties and a call for labor support in this.[36] On the other hand, when employer recalcitrance toward unionism was under consideration, the NRA appeared overburdened with difficulties in the face of this and a "power of enforcement" seemed "necessary" to make labor boards an effective means of bringing justice to industry.[37] This drift toward accepting government intervention in industrial conflict produced anxiety in the more staunch believers in tradition. In 1935, Matthew Woll, of the Photo Engravers, remarked that a tendency to rely on government to regularize economic affairs was becoming too general and unthinking.

> Most of those who today clamor for planning have government in mind as the agency for that planning. It seems not to dawn upon serious persons that a government that plans must have the power to enforce its plan, if anything is to be achieved. A government that plans and that has the power to enforce the plan must be possessed of a degree of power which labor cannot contemplate in contentment. Excessive or undue government planning leads almost surely to dictatorial power.[38]

Other leaders of the AFL exhibited a willingness to accept contradictory notions. On the one hand, editorials in the *American Federationist* called for voluntary and mutual recognition and cooperation between business and labor in the interests of, among other things, avoiding government intervention in industrial relations. Indeed, government roles of "coordination" and "chairmanship" are to be viewed in terms antithetical to intervention.

> Our industrial civilization requires planning and direction.
> Either the functional groups concerned will assume these re-
> sponsibilities under *government chairmanship* and endeav-
> or to maintain balanced economic progress or the govern-
> ment must assume *control*. There is no need of argument to
> prove that the best way for industry [all groups concerned]
> is through collective bargaining to promote the greatest good
> for the greatest number .... [Otherwise] the government
> may impose orders and use force to get compliance.[39]

On the other hand, employers have made it necessary for labor to consider the possibility that government intervention and increased powers of enforcement in the industrial sphere may be an unavoidable and even desirable means of affirming industrial democracy.

> With their control over employment, it is easy for employers
> to penalize those who join unions. The real measure of
> workers' rights to organize in unions is the effectiveness of
> the government in punishing infringements on these rights.[40]

> A labor board must have power to assure wage-earners the
> free exercise of their rights.[41]

And both these tendencies were even expressed in one editorial which stated:

> The past five years have shown us we were at the end of the
> period when we could permit industry to function without
> plans and without control in the interests of all. Accepting
> this conclusion, there is left only decision upon the kind of
> controls we wish to develop. We can choose from these pat-
> terns: dictatorship with governmental edicts deliberately ad-
> vancing the interests of labor or investors, or *self-govern-
> ment through balanced representation* for functional groups
> under supervision of an agent representing national well-be-
> ing .... [E]mployers continue to prescribe agencies
> through which employees they employ shall be represented
> for dealing with management. They and their represent-
> atives have sought to build up industrial relations boards in-
> dependent of the National Labor Relations Board and sub-
> ject to the code authority of their industry—a body which
> employers dominate. Out of some 550 code authorities only

23 have labor representatives. Only through the National Labor Relations Boards and the local agencies which it creates and supervises can Labor entrust compliance with this fundamental right. It is essential that such a board be maintained and Labor's rights should be protected by defining what constitutes invasion of the right. . . . The decisions of this board should be final and when compliance must be forced, should be referred to the courts for necessary action.[42]

It should not be supposed that the AFL's drift in two different directions at once led it to a consciousness of the contradictoriness in its viewpoint, for acceptance of government-enforced industrial democracy was intended to have clear limits. To the extent that government attempted to do more than protect labor's right to self-organization and union representation in collective bargaining, it was exercising illegitimate power over industrial affairs. As we have seen, this notion was never, really antithetical to voluntarism. Thus, the AFL's willingness to consider government protection of labor's organizing and bargaining rights a virtue does not deny traditional Federation ideology.[43] The idea, however, that labor boards with unprecedented powers to "legislate" in the industrial sphere might provide such protection is a departure from the Federation's past. Only the AFL anger at employer resistance to unionization and its realization that without government aid it might be relatively helpless to compel employers to deal with unions made it possible to overlook or obscure this fact. Yet because the Federation had always allowed for some form of government action friendly to unionism, its willingness to go farther and demand the institution of strong labor boards did not produce extreme ideological tension.

Now, it was stated in the Recovery Act that as a piece of legislation it "shall cease to be in effect and any agencies established hereunder shall cease to exist at the expiration of two years after the date of enactment of this Act." It could cease to be in effect sooner "if the President shall by proclamation declare that the emergency . . . has ended." Of course, the emergency had not ended.. But in general the purposes of the NIRA seemed to have failed. Indeed, this—in addition to the industrial warfare it was seen by so many in Congress to have provoked—became a reason why prospects for extending it beyond June 1935 looked so dim.

Finally, the constitutionality of the NIRA came to be tested before the Supreme Court. Its enemies had always doubted its constitutional validity; the Supreme Court confirmed their doubts in the famous Schechter case in 1935. In *Schechter Poultry Corp.* vs. *United States*, the Court ruled that counts against the poultry company did not fall under transaction in interstate commerce and that the government had exceeded its constitutionally set bounds in suing on grounds (wages and hours provisions in the Live Poultry Code) which actually fell under intrastate commerce.[44] It was clear that the industrial codes would not be upheld. On 27 May 1935 the NIRA had come to an end and liquidation of the vast code organization was accomplished by 24 December of that year.

With the end of the NIRA the Federation was left without Section 7(a) and in a particularly anxious mood to consider any further legislation which would sanction labor organizing. By this time the traditional ideological commitments of the AFL appeared also to have become so diluted, diffuse, or contradictory as to verge on having become unidentifiable. Unable to reason in voluntarist terms and unable to reject voluntarist premises, the Federation's ideological personality was losing coherence. Yet as events were to subsequently show, voluntarism still continued to influence AFL perceptions of the political universe, this while current contingencies continued to challenge its capacity to survive or to produce coherent Federation policy.

Notes

[1]These were the terms of the all important Title I of the act. Title II provided mainly for a public works program to be funded by Congress, for the purpose of expanding employment. Title III provided essentially for the amendment of the Emergency Relief and Construction Act. The NIRA was composed of these three titles. See Carroll Daugherty, *Labor Under the NRA*, pp. 2-5, for further specifications in the terms of the NIRA, especially Titles II and III.

[2]Ellis W. Hawley's *The New Deal and the Problem of Monopoly* indicates that this acclaim was the result of an administration publicity campaign to promote the act. While Hawley's is an excellent account of the NIRA period, I believe it underestimates public readiness to embrace a measure like the Recovery Act.

[3]See Irving Bernstein, *The Turbulent Years*, especially pp. 19-22, for a vivid account of the tenets and popularity of the overproductionist, or what Bernstein calls the "self-regulation of business," school of thinking. It is also stressed here that it was a generally accepted "business" point of view. That businessmen tended toward overproductionist explana-

tions for economic depression is also stressed by Philip Taft, *Economics* · *and Problems of Labor.*

[4]These three notions are intelligently analyzed by Ellis Hawley in some detail in his *The New Deal and the Problem of Monopoly.* There are resemblances between my own description of these trends of thought and those provided by Hawley. While the account which follows emphasizes their underlying compatibility with overproductionist assumptions and their character as economic strategies for control over business cycles, the Hawley account emphasizes instead their employment as strategies for gaining political influence. The difference in emphasis, however, does not imply incompatibility between these views of the matter.

[5]Thornton Oakley, "NRA," *American Federationist* 40, no. 10 (October 1933): 1076-77.

[6]*AFL Convention Proceedings*, 1933, p. 80. It might also be mentioned that some others, besides members of the AFL, thought of the NIRA as a healthy attempt to improve mass purchasing power. See the useful study made by Leverett Lyon, et al., *The National Recovery Administration.* There is one difficulty, however, with this careful, indeed indispensible, study. And that is its failure to see the number of streams of thought the NIRA (and consequently the NRA) could accommodate and the fact that it exaggerates the role of underconsumptionism in its acceptance.

[7]Hawley, *New Deal*, p. 446.

[8]A group loosely organized around "brains-truster" Raymond Moley, which included Bernard Baruch, Gerard Swope, Hugh Johnson, and others of the "cartelist" school, and one organized around Senator Robert Wagner (who also guided the NIRA through Congress), were the two major centers of actual formulating activity in the drafting of the Recovery Act.

[9]AFL, Executive Council Meeting, 1 May 1933, Minutes, as quoted in Philip Taft, *The A.F.L. from the Death of Gompers to the Merger*, p. 42.

[10]As a matter of fact, even before the NIRA was made law, when many suggestions for recovery measures were being bandied about and ardently debated, the AFL Executive Council gave evidence at the 1932 AFL Convention that a recovery measure which required conference and negotiation by all parties immediately involved in industrial enterprises would meet with the approval of organized labor (see *AFL Convention Proceedings*, 1932, p. 72).

[11]Executive Council Report, *AFL Convention Proceedings*, 1933, p. 60.

[12]*American Federationist* 40, no. 12 (December 1933): 1280-90. See also ibid., no. 7 (July 1933): 667-80.

[13]*AFL Convention Proceedings*, 1933, p. 73.

[14]*AFL Convention Proceedings*, 1933, p. 78

[15]See Saul Alinksy's interview with Lewis in *John L. Lewis: An Unauthorized Biography*, p. 67.

[16]Irving Bernstein, *The Turbulent Years*, pp. 38-39. There was also a rash of labor spy and strikebreaking "service" companies which sprouted in this period. See testimony before the Senate Subcommittee on Edu-

cation and Labor, *Violations of Free Speech and Rights of Labor* (in 1936), *American Labor Movement*, ed. Leon Litwak, pp. 95-112. For how workers were manipulated by company unions, see testimony before the same committee cited in *American Labor: The Twentieth Century*, ed. Jerald S. Auerback, pp. 278-85. All of this is in addition to the employment of thugs for beating (or occasionally murdering) union organizers. See examples from testimony before the same subcommittee (headed by LaFollette) in Auerback, *American Labor*, pp. 253-72, 286-304.

[17]The NICB sent brief inquiries to 10,335 concerns selected from *Thomas' Register* on the basis of an indicated capitalization of $500,000 or over in the field of manufacturing and mining. A total of 3,314 companies replied which together employed 2,587,740 wage earners (National Industrial Conference Board, *Collective Bargaining through Employee Representation*).

[18]National Industrial Conference Board, *Individual and Collective Bargaining*, p. 36.

[19]National Industrial Conference Board, *Employee Representation and Collective Bargaining*, p. 2.

[20]Lyon, et al., *National Recovery Administration*, p. 526.

[21]*AFL Convention Proceedings*, 1934, p. 41.

[22]See the Johnson and Richberg statements appearing in the *New York Times*, 3 February 1934, p. 19; and ibid., 4 February 1934, p. 25.

[23]One public member—Senator Wagner; three labor members—Leo Wolman, chairman of the NRA's Labor Advisory board, Gerald Swope of General Electric and Louis Kirstein of Filene's. William M. Leiserson was executive secretary and he grouped together a handful of mediators.

[24]See Bernstein, *Turbulent Years*, pp. 177-80, for a clear account of these and other cases leading to the impotence of the National Labor Board. This is not to say that the NLB had no successes at all. The NLB met its first test rather well. A recognition strike occurred early in the fall by the Hosiery Workers in the mills at Reading, Pennsylvania. The board arranged a settlement which allowed workers to return to work without discrimination, a secret ballot to be taken for determination of worker representatives, and allowance for bargaining on wages and hours. This settlement, known as the "Reading Formula" gave the board considerable prestige at first. But in the Weirton case, the company refused to permit an election under board scrutiny and instituted a company union ballot instead. The case of Budd Manufacturing involved the company's refusal to accept board decisions. The board stood powerless on both counts.

[25]Hawley, *New Deal*, p. 51.

[26]Ibid., p. 56.

[27]Businessmen Alvin Brown, Robert Lea, Kenneth Simpson, Arthur D. Whiteside, Clarence Williams, and Malcom Muir's names come up most frequently in NIRA studies (see especially, ibid).

[28]Lewis L. Lorwin and A. Ford Hinrichs, *National Economic and Social Planning*, p. 71. See also p. 85.

[29]Students of the code-writing process are virtually unanimous in noting the weakness of the labor provisions and the triumph of the business point of view. See Lyon et al., *National Recovery Administration*, pp. 93, 120-23, 346, 427-44, 458-61, 568-77; Lewis Lorwin and A. Ford Hinrichs, *National Economic and Social Planning*, pp. 71, 85-86; Arthur M. Schlesinger, Jr., *The Coming of the New Deal*, pp. 125-26; Herbert F. Taggart, *Minimum Prices under the NRA*, p. 22; and Bernard Bellush, *The Failure of the NRA*, pp. 38, 45-48, 56-57.

[30]Since the NIRA was passed in June and the AFL held its 1933 convention in October, criticism was already evident at the 1933 convention. See *AFL Convention Proceedings*, 1933, pp. 184-86, 189, 194-95, 198, 368, 417-19, 458. But hackles were certainly raised by the time of the 1934 convention for even the Executive Council's report contains criticisms, though soberly and mildly stated. See *AFL Convention Proceedings*, 1934, pp. 47-50, 89-110. This was in addition to a large variety of proposals, highly critical of the NIRA, the NRA, or both, raised from the floor by AFL delegates. Some of the proposals simply addressed the problem of eliminating company unionism. References to all of these are too numerous to make here. Almost anywhere in the *1934 Proceedings* one turns, there will be found some criticism of the NRA. See also the *American Federationist* 41, no. 1 (January 1934): 10-11; ibid. 41, no. 2 (February 1934): 129-33, 179-80; ibid. 41, no. 2 (February 1934): 129-33, 179-80; ibid. 41, no. 3, (March 1934); 268-70; ibid. 41, no. 5 (May 1934): 470-71; ibid. 41, no. 7 (July 1934): 751. Although many of the items in the *American Federationist* were editorials by William Green and bear his usual mildness as well as his continued hope that the NRA be fulfilled, the NRA reorganized and all parties reconciled.

[31]*American Federationist* 41, no. 3 (March 1934): 361.

[32]Ibid., p. 277. See also *AFL Convention Proceedings*, 1935, pp. 41-42, for continuing attacks on the absence of adequate labor participation in code making and attributions of NRA failure to this fact.

[33]Ibid., p. 278.

[34]*American Federationist* 42, no. 3 (March 1935): 241.

[35]Ibid., no. 5 (May 1935): 465-67.

[36]*AFL Convention Proceedings*, 1935, pp. 8, 23-24, 41-42.

[37]Ibid., p. 43.

[38]Matthew Woll, *Labor, Industry and Government*, p. 207.

[39]*American Federationist* 42, no. 1 (January 1935): 11-12 (italics mine).

[40]Ibid., no. 5 (May 1935): 465.

[41]Ibid., no. 1 (January 1935): 11.

[42]Ibid., no. 3 (March 1935): 242,244 (italics mine).

[43]In fact, the AFL waxed enthusiastic over the Railway Labor Act of 1926, which in some ways foreshadowed the Norris-LaGuardia Act of 1932. It guaranteed rights of labor self-organization for the railway industry and was approved in 1930 by the Supreme Court in *Texas & New Orleans Railway* v. *Brotherhood of Clerks*. But the act did not contain provisions for a strong railway labor board (although a Railway Labor

Board had been established by the Transportation Act of 1920. Its function, however, was essentially advisory).

[44]The Court's opinion, set forth by Chief Justice Hughes, may be found in Charles Roos, *NRA Economic Planning*, pp. 563-80.

Chapter 5

The Voluntarists and the Wagner Act

AFL voluntarism was heavily compromised by 1935, essentially because of the Federation's own willingness to consider with favor the institution of a strong national labor board to regulate industrial conflict. Many factors contributed to this condition. Probably most important, as was indicated in the previous chapter, had been fierce and effective employer opposition to unionism. Under its impact the AFL began to feel a need to rely on government aid in order to guarantee the survival of labor unions.

But there were some other factors as well. For example, despite the fact that the original National Labor Board established under the NIRA stood powerless before employer recalcitrance, it had created at least some reason for the AFL to believe that labor boards could regulate industrial conflict in terms favorable to organized labor. For one thing, the NLB had established a precedent with its decision in the Reading case that union membership could not be a basis for discriminating against employees. For another, while the NLB stood embarrassed before employer noncompliance in the Weirton case, it had made a decision nonetheless that employee desires with respect to representation were decisive. And in yet other cases, the NLB elaborated on secret ballot procedures for elections to be held among employees, under NLB scrutiny, to help determine employee preference as to representation.[1] And lastly, even the new NLRB created by Public

Resolution 44 basically followed its NRA predecessor in this pattern of decision making. In fact, it went a bit further by adding to the decisions made by the older NLB a cautious encouragement for the majority rule principle, even though it was hampered from taking an overt and strong stand by the Johnson-Richberg position. The majority rule principle meant that if a majority of workers selected a given trade union to be its freely chosen representative, that union should have exclusive bargaining rights with the employer.[2]

All of this had the effect of adding some precedent favorable to labor in the developing industrial common law proceeding out of NLB and NLRB decisions. The fact that some belief in the value of these board actions was growing, even in AFL circles where the impotence and untrustworthiness of labor boards was being widely proclaimed, is attested to by the role that William Green played in bringing about the creation of the NLRB in 1934. For though it was established under the president's public resolution, Green had indicated to Roosevelt just before its establishment that the strike impending in the steel industry looked ominous and the parties looked irreconcilable. Strong labor board action would be needed to ward off fierce industrial warfare. The AFL's Amalgamated Association of Iron, Steel, and Tin Workers, a craft union, had opened its doors to an influx of new and militant members. Simultaneously, the steel companies were trying to establish company unions in all their plants. Moreover, the steel management was preparing for a showdown with the Amalgamated, purchasing ammunition and stringing barbed wire. Green had become frightened that an ultimate confrontation would destroy the union and sought to forestall a showdown conflict. This motivated him to contact the president, urging him to intervene and asking that the matter be arbitrated by a labor board. Roosevelt informed him that arrangements were being made to allow for the creation of a steel labor board.[3] But the situation in steel looked so disastrous that the president promptly sent his Resolution 44 to Congress.

Finally, important congressional voices were being raised on behalf of a strengthened labor board which had the effect of encouraging and deepening AFL commitment to the idea. The most notable and influential of these was Senator Robert Wagner, who had been formulating and pressing for appropriate enabling legislation at least since 1934. Even before the president's public resolution had been approved in June, Wagner introduced his Labor Disputes Bill on 1 March 1934. Title I of this bill stated the need to aid the workers in efforts at self-organization as a means of removing obstructions to interstate commerce and as a means of aiding the public welfare by promoting a balance of power in industry. Title II of the bill called for creation of an independent tripartite national labor board of seven—three public members, two labor members, and two employer members—to be appointed by the president with Senate advice and consent. Title III called for the use of the Conciliation Service in the Department of Labor (which had been created as early as 1913, but no labor statute had previously called for its use).[4]

Slowly but surely the AFL rallied around Senator Wagner. By 1935 the AFL had proclaimed his efforts to the nation as a great contribution to the cause of industrial justice and American democracy. And when finally Wagner's later National Labor Relations Act succeeded in passing through Congress in 1935, the Federation was very nearly jubilant.

One motive for this AFL position on Wagner's ultimate labor bill may also have been concession to what could have appeared as inevitable. For in November 1934 the Democratic party won resounding congressional election victories.[5] And Senator Wagner tried to take advantage of an atmosphere that appeared promising from the point of view of reestablishing the principle of Section 7(a) in permanent legislation after the demise of the Recovery Act. He also sought to include in this legislation a section which would provide for enforcement procedures against employers so that the terms of a labor provision would not be destroyed by employer refusal to deal with labor unions. He worked closely with a legal staff and was diligently focused on drafting legislation likely to meet even constitutional tests of validity.

But it is much more likely that the AFL was, in fact, drifting rapidly away from voluntarist orthodoxy. For the inevitability of getting legislation through Congress that provided for stronger administrative procedures in dealing with industrial conflict, especially for dealing with employer arrogance, was, in fact, uncertain. And despite the fact that the Congress had been potentially unified by strong Democratic gains in both houses, Wagner worked in an atmosphere of some uncertainty. He had tried, for example, to get the president's support for his bill prior to its introduction in the Senate. But in the words of one student of the situation:

> Despite his determination to exploit the election by pressing hard for a program of reform in 1935, Roosevelt declined to

back this measure. This response may have been influenced by the fact that neither the Department of Labor nor the NRA gave evidence of enthusiasm.[6]

If the administration lacked interest in Wagner's bill, and did little to promote or aid it, the AFL hardly had reason to believe that such a measure was inevitable.[7] There is, then, probably no challenging the fact that the AFL had come to accept the idea that a bill which promised both labor recognition and a stronger labor board for purposes of curbing employer power was an absolute necessity and posed little danger that should be allowed to interfere with support of the legislation. Indeed, William Green wrote to Roosevelt asking him to convert the principle of Section 7(a) into new legislation and to support Wanger,[8] The pages of the *American Federationist* came in 1935 to be filled with this call for a new statute to embody both Section 7(a) and better enforcement procedures than had been included under the NIRA.[9]

While all of this pointed to an ideological about-face for the AFL, the Federation made little effort to confront the fact and merely ignored its old voluntarist revulsion for the use of government machinery in industrial relations. This problem was not raised at the time the Recovery Act passed in 1933, for Section 7(a) could be interpreted to mean that labor itself was called on to determine terms of life in the industrial sphere. Labor boards were set up only afterward to implement the terms of the act. If there were disappointment with the boards, there seemed no necessity to hold the act itself at fault. But acceptance of legislation involving clear provisions for government regulation of industrial relations themselves (not of pricing or production standards, something more or less acceptable to the AFL, especially if unions aided in their formulation) had to indicate a change of heart for the defenders of voluntarist notions. Bernstein has written of the AFL call for the Wagner Act that "the AFL was now firmly committed to legislation, voluntarism, like last year's bonnet, being cast into discard."[10]

Some AFL skepticism was expressed and questions arose about the willingness of the courts to validate the constitutionality of the 1935 Wagner Act. But essentially the pages of the *American Federationist* rang with enthusiastic anticipation of defeating company unionism with Wagner's legislation and firmly rooting labor unions into American society with it. A bit of the questioning element also mingled with the warm support in the report of the Executive Council to the 1935 AFL convention. For despite the support enthusiastically given to the Wagner legislation, the council did not fail to record its disappointments with the older NLB, NLRB, and various boards set up in specific industries under the NIRA, noting especially the concessions these so often made in decisions and public statements to the Johnson-Richberg formula for proportional representation of all labor organizations in a plant or industry.[11] Thus, AFL support for the new Wagner Act would, in fact, be given with some "wait and see" reservations. Still, the act would be heralded as an important victory for the labor movement.

Despite the fact, however, that all appearances indicated that in 1935 the AFL was decidedly drifting away from its older voluntarist attitudes and policies, these were to be affirmed once again for some surprising reasons, and with renewed vigor, as a new National Labor Relations Board worked to carry out the terms of the Wagner Act. The result was that ideologically the AFL remained in the same state of confusion in which it had lived since its 1932 convention. To understand the reasons why the Federation remained unable to abandon its voluntaristic predilections, while at the same time unable to support them with any conviction, it is necessary to understand the major purposes and features of the Wagner Act and to examine its impact on the labor movement in the years after its passage.

Wagner introduced his bill in the Senate on 21 February 1935. A companion bill was also introduced in the House by Representative Connery on 28 February. Extensive hearings were held before the Senate Committee on Education and Labor, and before the House Committee on Labor, at which representatives of employers, labor, and the general public appeared and stated their views.[12] On 2 May the Wagner bill was reported by the Senate Committee with minor amendments, and after some debate, was passed by the Senate on 15 May. It was sent to the House where, after more extensive debate, it was passed on 27 June. The National Labor Relations Act (NLRA), formulated by Senator Wagner and his staff, was signed by Roosevelt and became law on 5 July 1935.

The Wagner Act was considered by its supporters to have brought to fruition what they considered to be a revolutionary national policy begun with Section 7(a) of the Recovery Act. That policy was seen to demand that workers were to be protected by law in their right to organize and bargain collectively through freely chosen representatives, so that labor would be guaranteed the necessary strength to engage in private negotiations with employers and set the terms of industrial peace acceptable to both. The act itself was simple with limited purposes. These are set forth in a statement of findings and policy at the outset:

> Section 1. The denial by employers of the right of employees to organize and the refusal by employers to accept the procedure of collective bargaining leads to strikes and other forms of industrial strife or unrest, which have the intent or the necessary effect of burdening or obstructing commerce by (a) impairing the efficiency, safety or operation of the instrumentalities of commerce; (b) occurring in the current of commerce; (c) materially affecting, restraining or controlling the flow of raw materials or manufactured or processed goods from or into the channels of commerce; or (d) causing diminution of employment and wages in such volume as substantially to impair or disrupt the market for goods flowing from or into the channels of commerce.
>
> The inequality of bargaining power between employees who do not possess full freedom of association or actual liberty of contract, and employers who are organized in the corporate or other forms of ownership association substantially burdens and affects the flow of commerce, and tends to aggravate recurrent business depressions, by depressing wage rates and the purchasing power of wage earners in industry and by preventing the stabilization of competitive wage rates and working conditions within and between industries.
>
> Experience has proved that protection by law of the right of employees to organize and bargain collectively safeguards commerce from injury, impairment or interruption, and promotes the flow of commerce by removing certain recognized sources of industrial strife and unrest, by encouraging practices fundamental to the friendly adjustment of industrial disputes arising out of differences as to wages, hours or other working conditions, and by restoring equality of bargaining power between employers and employees.
>
> It is hereby declared to be the policy of the United States to eliminate causes of certain substantial obstructions to the free flow of commerce and to mitigate and eliminate these obstructions when they have occurred by encouraging the practice and procedure of collective bargaining and by protecting the exercise by workers of full freedom of association, self-organization and designation of representatives of their own choosing, for the purpose of negotiating the terms and conditions of their employment or other mutual aid or protection.

The first purpose of the act, then, was to affirm that industrial concentration had destroyed labor's bargaining power, and that it would be to the economic benefit of the whole community if labor could act collectively to improve its economic position. For improvements in mass purchasing power that could flow from labor's increased capacity to bargain for better terms of work was a necessary deterrent to depression. Second, the act would remove a primary cause of industrial conflict by establishing labor's right to associate for self-improvement. And all of this can be seen to have been phrased with one eye on the Supreme Court and testing of the act's constitutional validity. For the argument, for example, that deterrents to mass purchasing power and collective bargaining have a detrimental effect on interstate commerce (in view of a resultant outbreak of strikes) is a clear address to the constitutional problem. This was an attempt to appeal to the constitutional provision that Congress had the power to regulate or prevent activity, which, if unrestrained, would affect or burden commerce between the states and thus sidestep the difficulty other pieces of legislation were in (like the NIRA) when they were struck down by the Supreme Court's employment of this provision against them.
them.

It should be noted that the constitutional consideration was also motivated by a practical and immediate need to find a formula for dealing with the NAM, the American Liberty League, and employers by the thousands who were arrayed against the act. These were preparing to defeat it in any way possible, and their reliance on propaganda about the act's questionable constitutionality was a seemingly strong start. For example, lawyers from the Liberty League opposed to the act argued:

> Production is not commerce. The processes and incidents of production, such as labor, are not commerce, even though the products of such activities subsequently find themselves in interstate movement. Although production may have some impact on interstate commerce, the effect on commerce of labor expended in production is remote and indirect. Remote consequences cannot justify federal action, because federal power is limited to interstate commerce and cannot, by a pretext, intrude into local activities.[13]

The act, however, was not intended to deal with all types of labor relations questions, with the prevention of industrial conflict in general. The Wagner Act gave to the National Labor Relations Board, established under the act to administer it, only limited powers—to prevent employer practices which interfere with the right of workers to freely organize and bargain collectively, and also to determine questions of fact as to whether groups of workers had freely chosen labor organizations to represent them in dealing with their employers. This was intended to come to grips with the company union problem. Toward this end, the basic rights of employees were defined in Section 7:

> Employees shall have the right to self-organization, to form, join or assist labor organizations, to bargain collectively through representatives of their own choosing and to engage in concerted activities for the purpose of collective bargaining or other mutual aid or protection.

In addition, five unfair labor practices were defined (in Section 8) and specifically forbidden to employers: (1) any interference, restraint or coercion of employees in the exercise of rights guaranteed by law; (2) domination or interference with the formation or administration of a labor organization by contributing financial or other support to it; (3) any discrimination for the purpose of discouraging union membership; (4) any discrimination against an employee for filing charges or testifying under the Wagner Act; and (5) refusal to bargain collectively with the legal representative of the employees constituting an appropriate bargaining unit.

A National Labor Relations Board (NLRB) of three members, appointed by the president (with the advice and consent of the Senate) was to administer the act. Like other independent administrative agencies, the board was to investigate, to hold hearings, and to issue orders. Its orders were not self-enforcing, but the board could petition a circuit court of appeals for the enforcement of an order in cases involving unfair labor practices (though similarly, any person aggrieved by such an order could petition the circuit court for review). The board's findings of fact, supported by evidence, was to be controlling in the courts. While there were no actual penalties imposed by violation of the act, there was power to prevent the continuation of unfair labor practices by employers, since the board could issue cease-and-desist orders to be upheld in court. Moreover, the board might require the employer to take affirmative action; for example, the reinstatement with back pay of employees who had been discharged or otherwise discriminated against because of union activity. The board could even order the instatement of employees who were never hired and who were refused employment because of their union affiliation. In addition, the board could order the employer to disestablish a company union and it could withdraw recognition from any union with whom the employer bargained, if that union had been set up with employer aid or funds. Finally, in cases in which it was found that the employer refused to bargain with a union which had been established as the duly chosen representative of his employees, the NLRB could order him to bargain upon request of that union. Clearly, the National Labor Relations Board established under Wagner's National Labor Relations Act had been endowed with powers that went well beyond those allotted to its predecessors, and these powers were meant to effect the purpose of the act—to grant recognition and collective bargaining rights to labor unions.

The Wagner Act, however, was limited in intent as compared with the Recovery Act. Nothing like rejuvenating or reorganizing industrial society was contemplated or attempted. All that was involved was the extension of rights of self-organization for purposes of collective bargaining to working men who desired them. From this, most supporters of the act expected only a measure of industrial peace. And yet a broad concept of what democracy in industrial society was about underlay the legislation.

For many years Senator Wagner argued that men who have been insufficiently exercised in self-expression are men who grow both servile and frustrated. To deny to workers their right to appropriate forms of self-expression is to leave them, as it is to leave anyone else, dependent and angry. Whoever imagined that this fact was of little consequence, was deceived by a mad illusion. For ambitious individuals who sought to capitalize on the frustration and anger of citizens left helplessly dependent on "superiors" will be able to do so for any number of purposes detrimental to freedom in a society. Wagner argued that to leave so large a portion of the citizenry weak and resentful is to give self-seeking dictators who promise frustrated men their revenge and redemption a base of support. Further, he felt that people lacking in the habits of responsible self-assertion will follow such tyrants, even to the destruction of liberty for the whole society. Accordingly it is best to encourage habits of self-assertion, and since the worker can only acquire them where he spends most of his time, on the job and with fellow workers, self-assertion in the work setting ought to be promoted. Unions functioned to promote this and thus played a part in preserving democracy and freedom.

Wagner's views on this subject were perhaps best stated in 1937 for the *New York Times Magazine* but restatements of the same idea are to be found running through his arguments during the whole period when the act was under consideration. In 1937 he said:

> The struggle for a voice in industry through the process of collective bargaining is the heart of the struggle for the preservation of political as well as economic democracy in America. Let men become the servile pawns of their masters in the factories of the land and there will be destroyed the bone and sinew of resistance to political dictatorship.
>
> Fascism begins in industry, not in government. The seeds of communism are sown in industry, not in government. But let men know the dignity of freedom and self-expression in their daily lives, and they will never bow to tyranny in any quarter of their national life.[14]

Thus, despite the limited intentions and application of the Wagner Act, it was, after all, meant to have some effect on the quality and direction of American society in general.

Now, of course, the question arises, given that the AFL found all of the terms of the Wagner Act acceptable and had drifted far from its voluntarist course in accepting strengthened government machinery for dealing with industrial conflict, what happened to revive the more "classic" voluntarist position and leave the Federation, once again, torn in two directions at once? Certainly the NLRA had stated prolabor purposes and endowed a labor board with powers sufficient to effectuate them. This fact should have acted to keep AFL leaders oriented positively toward legislation, government, and, at the very least, the National Labor Relations Board established under the NLRA. And yet, this was not to be the case.

In some sense, of course, a law which validated the right of people conscious of some common interest among themselves to organize for self-improvement enabled the AFL to accept the Wagner Act on traditional grounds. That is to say, even its support of the enlarged role in industrial relations to be played by the government did not totally obscure the voluntarist viewpoint. For ultimately, Gompers had long ago reminded, the recognition of labor unions in the society generally and by employers specifically, would eventually make any enforcement machinery superfluous, and both employers and workers might proceed to define the industrial realm among themselves. Acceptance of unions, regardless of how achieved, would eventually bring the habit of accommodating interests in the industrial sphere as a matter of course. Indeed, one scholar has even been willing to say of the AFL's attitude to the Wagner Act that

> The. . . approval given by the A.F. of L. to the N.L.R.A. was not, as such, a reversal of policy. In even its purest form, voluntarism can be reconciled with legislation which would guarantee the right of labor to organise. As a matter of fact, *it is only after this right is given, that voluntarism can begin to operate effectively.* . . . All that labor asked under voluntarism, and all that it would tolerate by and large, was freedom for itself as one of the principal groups in the economic system to pursue its own economic ends without let or hindrance and to bargain collectively.[15]

But the fact is that acceptance of labor legislation safeguarding union organizing and collective bargaining rights did not constitute a departure from voluntarism, while the acceptance of a labor board with specific power to intervene in the industrial realm *did*. This is why the vitality of AFL voluntarism was still so strikingly evident in AFL support of the National Industrial Recovery Act in 1933. In 1933 the AFL did not have to confront a projected government role in industrial relations. The NIRA provided the president with powers to act through "duly authorized" agents to press code making upon heads of industry. And even this he would do only if industrialists proved slow to undertake the task themselves. The NIRA set no standard that had to be met per se, and the labor provision enabled the AFL to see itself as vested with rights to participate in the general activity. No standard then, would be set without its approval and participation. All government was seen to be doing was to require that industrial cooperation be undertaken. The terms would be set by the participating parties. That labor boards became involved in the process was unanticipated in 1933. But the fact that difficulties would force the AFL to live with them until 1935 provided a basis for a change of view. Confronting a piece of legislation specifically promising government intervention in industrial relations is a different matter. AFL acceptance of such legislation did indicate the weakening hold of voluntarism on the leaders of the AFL.

Of course, the AFL also supported all of the terms of the Wagner Act because antiunion elements opposed it so vociferously. Harassment in the form of unending criticisms from congressmen and and industry confronted the board for years after its formation. The fight on the constitutionality issue consumed much of the board's energies. When that issue was settled with a favorable ruling by the Supreme Court on 12 April 1937,[16] the major associations of industry began a drive for amendment, which continued during World War II, and succeeded finally in 1947.[17] The three lengthy congressional investigations in both House and Senate in 1939 through 1940 took much time and harassed the board at a period when it was overwhelmed with a heavy case load and was understaffed. A minority report from the House Committee on Labor even said:

> Justly or unjustly, the consensus of public opinion is that the Board is biased, prejudiced, and has been guilty not only of grabbing and using power never delegated to it by the act, but that it has been unfair and unjust in its actions.[18]

And when this attack upon the act failed to result in amendment, congressional opposition took the form of hostility in the appropriations committees where only inadequate funding, in view of the board's vast case load, was provided for the board's functioning.[19] Again at the close of World War II, the drive for repeal or amendment was renewed and actively promoted by the NAM. And Congress continued to allow scant appropriations. A large share of the board's time and energy continued to be absorbed by the necessity of supplying material for investigating committees and in order to justify requests for better congressional funding. For much of its life, the board established under the Wagner Act worked in a hostile atmosphere in which opposition was also promoted by much of the press. And yet, even if employer hostility was a factor in promoting labor support for a bill that provided for an expanded government role in industrial disputes, the fact remained that such support was unprecedented. Business hostility had not moved the AFL to such a position before.

Now having noted all of this, and having conceded the bases on which the AFL drifted away from the voluntarist past, it becomes rather startling to find John Frey in 1937 announcing about the National Labor Relations Board:

> I now want to charge the Board itself with having done more

during recent months to destroy the practice of collective bargaining, to interfere with its progress, than all the efforts of the anti-union forces in the country combined.[20]

At first sight, it might be thought that Frey, being such a stubborn traditionalist, is speaking out of some particular discontent of his own. But the Executive Council of the AFL joined him in its report to the 1937 convention:

> There is considerable opportunity for abuse of discretion by the Board in determining representation. Our theory is that representation should be determined by elections supervised by the Board by secret ballot and the Board really has no authority to determine representation otherwise. . . . The Federation has consistently taken and tried to maintain the position that the Board was not created to resolve the internal disputes of labor organizations, nor to interfere with existing contracts between employers and unions.[21]

The council went on the charge the board with arbitrariness and prejudice. And after 1937 the AFL's disupte with the board became, if anything, more antagonistic. In 1937 and 1938 AFL conventions were virtually devoted to criticism of the board and elaboration on board maladministration.

Why had this antagonism of the AFL to the National Labor Relations Board broken out and become so severe? The congressional and employer enemies of the Wagner Act and the NLRB had reviled them just because of the sympathy for and protection of labor which they were considered to have provided. The board, in fact, was consistently charged with an antiemployer bias. How could friends of the Wagner Act from the organized labor movement be so moved as to hurl such critical charges at the board carrying out its terms?

It should be made clear in all of this that the AFL did reserve its bitter attacks for the board itself. It did not reverse its position on the Wagner Act. Still, its attacks on the board were strongly reminiscent of the voluntarism of old. A close student of the Labor Board's history observed about the AFL's response to the NLRB: "The Federation clings tenaciously to the doctrine laid down by Gompers, and it hews to the 'voluntarist' philosophy with ardor."[22]

To understand why the AFL experienced a revival of voluntarist feeling after 1935, it is necessary to consider some developments of major importance that occurred within the labor movement at the time. Ever since Section 7 (a) and the organizing efforts launched by the AFL in 1933, criticism had been mounting within Federation ranks of the Executive Council's organizing policies, essentially castigating the national leadership for timidity and excessive attachment to craft unionism. Led by John L. Lewis, the critics within the Federation came increasingly to espouse more militant labor organizing on an unrestricted industrial unionist basis. In supporting their demands for policy and structural change within the organized labor movement, they contended that mass production industries had made the "composite" worker typical, an individual who, in the course of a working day, might be called on to perform tasks coming under the jurisdiction of several craft organizations, causing disrupting, disunifying jurisdictional disputes among unions. Moreover, the mechanization and large-scale nature of American industries had created a vast unskilled or semiskilled work force which was crying out for unionization, this while the craft oriented Federation had grown fearful of or indifferent to this human mass of millions. Thus, for the sake of labor unity and so as to swell the ranks of the Federation, a modification of organizational principles, as well as militant organizing drives in the mass production industries were called for. The AFL Executive Council proved alternately equivocating, ambivalent, or hostile to the appeals of the industrial unionists. At the AFL's Atlantic City convention in 1935, the tension reached an intolerable point, and when the convention voted against unrestricted industrial unionism in the mass production industries, the industrial unionist faction of the Federation was irrevocably alienated. The Committee for Industrial Organization was formed in November 1935, several weeks after the convention decision, and rapidly became an organizing center for the dramatic and successful campaigns among the steel, automobile, and rubber workers that followed. By November 1938, the Committee was renamed the Congress of Industrial Organizations (CIO), had held a founding convention of its own, and formalized the split in the labor movement. Thus, after 1935, two great labor federations, opposed in organizational philosophy and strategy, vied for leadership of the labor movement.

When the Wagner Act was passed in July 1935, organized labor had meant the American Federation of Labor. Some few non-AFL unions were then more or less insignificant organizations. Consequently, the AFL, in its drift away from voluntarism toward a strengthened national labor board, had no thought that board rulings favorable to labor in industrial disputes would mean anything more than rulings favoring the AFL. By the end of 1935, however, the CIO became a significant rival of the AFL. And while the CIO's victories in steel and automobiles were not secured by use of the Wagner Act's machinery, the CIO soon proved that the Wagner Act was something quite different from a convenience to the AFL. This, in turn, led to considerable antagonism toward the NLRB by AFL officials. Section 9(a) of the Wagner Act provided:

> Representatives. . . selected for the purposes of collective bargaining by the majority of the employees in a unit appropriate for such purposes, shall be the exclusive representatives of all the employees in such units for the purposes of collective bargaining.

This provision represented acceptance of the majority rule principle long favored by the AFL. To implement majority rule the Labor Board was empowered, in representation cases, to determine majority preference and to rule in favor of the bargaining agent preferred by a majority of workers in any given plant. In order to determine if a given union was the representative of workers in a plant, the NLRB generally held elections among the workers. The names of the union or unions that were seeking certification were placed on the ballot along with the designation "no union." If a union won a majority of these votes, the board certified it as the bargaining agent with whom the employer concerned had to bargain as the workers' exclusive agent. If "no union" received a majority, no certification was made. If, however, there were one or more contesting unions and no majority was received by any of them, the board had to devise a system of runoff elections.[23]

But clear and simple as the matter of determining majorities appeared at first to be, time was to show that it was one of the most difficult, entangling and discouraging problems the Labor Board would have to deal with and the AFL would have to confront. Francis Biddle, who had been chairman of the previous NLRB, foresaw some of the difficulties that would arise when he testified at congressional hearings held on the Wagner Act:

> The difficulties sometimes involved can readily be made clear where the employer runs two factories producing similar products: shall a unit be each factory or shall they be combined into one? Where there are several crafts in the plant, shall each be separately represented? To lodge the power of determining this question with the employer would invite unlimited abuse and gerrymandering the units would

defeat the aims of the statutes. If the employers themselves could make the decision without proper consideration of the elements which should constitute the appropriate units they could in any given instance defeat the practical significance of the majority rule; and, by breaking off into small groups, could make it impossible for the employer to run his plant.[24]

While Biddle felt certain an impartial labor board could resolve these difficulties with dispatch, they proved, in fact, elusive and resistant to sound and rapid solution. Nevertheless, Congress had delegated these problems, known as questions of the "appropriate bargaining unit," to the NLRB, giving it almost unlimited authority in Section 9(b) of the Wagner Act:

> The Board shall decide in each case whether, in order to insure to employees the full benefit of their right to self-organization and to collective bargaining, and otherwise to effectuate the policies of this Act, the unit appropriate for the purposes of collective bargaining shall be the employer unit, craft unit, plant unit, or subdivision thereof.

This wide authority was given to the NLRB in the belief, based on experience of the NRA labor boards, that the various problems which arose were not foreseeable and could best be determined by the NLRB. The AFL supported this viewpoint, not, of course, being able to predict that a full-fledged rival would arise to have equal status and different views on bargaining unit problems.

The problem of determining the appropriate bargaining unit as a means of operationalizing the majority rule principle arose, however, somewhat slowly. Indeed, it arose as a result of gains in strength and militancy of the CIO. And it was slow to become a source of friction and confusion, also because the NLRB chose for a time to keep its distance from disputes involving interunion competition. As late as 1936, the board exhibited an inclination to steer clear of internal union disputes. For in June of that year, in the *Aluminum Company of America* case,[25] the NLRB was petitioned to intervene in a jurisdictional dispute between two affiliates of the AFL. The Labor Board declined to intervene. The case had been presented as a "representation" case, that is, as a case involving the entitlement of one affiliate over the other to exclusively represent the workers in collective bargaining with the employer. The NLRB argued that this was not a representation case in the terms spelled out by Section 9 of the Wagner Act. It was in reality a jurisdictional dispute between affiliates of the same labor organization and therefore ought to be resolved by the AFL itself. In this same year, the NLRB was also petitioned to decide in another case, *Axton-Fisher Tobacco Co.*[26] Here, again, two AFL affiliates were involved in the contention. Again, the board reasoned that the vocabulary of Section 9 of the act meant to settle representation cases involving freely chosen collective bargaining agents to deal with employers and that it did not apply to internal jurisdictional disputes within the AFL itself. The board stated that this was a matter of internal union government, to be decided by the AFL alone. The Wagner Act, the board noted, was not set up for the purpose of drawing appropriate jurisdictional lines between unions in the AFL. The authority to draw these boundaries was peculiarly a matter of interest to labor. Such interests, the board reminded, were subject to labor's own decisions.

The understanding which guided the Labor Board's decisions in these cases clearly rested on the assumption that internal union disputes were a matter of internal union governance. The contenders in these disputes had, in the heat of rivalry, attempted to cast jurisdictional issues as representation issues, but the board regarded the latter to be valid only in cases which required that it determine between employer-preferred or labor-preferred collective bargaining agents in a plant or industry. But one year after the board declined to make decisions in disputes it regarded manageable by internal union procedures, it did intervene in AFL-CIO disputes.[27] It intervened in spite of the fact that the CIO had not yet held its first convention; neither had it formally constituted itself a fully independent federation. It was still a "Committee," not yet a "Congress" of Industrial Organizations. In its intervention, the board took little care to consider the events and circumstances leading to the split in the labor movement. It could have, but it did not consider the possibility of defining AFL-CIO disputes as being of a jurisdictional character and requiring settlement through procedures the AFL or the CIO might have devised for the purpose between themselves. It intervened on the ill-considered grounds that the conflict between the two great labor bodies presented a situation where no one parent body existed to which the conflict might have been referred. Thus, the board assumed a right to intervene in loco parentis.[28] This interventionist policy, which it did not abandon even when AFL rivalry with the CIO became extreme and destructive, added to the difficulties of reuniting the two labor federations. It is highly conceivable, at least in retrospect, that a policy of nonintervention in cases involving AFL contention with the CIO might have helped strengthen labor unity, especially because on several occasions during 1937 and 1938, moves toward conciliation were contemplated by leaders in the AFL and the CIO. At any rate, thus it was that the Labor Board became embroiled in labor controversies and even played a role in the debate on the merits of craft unionism and industrial unionism.

Provisions for "majority rule" had been in the Wagner Act, as noted above. This was to facilitate choice of the exclusive representative for collective bargaining purposes. This aspect of the Wagner Act, in 1935, had been particularly pleasing to the AFL out of its recent and distasteful memories of the Johnson-Richberg policy of encouraging a proportional representation solution to representation problems. Identifying this approach with toleration of company unionism, the AFL was especially eager that a majority rule principle be employed so that exclusive representation rights in collective bargaining could be guaranteed to all of its local units. Proof that a majority in a plant, or among a group of craft workers in a plant, had freely chosen AFL bargaining representatives was then to be shown by AFL locals when a petition was filed asking the board to determine a question of representation. In early cases, evidence introduced in hearings before the board was considered sufficient. This evidence was largely composed of testimony of employees, the submission of petitions signed by a majority of employees in a given plant, or, if only one group was organized out of a larger work force in the plant, a majority of employees belonging to that group of workers. If the board entertained doubts about the validity of this proof, which could happen if an employer claimed that signatures or testimony were the result of coercive pressure exerted on employees by the union, the board could call for and direct the holding of a secret ballot election (eventually the board relied primarily on this method).

Now before it could be known whether a majority of the employees had, in fact, freely chosen their own collective bargaining representative, it had to be determined what constituted a majority. Was a majority constituted in a given case by a simple majority of workers in a plant who might desire affiliation with an industrial union permitting membership to all in the plant regardless of trade or craft differences, skilled or unskilled? What if a number of groups desired affiliation with a number of craft unions, each group being a minority, yet together comprising a substantial force, and these existed in a plant where the rest of the work force desired affiliation with an industrial union? What if the latter constituted the largest group and the former a series of small minorities which only together comprised a majority? They could coexist, perhaps, but what if all of these (as they did) claimed entitlement to exclusive representation rights? Disputes did arise involving the request of small groups of skilled employees for small AFL craft units as against the claims of groups in a plant who wanted a unit having no craft distinctions for membership, who wanted an industrial union (some of these were at times craft workers as well). Were both perhaps entitled to "self-organization" if workers had freely chosen the desired unit of affiliation? And what of the effectiveness of collective bargaining if employees were represented by different units?

The board became enmeshed in determining the appropriateness of claims for desired affiliation in an effort to establish the majority principle. This was a problem originally expected to arise between company and labor unions. Now the board took on the additional task of determining the legitimacy of claims between workers desiring affiliation with craft or with industrial plant units. It pondered the nature of an appropriate unit that would support a majority principle. It considered the duties, skills, wages, hours, or other conditions of work held in common by a majority of workers, the history of unionism in given trades or plants, the type of self-organization workers desired, the relation between a desired unit and the character of administration or organization of an employer's business. The situation became crucial as AFL and CIO unions brought petitions in increasing numbers before the board.

Finally, a precedent-setting case arose in 1937 where the leadership of one craft union rivaled with the heads of another craft union, the former desiring a craft union and the latter an industrial union affiliation. This occurred in a plant where the employer had just concluded a plantwide agreement with the CIO, and yet where both craft and industrial unions had previously engaged in collective bargaining with the employer. Precedents for craft unionism and industrial unionism thus existed side by side. In the case of *Globe Stamping Machine and Company*, the board decided that both craft and industrial unions had an equal claim to exclusive representation.[29] An election among the employees themselves, then, should be the final determining factor in settling the representation dispute. The board, therefore, ordered an election in which the two craft units would vote independently of each other. If the industrial unit was preferred, then both craft unions would be included in a plantwide unit. If the members voted for craft unions, then they would be given separate craft union status. In this case, the industrial union won a majority and both craft units were brought into the larger plant unit.

This procedure became known as the "Globe election" and it came to be increasingly relied upon in a great number of cases, especially as the CIO made gains among less-skilled workers in areas where only one skilled AFL craft unit existed. Wherever the board felt that evenly balanced factors existed that made smaller craft units as acceptable as larger industrial units, it resorted to the Globe election technique of resolving disputes. The board members, however, always argued sharply over where it should be applied and it remained a problematic procedure in any event.

This vexed question of the appropriate unit became the source of the AFL's fury with the Labor Board. By 1938, even the usually conciliatory William Green lashed out at the board mainly for what he took to be its bias in favor of the CIO as it decided appropriate bargaining unit cases:

> The Board has given an insurgent group the rights of belligerants. . . . Every agency of government that gives status to the CIO gives the same recognition. Surely this is not freedom for the workers to choose their own unions and representatives for collective bargaining, but union development under government patronage.[30]

Statements of this critical nature are innumerable in AFL publications and at AFL conventions whenever the labor board is mentioned after 1936. From 1937 onward, the AFL actively sought either amendment of the NLRA, curtailment of the extent of the board's discretionary power, or replacement of board members themselves for displaying a pro-CIO bias.

In examining, however, the actual outcome of NLRB decisions in cases involving AFL and CIO rivalry, there appears to be no basis for the rage of the AFL against the labor board on the basis of a pro-CIO basis. For decision making did not actually favor the CIO over the AFL. Table 2 indicates that this was the case. These figures account for cases until 1939. Another study of this issue indicates very similar results for the later years of 1943-47.[31] The source of AFL discontent, then, cannot be fully and precisely indicated when AFL leadership charges the board with "bias" and pro-CIO prejudice.

Table 2

UNIT ISSUES INVOLVING AFL AND CIO
UNIONS TO 1 DECEMBER 1939

A. Cases in which there was agreement between the AFL and CIO on the unit:

(a)	Complete agreement:	131
(b)	Substantial agreement:	56
		187

B. Cases in which there was important disagreement on the unit between AFL and CIO:

(a)	AFL contention upheld:	51
(b)	CIO contention upheld:	45
(c)	Contentions of each in part upheld:	14
(d)	No decision necessary:	2
		114

Total cases decided by the board in which both AFL and CIO unions participated where the question of appropriate unit was involved: 301.

Source: Bowman, *Public Control,* 172.

It is possible that AFL antagonism to the board stemmed merely from its unwillingness to recognize the CIO as a legitimate labor organization. Just as likely, however, is the fact that the "Globe doctrine" as a basis for board decision making affected the AFL adversely in spite of the fact that, in total number of cases, the CIO appears not to have received undue favor from the board. For example, the AFL craft organization of a trade allowed for cases where a single individual in a given plant might constitute an acceptable bargaining unit within the Federation. It is difficult to say how many such "single-employee" units there existed in the AFL, but judging from the Federation's reaction to board rulings, there could not have been so very few.[32] For the Labor Board held that one individual cannot constitute a bargaining unit. This decision was reached in the *Luckenbach* and *Shick* cases.[33] The *Finch* case appeared to have been a last straw for the AFL on this question.[34] Clearly this pattern of board decision making removed any number of "units" from the AFL's jurisdiction. It is difficult to say if this had a significant effect on AFL membership figures, but it reduced the capacity of the AFL to represent as great a number of units as it had in the past. More than loss of membership, however, the AFL feared the capacity of the board to use these instances as precedents for broader application.

Of course, the AFL also feared that the skilled worker would become submerged in an industrial union mass, therefore losing his power to exert pressure on his employer by withholding skills the AFL considered indispensable to industrial functioning. This harkened back to its nineteenth-century conception of the skilled worker, and was an attempt to preserve a "vanguard" role for the skilled worker as the labor pacesetter in wages and hours contracts with employers. Thus, the "Globe doctrine," as applied by the board, which tended to merge the smaller craft units with larger units, was bitterly resented as a practice that would weaken the labor force itself. At the least, the AFL demanded that a separate unit should exist for craft and industrial unions where a plant had one or more craft workers and where both these and the rest of the plant employees desired separate units.[35] Therefore, the board's discretionary power would yield to true worker self-determination.

However that may be, it might be thought in all of this that the CIO would be lacking in critical estimation of Labor Board decisions. But the fact is that even the CIO resented the board's application of the Globe doctrine.[36] The CIO's objection, however, was that, essentially in applying the Globe doctrine, the board was demonstrating a lack of resolve. For it permitted the possibility of carving out craft units from an industrial unit by virtue of the fact that, under the Globe doctrine, the board could permit one, two, or many small groups of craft workers in a plant or industry to vote on craft affiliation, regardless of the fact that a majority (likely to be made up of the unskilled) would probably be eroded in this way. If any number of groups desired craft affiliation, each having only a minority preference, but together reducing the possibility of a plant majority emerging in an election, the result would be, if all attained recognition, sheer fragmentation and disunity. Workers would be driven by different interests and make different claims on employers. Unless craft units already predominated in given plants, workers desiring to institute them should be willing not to vote and allow the rest of the work force to render a majority opinion by ballot on the matter. The board should establish this as normal procedure.

The CIO's position proceeded from its need to become a major force by aggressively promoting the power of unskilled majorities to determine preferred representation agents wherever possible. Under the circumstances, the AFL fought a defensive battle to retain all of its units, even if they be made up of single individuals, so that the prestige of the AFL would not be lost and so that it could retain a foothold wherever it already possessed one in a given industrial organization. The CIO, therefore, stressed a preference for the board to devise election procedures which would prevent minorities desiring craft affiliation from participating in the determination of appropriate bargaining units. The only instance in which such workers could be granted undisputed self-determination was in areas where they had already been represented by craft unions for a long time, and where together, they made up a majority of the working population of a plant. The CIO urged, then, that the board take a stronger position and exert more influence in enforcing the majority rule principle.

Despite the criticisms leveled by the CIO, it supported the board warmly and urged worker support of both the board and the Wagner Act in many issues of the *CIO News* which it had begun to publish in 1937.[37] In fact, when Senator Wagner introduced an additional bill in Congress that was intended to extend the terms of the Wagner Act to all employers holding government contracts, the CIO took up the cudgels for this bill, while the AFL did not do so. The CIO eventually charged:

> The passage of the bill was seriously threatened by President Green of the AFL, who, assuming his customary role of flaying legislation favored by the majority of union workers, had called for an amendment to the bill requiring administration of its provisions by the court rather than the NLRB. This amendment was supported by witnesses for contractors and surety companies who opposed the bill.[38]

The AFL, on the other hand, drifted back to a voluntaristic demand that workers themselves determine the shape and destiny of their own organizations. The original purposes of the Wagner Act came to be seen as involving precisely the carrying out of this voluntarist mandate. In protest against government interference in labor affairs, there ought to be, it was argued, a general return to the purposes of the act. The act was now seen to be a measure that provided for worker self-organization and no board ought to interfere with the purposes of such an act:

> Return to the purposes and functions prescribed in the Na-

tional Labor Relations Law is the essence of the recommendations adopted by the Houston Convention. The law was intended to assure to wage-earners the right to membership in unions of their own choosing for the purpose of collective bargaining through their duly chosen representatives. That means Society through its administrative agents assures voluntary institutions and practices. The Act is intended to underwrite the economic right of wage-earners to union membership to advance their rights and interests.

Nothing was further from the purposes and intentions of those promoting the legislation than efforts to coerce workers into membership in unions not of their own choosing or to control the structure of union organization or to regulate union practices in collective bargaining.

The first months of administration of the Act held great promise, but unfortunate developments came when administrative duties required greater experience in the field of labor problems and greater maturity of judgment than the administrative staff possessed. The spirit of partisanship to a special form of union organization early began to interfere with impartial administration.

The Executive Council reported to the Houston Convention that the National Labor Relations Board had been administering this Act contrary to its letter and spirit and intent, with manifest bias and prejudice against the American Federation of Labor and in favor of rival and dual organizations. We have repeatedly condemned in vigorous terms the fact that a three-man board, with no direct labor experience or responsibility should undertake to determine the form and structure of our labor movement through decisions clothed with judicial authority.[39]

And at the 1938 convention, a traditionally voluntarist orientation was clearly influencing the thinking of the AFL leadership. The Committee on Resolutions, of which Matthew Woll was the chairman, went so far as to extend itself beyond its usual duties and formulated a report entitled "Present-Day Trends and Tendencies."[40] The report was a dire warning against allowing government any further "control" over labor, and, indeed, stressed the desirability of eliminating such control as it already possessed. It was clear that workingmen needed to be on their guard:

The tendency of today is for the state to take over more and more functions which we believe belong to labor itself. . . . Already the state is seizing control of our destiny through a National Labor Relations Board which has and uses the power to define the boundaries of our unions, to determine what shall be their character and even when and where there is or is not a strike in effect.[41]

This entire tendency, the report warned, endangers the traditional principles of organized labor, which wants little beyond its own independence.

> We set up a principle in our infancy. It was that we want nothing from the state that we can do for ourselves through voluntary collective action. We set up another principle which was that the labor movement must make its own policies and control its own destinies.[42]

Matthew Woll was an extreme tradtionalist, however, and something less than fully representative of AFL thinking, even of the Executive Council. Even if we grant that John Frey, also on the Resolutions Committee, would jump to support this report (which he did), we might justifiably ask if all national leaders of the AFL would go quite so far. William Green, for one, could be seen to be hedging. This became obvious after one of the delegates to the convention from the Pattern Makers union made strong objections to the Resolution Committee's report. According to delegate Lynch, the report was not "practical" as a guide to immediate action, and besides suffering from an excess of philosophizing, it constituted an attack on the Roosevelt administration which he was not willing to support. Woll assured the delegate that nothing in the report could be construed as an attack on the sincerity and good intentions of the administration. But then, Green himself submitted that the report was, in fact, somewhat "confused" on this point.

Green's hedging response was not merely a reflection of his rather tepid personality. It represented the temper of a majority of AFL leaders, national and local, present at the 1938 convention. For despite AFL anger with the criticism of the National Labor Relations Board, it had not gone so far as to renounce the existence of a national labor board on principle. One of the AFL's vice-presidents, Gainor, cautioned the Federation to stay flexible on this matter:

> Let us go along as our common sense demands; let us follow the course as America has followed it from the beginning.[43]

An amendment to modify the Woll report and a motion to refer it back to the Executive Council for "further study" was offered by a delegate from the Lathers. Even Woll backed down a bit in the face of a largely skeptical response to the report and defended it only on the grounds that it raised vital issues for Federation consideration and was intended to do little else.[44] Numbers of delegates urged a cautious but "flexible" attitude toward government generally and labor boards specifically, and warned Woll to take great care not to sound like the NAM and other business enemies of the Wagner Act.[45] Moreover, it should be stressed that for all the grievances and anger the AFL harbored against the NLRB, it did refuse to join a chorus of employer and congressional opponents of the Wagner Act in demands to repeal it and confined itself mainly to insisting on amendments that would reduce the discretionary power of the board.

In 1938, then, voluntarist rhetoric continued to appear in the statements and comments of AFL leaders. And yet, for fear of joining employers in their resentment of labor legislation, voluntarist notions were not pressed very far, and the AFL called only for modifying rather than rejecting outright the government's role in dealing with industrial disputes. After all, whatever aid and comfort the CIO received from the National Labor Relations Board, it is true that company union growth had fallen off seriously and was on the decline, in no small part due to the work of the board, while the organized labor movement as a whole continued to make impressive gains in strength and numbers. The result was that the Federation neither really accepted the labor board institution nor really rejected it, its leaders counseling that labor maintain a "flexible" attitude.

This ambivalence is evident in an address given by William Green to the Economic Club of Chicago on 15 December 1938. On the one hand, Green expounded at great length on the NLRB's tyrannies and errors. Indeed, he insisted, the American people as a whole, including labor, are mortified by the Labor Board's performance to such an extent that popular doubts about the value of the board's existence are pervasive, and that he, Green, would find it no loss to labor if the board were abolished. On the other hand, Green contended in the same breath that:

> Government regulation to prevent abuses or public exploitation by industrial and financial organizations has long since become a part of the national policy. Indeed such regulation has been and will ever continue to be a function of government itself.[46]

And so, "flexibility" both sustained and diluted the voluntarist stance and the AFL remained as unclear and ambivalent in its outlook as it had been since 1932. Meanwhile, the CIO was drifting rapidly away from the voluntarist past. The effects of this on the AFL and labor ideology will be the subject of a later chapter.

Notes

[1] U.S., Executive Office, *Decisions of the National Labor Board* (Washington, D.C.: Government Printing Office, 1934), pt. 1, "Berkeley Woolen Mills and Textile Workers," pp. 5-6.

[2] Ibid., "Houde Engineering and Auto Workers Federal Labor Union," p. 87.

[3] Robert R. R. Brooks, *As Steel Goes. . . . Unionism in a Basic Industry*, p. 66.

[4] The NAM and the steel companies came out in force against Wagner's bill. The press opposed it. But the AFL supported the bill. Wagner felt pressured into reformulating it. This was accomplished through the Senate Committee under Walsh, its chairman, who reported it out of committee on 26 May under Walsh's title, the National Industrial Adjustment Bill (NIAB). The revised bill received the endorsement of Wagner, Johnson, Richberg and Frances Perkins, secretary of labor. Green was ambivalent about its modifications and the press remained cool to the NIAB. The NAM remained unrelenting. Under these circumstances, even the modified version of the bill stood little chance of passing both houses of Congress.

[5] *New York Times*, 7 November 1934, pp. 1, 3, 8, 9, 11, 15.

[6] Irving Bernstein, *The New Deal Collective Bargaining Policy*, p. 89. See also Raymond Moley's *After Seven Years*, p. 304.

[7] There is much evidence that Roosevelt evinced little interest in the Wagner Act. Frances Perkins, who was Roosevelt's secretary of labor throughout his term of office, has said of the president's relation to the Wagner Act: "It ought to be on record that the President did not take part in developing the National Labor Relations Act, and, in fact, was hardly consulted about it. It was not a part of the President's program. It did not particularly appeal to him when it was described to him. All the credit for it belongs to Wagner" (*The Roosevelt I Know* [New York: Viking Press, 1946], p. 239). Raymond Moley, at the time still in good standing with the administration, corroborates Perkins's statement. He also indicates that Roosevelt's last-minute adoption of the act occurred because the president "needed the influence and votes of Wagner on so many pieces of legislation and partly because of the invalidation of the N.I.R.A." (*After Seven Years*, p. 304). The most thorough research into the New Deal labor and collective bargaining legislation has been done by Irving Bernstein. After an exhaustive study of the relevant documents

and all the key personnel he records the president's lack of interest in the Wagner bill (*New Deal Collective Bargaining Policy*, pp. 25, 56, 89, 114). Finally, it is interesting that in the hearings before the Senate Education and Labor Committee, administration spokesmen, like Perkins or Biddle, played a minor part in all the proceedings (though Biddle proposed the fifth unfair labor practice recognized by the bill). Nevertheless, the administration made no comment on the Biddle proposal. It should be said for Roosevelt, however, that when he did manage to accept the Wagner Act, he did not sway under the pressure exerted both by congressional or business enemies of the act.

⁸Bernstein, *New Deal*, p. 89.

⁹*American Federationist*, 41, no. 3 (March 1935): 243-44, 249.

¹⁰Bernstein, *New Deal*, p. 83.

¹¹Report of the Executive Council, *AFL Convention Proceedings*, 1935, p. 52.

¹²Hearings were held during March and April. See U.S. Senate, Committee on Education and Labor, *Hearings, National Labor Relations Board*, 74th Cong., 1st sess., 1935. The full title of the act was: "A Bill to Promote Equality of Bargaining Power Between Employers and Employees, to Diminish the Causes of Labor Disputes. . . and for Other Purposes."

¹³National Lawyers Committee of the American Liberty League, *Report on Constitutionality of the National Labor Relations Act*, New York, 1935; reprinted in E. David Cronon, ed., *Labor and the New Deal*, p. 31.

¹⁴"The Ideal State—As Wagner Sees It," *New York Times Magazine*, 9 May 1937, p. 23.

¹⁵George G. Higgins, *Voluntarism in Organized Labor*, p. 85 (italics added).

¹⁶The first decision of the Supreme Court on the validity of the NLRA and its application by the NLRB was handed down on 12 April 1937. The case arose during a dramatic period in which Roosevelt, frustrated by the Court's decision on a number of matters, notably the NIRA, suggested the reorganization of the court to include "younger" and "more" members on the bench. This "court packing plan" is generally felt to have influenced the Court's decision in April. The specific case involved, however, was *National Labor Relations Board v. Jones and Laughlin Steel Corporation*. In this case, a union affiliate of the Amalgamated Association of Iron, Steel and Tin Workers of America charged the steel company with discrimination against union members. The corporation failed to produce evidence to refute this charge. But it did contend that the NLRA was unconstitutional and thus refused to comply with the Labor Board's order to cease and desist in its discriminatory practices. Consequently, the board petitioned the Circuit Court of Appeals, as provided in Section 10(e) of the act, requesting that the Court enforce its order. The Court declined and thus the Board took the case, on a writ of certeriori, to the Supreme Court. For elaboration and extensive citation of arguments in this case, see Charles Aiken, ed., *National Labor Relations Board Cases*, pp. 19-20.

[17]Chamber of Commerce of the United States, *Federal Regulation of Labor Relations*, p. 4. Also National Association of Manufacturers, *Why and How the Wagner Act Should be Amended*, pp. 19-20.

[18]U.S., Congress, House, Committee on Labor, *Minority Report Proposed Amendment to the National Labor Relations Act*, 76th Cong., 3d sess., 1940, H. Rept. 1928, pt 3, p. 10.

[19]Harry A. Millis and Emily C. Brown, *From the Wagner Act to Taft-Hartley*, p. 34n. Appropriations figures were taken from the annual reports of the board.

[20]*AFL Convention Proceedings*, 1937, p. 489.

[21]Ibid., p. 127.

[22]Dean O. Bowman, *Public Control of Labor Relations: A Study of the National Labor Relations Board*, p. 207.

[23]Early in its life the NLRB was forced to determine whether a majority was constituted by those eligible to vote, or a majority of those who actually voted. At first it adopted the former interpretation, but it soon found that this inspired coercion to keep employees from voting. The NLRB then changed its policies and certified unions if they received a majority of the votes cast. This proved wise, for it compelled all interested groups to vie in getting into the vote.

[24]Cited in the *American Federationist* 42, no. 4 (April 1935): 386.

[25]1 NLRB 530 (1936).

[26]1 NLRB 604 (1936).

[27]The first case in which the NLRB intervened in the AFL-CIO disputes was the Interlake Iron Corporation case, 2 NLRB 1036, decided in June 1937. For Madden's statement see U.S., Congress, *Congressional Record*, 75th Cong., 1st sess., 1937, 81, pt. 3:3216.

[28]Application of this reasoning may be seen in 2 NLRB 1036 (1937): 3 NLRB 257 (1937); 13 NLRB 1303 (1934); 13 NLRB 1308 (1939); and 13 NLRB 1322 (1937) among others.

[29]3 NLRB 294 (1937).

[30]*American Federationist* 45, no. 8 (August 1938): 802.

[31]Millis and Brown, *From the Wagner Act to Taft-Hartley*, pp. 143-47.

[32]U.S., Congress, House, Committee on Labor, *Hearings on Proposed Amendment to the National Labor Relations Act*, 76th Cong., 1st sess., 1939, vol. 3, pp. 863-67 and 1064-67.

[33]See Bowman, *Public Control*, pp. 166-67 for a discussion of 2 NLRB 181 and 4 NLRB 246.

[34]Ibid., pp. 167-68 for discussion of 10 NLRB 896.

[35]House, Committee on Labor, *Hearings on Proposed Amendment*, 76th Cong., 1st sess., 1939, 3:756-73.

[36]U.S., Congress, Senate, Committee on Education and Labor, *Hearings to Amend the National Labor Relations Act*, 76th Cong., 3d sess., 13 August-16 September 1940, pp. 4265-76.

[37]*CIO News*, 29 January 1938; ibid., 5 February 1938.

[38]Ibid., 26 March 1938.

[39]*American Federationist* 45, no. 11 (November 1938): 1171-72.

[40]*AFL Convention Proceedings*, 1938, pp. 457-63.

[41]Ibid., p. 457.

[42]Ibid., p. 457. It might also be said that William Green went on for years delivering speeches on the need to return to the true purposes of the Wagner Act. See his "Amend the National Labor Relations Act, Address to the Saturday Discussions Committee of the New York Republican Club in New York," *Vital Speeches of the Day*, 1 March 1940, pp. 311-14.

[43]*AFL Convention Proceedings*, 1938, pp. 461-62.

[44]Ibid., p. 462.

[45]Ibid., p. 462.

[46]This address was reprinted in *Vital Speeches of the Day*, 15 January 1939, pp. 208-10. See especially pages 209-10. It should be pointed out that Green's ambivalence did lead him to propose the *abolition* of administrative boards like the NLRB in settling industrial conflict and to suggest that Congress fulfill this "regulatory" function directly through statutory enactment. In this way, Green sought to reconcile an antilabor board position with one that accepted a government role in industrial affairs. This did not, however, become a general demand of the AFL which tended rather to confine itself to demands for amending the Wagner Act to reduce the board's power.

Chapter 6

The Challenge
of Social Security

If events around passage and administration of the Wagner Act highlighted an AFL propensity toward ideological modification on the one hand and resistance to this tendency on the other, Federation reactions to the Social Security Act, which was passed in 1935, revealed how pervasive ideological uncertainty had actually become among the AFL leaders. Indeed, were it not for the fact that the leadership of the CIO exhibited a bold willingness to cast some traditional notions to the winds, at least after it began to publicize its independent legislative views between 1937 and 1938, the organized labor movement in America might never have developed a clear position or deeply felt stake in economic security legislation. For AFL leaders influenced by the Gompers creed were developing, and even cultivating, the habit of making elusive statements aimed at preserving valued traditions on the one hand, while conceding to distasteful but overpowering circumstances on the other. Such a habit would do little to fan enthusiasm for social security. In any event, it would certainly reveal how obscure voluntarist traditions were becoming by virtue of AFL inclinations to think and even act in contradictory ways at the same time.

The Social Security Act became law in 14 August 1935, and was the outcome of the Roosevelt administration's application of a new strategy to the problem of economic recovery from the severe depression which, despite occasional upturns, had continued to haunt the nation since 1929. In essence, it was a measure that affirmed the right of all citizens to claim economic aid from the American government when they became incapable of full self-support through no fault of their own. That is to say, the disabled, the aged, the involuntarily unemployed, dependent children, those unable to secure gainful work, and those left without an adequate source of income became entitled by the law to some measure of aid from the government of the nation, sufficient at least for their bare survival.

The titles of the act, while intended to cover broad areas of economic need, nevertheless distinguished between two groups of beneficiaries and were formulated so that each would secure benefits by different methods. One group of beneficiaries would contribute, through a minimal tax on incomes, to the general fund from which payments would be made. The other group would be noncontributing. The contributing group (which excluded farm and domestic labor) would constitute a vast public serviced by a social insurance program in which payments were made to individuals upon their retirement from the job market in old age, during periods in their working lives when they found themselves temporarily and involuntarily unemployed, or to their survivors in the event of death (health insurance was not made available at that time). The payments were received as a matter of right by virtue of tax contributions recipient individuals had made in the course of their income-earning years. The noncontributing group would be made up of all those who lived in a state of extreme dependency and in no position to alleviate this situation. They were to be serviced by a public assistance program, which did not make eligibility for aid dependent on prior tax contributions and under which payments would be made after determination of the extent of an aged, impoverished, or disabled person's need. It might be mentioned, however, that although the act set up both social insurance and public assistance systems, popular usage has tended over the years to equate "social security" with the social insurance system. But the act defined categories of need within both systems and provided for state and federal methods of distribution.

While the institution of social security reflected a slowly changing American attitude toward poverty and unemployment—individuals rendered economically dependent by circumstances beyond their control were no longer to be abused with charges of personal failure and moral delinquency—it was not intended to significantly alter the distribution of wealth in the nation. It was in fact intended to do little more than improve mass purchasing power toward the end of national recovery and to keep it stable enough to minimize the most destructive effects of depression. Payments made to any beneficiaries were to be kept at minimal levels and would under no circumstances be allowed to equate or even approach income standards derived from gainful employment. Much effort was expended by the framers of the act to guarantee to the public, and especially to businessmen of all sorts, that socialism was not insinuating itself into American life through the Social Security Act, and that the Puritan ethic no less than the spirit of capitalism were safe from destruction. The limited character of the law was often and candidly discussed by one of its most important founding fathers, usually with the purpose of assuaging business suspicions or opposition. For example, as late as 17 June 1938, Edwin Witte was still explaining to the Wisconsin Alumni Institute:

> Social Security is not a remedy for all economic ills. It does not even attempt to deal with the most serious difficulties in our economic system, which are associated with its violent fluctuations and apparently increasing severity of depressions. Only to a very minor degree does it modify the distribution of wealth and it does not alter at all the fundamentals of our capitalistic and individualistic economy. Nor does it relieve the individual of primary responsibility for his own support and that of his dependents. . . . It would be killing the goose that laid the golden egg if in seeking to establish social security we burdened enterprise so that it cannot function.[1]

Businessmen's fears may have been somewhat soothed by statements like Witte's. But how would an organized labor movement confront legislation that implicitly denied the validity of its voluntarist traditions, traditions that regarded social security as an obstruction to union growth and strength? It would be reasonable, certainly, to expect that a union movement which had made it a matter of principle that all distributive functions be centered in its own constituent locals would be reticent toward, if not violently opposed to, the Social Security Act of 1935. For Gompers and other founding fathers of the AFL would have regarded social insurance as a matter to be negotiated privately between employers and workers through representative unions, insofar as it was acceptable at all, and public assistance would have been seen as a public bribe to prevent unions from organizing the unorganized labor force (although the AFL traditionally favored some form of old-age assistance). The first reaction of the AFL, at least as stated by its leadership, to the Social Security Act on the occasion of its passage, seemed rather congenial:

> On August 14, President Roosevelt signed the Social Security measure by which we hope to provide dependable incomes for some of the emergencies of life that frequently overtake us. This act seeks to express as a national policy and practice our sense of obligation for those victims of forces beyond their control.[2]

Indeed, on the basis of this Federation statement, it would be easy to assume that all traces of traditional voluntarism were consigned to the past as irrelevancies in the face of contemporary conditions. No hint of fear appears to exist here that union building might be weakened by a government policy of income supplementation; either is there any suggestion that worker morality will suffer impairment as a consequence. Social insurance seems proper government business and public assistance will aid the human victims of a capitalist economy. It is, of course, possible that the minimal character of the act allowed the AFL to feel that its role in securing better wages for workers was not significantly curtailed, and that a national social security system was less of a threat than had been traditionally assumed. Still, if one compares this statement with those made by the AFL on behalf of the Wagner Act, also passed in 1935, one will surely notice that the former is strikingly bland in contrast to the latter. And this is rather revealing. In fact, investigation of AFL behavior in relation to a variety of legislative proposals for social insurance, as well as the one which finally became national law, indicates that the AFL's statement in support of the Social Security Act is not to be taken too seriously at face value. Let us retrace some of the steps that led up to it in order to demonstrate that fact.

Two bills had been under congressional consideration since 1934, each of them designed to bring some kind of economic assistance or social insurance system into effect. These were the Wagner-Lewis bill and the Dill-Connery bill. The Dill-Connery bill had, in fact, been before the Congress since 1932. It had even passed the House of Representatives in both 1933 and 1934. And while it won favorable comments in the Senate, it did not come to a vote in that body. It had been a bill designed to give federal aid to the states for old-age assistance and had been one of a number of measures promoted by the American Association for Social Security. It was motivated in part by the fact that the number of states which had passed their own old-age assistance laws had increased from seven to twenty-seven between 1928 and 1933, and state budgets were gradually becoming strained by the burdens of supporting these assistance measures.

In February 1934, the Wagner-Lewis bill (which had been drafted by Thomas Eliot, then the assistant solicitor of the Department of Labor) had been proposed in both houses of Congress. It was a measure which aimed mainly at instituting both unemployment *and* old-age insurance. It might be mentioned that Edwin Witte, a major figure in the ultimate creation of the Social Security Act, speculates that Supreme Court Justice Louis D. Brandeis formulated the terms of the bill proposed by Wagner and Lewis. He indicates that the bill came to Senator Wagner after drafting in the Department of Labor and that the essence of the bill was proposed to Secretary of Labor Perkins by Elizabeth Brandeis and Paul Raushenbush, the daughter and son-in-law of Justice Brandeis.[3]

However that may be, the Wagner-Lewis bill was preferred over the Dill-Connery bill by the administration. The president even sent a public letter to Chairman Doughton endorsing the Wagner-Lewis bill when hearings were held on it in the spring of 1934 before a subcommittee of the House Ways and Means Committee. Reasons for the president's preference are unclear. Witte, in fact, even notes that many administration leaders favored the Dill-Connery bill.[4] It is possible, however, that Roosevelt's preference stemmed from the fact that the Wagner-Lewis measure proposed the institution of a *social insurance* system for handling payments to the unemployed and the aged. Thus, vast revenues could be raised by taxing business *payrolls* and as such would permit the raising of monies for ecnomic relief more readily and directly than would be the case for a *public assistance* scheme. Moreover, the terms of the Wagner-Lewis bill were obviously more comprehensive than those of the Dill-Connery bill. And in addition, the Wagner-Lewis bill seemed well designed to withstand tests of constitutional validity. For it divided taxing and administrative powers along federalist lines. That is, it did not give to the national government sole responsibility for collection and distribution of monies, something which enemies of social security notions could charge constituted improper federal intervention in the financial affairs of the states. Rather, it sought to induce state governments to enact and administer compensation laws within guidelines proposed in a national law. More specifically, it provided for a levy of an excise tax of 5 percent on employers of ten or more employees against which an offset was to be allowed for payments made during the taxable year to "reserve" or unemployment insurance funds established pursuant to a state law which satisfied standards prescribed in the national law. And under the old-age provisions of the bill, the states were to make payments to eligible individuals (those seventy years or older) not to exceed $30 per month, but to which the federal government would contribute $15.

Now it was the Wagner-Lewis bill that came to occupy congressional attention, probably because the president favored it over the Dill-Connery bill. And it is likely that for this reason, the AFL also gave its attention to the Wagner-Lewis measure over the Dill-Connery bill. Yet examination of congressional hearings held on the bill, at which Federation opinion was represented by William Green, shows that the AFL was far from satisfied with it. For the Wagner-Lewis bill, in its allowance that the states may pass laws on unemployment insurance within certain guidelines provided in the bill, could include state laws which levied a tax, however slight, on workers' salaries as well as on employer payrolls. Under the circumstances of the Depression, this had to amount to an injustice. First, worker salaries would be depleted, even if only slightly, at a time when this could not be afforded. Second, employers paying the payroll tax would pass on the costs of it to the public in the form of higher prices. The cost to labor would thus be borne twice over. And as if this were not bad enough, the states would be left free to adopt either "industry reserve" or "state-pooled" schemes for unemployment insurance. This was no small or merely technical matter. For under an industry reserve (sometimes called individual company reserve) scheme, employers could, if they decided to, manipulate workers against unions. This would not be possible under a pooled-fund arrangement. Green was very emphatic on this point:

> I recommend that neither company reserves nor industry reserves shall be permitted, but that the bill shall provide for State-pooled funds only. In regard to the danger of individual company or industry reserves I cannot be too emphatic. Such reserves will be of benefit only to those employers whose risks are low and will

be taken advantage of only by those employers. Plant, company or industry unemployment reserves are not unemployment insurance. . . . We have seen company reserves tried as a method of unemployment insurance. There is no reason why experimentation should go so far as to try again something which has not, and of its very nature cannot, prove satisfactory. . . . The withdrawal of the "better" employers and industries from the State-pooled funds would seriously weaken State funds and endanger the employees who are working for the companies left in the pool. . . . Employers who are strongly opposed to . . . trade unions will be able to use their company or industry reserve as a weapon. . . . They might offer slightly higher benefits, or pay benefits for a little longer period, upon the understanding that their employees remain unorganized.[5]

In brief, the AFL was skeptical because the bill permitted reserve schemes under state law and these allowed individual companies, or the employers in a given industry within a state, to file accounts for their workers on an individual basis. Because of this, an employer might deal with his workers individually and arrange with them to be compensated in ways cheaper to the employer than the cost of state taxes might be. Or he might find ways to encourage employees to think that he would protect their unemployment insurance file as long as they agreed not to unionize his plant. He might even find ways to fire individual employees (especially if they are known for prounion sentiments) and avoid paying tax on their accounts at all. The employer might innovate in a variety of ways under a reserve system in order to forestall or avoid unionization of his plant. Taxes paid into an impersonal state pool, however, would not be open to such manipulation.

AFL leaders, however, did not publicly state whether they felt that the proposed measure would have a weakening effect on trade unionism in other ways. In the first place, the AFL had already gone on record publicly in favor of unemployment insurance at its 1932 convention. While AFL leaders had expressed favorable attitudes toward at least a limited insurance program, largely to forestall a movement of dissidents within the Federation from gaining power over the organization, their traditional notions were not unaffected by this development. Thus such notions lost a former certainty and clarity and acquired an indistinctness which no longer permitted decisive rejection of some form of social insurance. In the second place, the dissident movement which had become influential within AFL ranks in 1932 was far from dissipated in 1934 when the Wagner-Lewis bill was under congressional consideration. For at the 1934 AFL convention, AFL leaders were confronted by a resolution, introduced by delegates Raymond Lowry and Florence Hanson of the American Federation of Teachers (both these delegates consistently raised resolutions that seemed radical given AFL traditions), which affirmed in principle the need for broad social security legislation to cover old-age, health, disability, and unemployment insurance, as well as public assistance for the needy. They called on the AFL to initiate a campaign for "Federal Social Legislation including unemployment, old-age, sickness, injury, and maternity insurance."[6] Moreover, other proposals had also been raised from the floor calling for these items individually. The AFL Executive Council was, therefore, hardly in a position to reverse its 1932 stand and not likely to deal harshly with social security proposals under the circumstances.

This was especially true because the dissident movement within the AFL was moving fast and furiously to sympathy with a specific measure which was more radical than even the Wagner-Lewis bill. This situation provided AFL leaders with an additional motive for offering at least tepid support for the Wagner-Lewis bill. The socialist congressional representative, Ernest Lundeen of Minnesota, had proposed an unemployment insurance bill in Congress which was simple but unprecedentedly generous and becoming popular with left-wing groups throughout the country. It was introduced in the House on 3 January 1934, and Lundeen was giving it wide publicity through hearings he was holding on the bill. The Lundeen unemployment insurance bill proposed that compensation for unemployment be equal to whatever a worker's wages were in any given locale, but that it would never be below $10 per week, plus $3 additional per week for each one of a worker's dependents. Workmen's compensation for injury was also included in the bill. Money for this insurance plan was to come, not from payroll taxes, but from the Treasury, from funds not otherwise appropriated, from levying taxes on inheritances, gifts, and individual and corporation incomes over $5,000. All kinds of labor would be covered by the bill, including factory, farm, and domestic labor (unlike the Wagner-Lewis bill). Self-employed persons would be included also. Moreover, the plan, once instituted, would be administered by workers and farmers under conditions prescribed by the secretary of labor through unemployment insurance commissions. The personnel for these commissions would be elected by workers' and farmers' organizations. The left-wing clamor for the Lundeen bill was getting through to the AFL rank and file. And this agitation was to convince the AFL leadership that it ought, despite its own feelings or traditions in the matter, support some kind of social security measure.

At hearings held on the Lundeen bill, F. Elmer Brown, chairman of the National Congress for Unemployment and Social Insurance and a member of the Typographical Union in New York City, the largest local within the AFL's international, warmly expressed his support and explained that workers in the printing industry, fed up with the failures of the Recovery Act, were ready to join in the fight for the Lundeen bill.[7] Dozens of witnesses from labor and farm organizations, as well as unemployment councils, gave testimony favorable to the Lundeen measure. Louis Weinstock of the AFL's Brotherhood of Painters, Decorators, and Paperhangers of America, enthusiastically supported Lundeen and stated that three thousand AFL locals supported him.[8] Weinstock submitted a list to the committee of endorsing organizations,[9] and repeated in no uncertain terms that labor supported the "workers' bill" put forward by Lundeen:

> The rank-and-file members of the American Federation of Labor unions, in spite of definite instructions received from the top officials to endorse the Wagner-Lewis bill, were not ready to follow without analyzing the measure proposed. Wherever they had an opportunity to compare the worker's bill and the Wagner-Lewis bill, the result showed that they favored the workers' bill and rejected the Wagner-Lewis bill. . . . The convention of the Amalgamated Association of Iron, Steel and Tin Workers of America [was] held in April in 1934 in Pittsburgh. . . . At present this organization has a membership of over 100,000. The workers' bill was unanimously endorsed by the delegates present...and [they] instructed their officials to support the workers' bill at the American Federation of Labor convention in San Francisco. The convention of the United Textile Workers, an organization with hundreds of locals all over the country, held [in] August 1934, in New York City, went on record for the workers' bill by a great majority. The delegates gave similar instructions to its officials to support the bill at the American Federation of Labor convention. . . . [The] Mine, Mill and Smelter Workers' Union. . . at its convention in August 1934 held

in Salt Lake City. . . unanimously endorsed the workers'
bill, decided to notify every local of this action, and
ask[ed] for their approval of the convention decision.
This was done and the locals gave full support to the action of the convention decision. Scores of central labor
bodies, district councils, state federations of labor and
other bodies have endorsed the workers' bill.[10]

Not only this, but Weinstock indicated that worker delegations
had visited the AFL Executive Council, and that the council had
sidestepped demands for any kind of social security measure and
even avoided mentioning the Lundeen bill.[11]

The Lundeen bill never came to a vote in Congress and it is
presently impossible to determine if the measure, during the
short time it attracted labor's attention, was popular with a majority of AFL members. But in view of such support as was clearly
given to the "workers' bill," it is no surprise that Federation leaders accepted the more conservative Wagner-Lewis bill, and did
not pursue their doubts or objections beyond criticism of the bill's
provisions for modes of distributing unemployment compensation. Neither should it be surprising that there was a striking pau-
city of public statements about social security of any type of the
part of AFL leaders, and a bland "all purpose" rhetoric employed
by them in stating such support as they gave for administration
social security measures.[12] This kind of tepid response to the
whole social security issue in 1934 is nowhere better illustrated
than at the AFL convention of that year. On that occasion, the
Committee on Resolutions had taken upon itself responsibility for
the formulation and presentation of a proposal that recommended
that the matter of social security be assigned to the Federation's
Legislative Department for its consideration. Moreover, it was
agreed that such concrete action as was warranted to promote
social security in America could, actually, at least for the present,
be fulfilled by "strengthening" the AFL's Legislative Department.
Thus, in response to the social security issue, the committee stated:

> Your committee is of the opinion that labor's legislative
> necessities are becoming more and more urgent, and
> must continue to be so because of the far-reaching in-
> dustrial problems being made a matter of national leg-
> islation; therefore, the Legislative Department of the
> American Federation of Labor should be strengthened
> as may be required by the Executive Council. . . . This

necessary end may be secured by increasing the numbers of the Legislative Committee. . . . and any such other methods as the Council may determine. . . . Your Committee therefore recommends that the Executive Council be instructed to give immediate consideration to the steps necessary to carry out the recommendations of your committee.[13]

A very similar response was made to the Social Security Act before it passed Congress in 1935, when it was still in stages of formulation and congressional investigation. While the Wagner-Lewis bill was being considered by Congress, the president held a cabinet meeting in May 1934, at which time a decision was taken to make no further efforts to secure the Wagner-Lewis bill, but to prepare an even more comprehensive social security program for presentation to Congress when it convened after the November elections.[14] Roosevelt signaled this intention in the first of several messages to Congress urging consideration of a social security program on 8 June 1934. The president also announced his intention to create a Committee on Economic Security to study the entire problem and make recommendations to him on the program he would be presenting to the next congress. On 29 June 1934 Roosevelt established the Committee on Economic Security by executive order. According to Edwin Witte, who was himself executive director of the committee, it consisted of:

five top Cabinet members, with Miss Perkins, Secretary of Labor, as chairman. The Committee had a staff of less than fifty research, statistical and actuarial employees, who included, however, a majority of all people in the country who were considered to be specialists on any aspect of social security. In addition, there were nine advisory committees, composed of people (not on the staff) interested in some or all of the problems with which the Committee had to deal. The most important of these advisory committees was the Technical Board, composed of government officials and employees, headed by Arthur J. Altmeyer, then an Assistant Secretary of Labor. This Board, acting as a group through subcommittees, kept in close touch with the staff and the Committee on every phase of its work and probably had more to do with the final recommendations than any other group or individual not a member of the Committee. More publicized, but distinctly less important, was the Advisory Council on Social Security, appointed by the President and composed of people representing leading nongovernmental organizations interested in social security. The other seven advisory committees were more specialized, concerned with specific problems or aspects of the social security program. There was also a two day National Conference on Economic Security, attended by several hundred men and women from all parts of the country, at which specialists not otherwise connected with the Committee presented differing views on major social security problems. Literally almost everyone in the country who had ever discussed any aspect of social security had some part in the work of the Committee on Economic Security, although all decisions reached were those of the Committee.[15]

In all of this structuring and mobilization of committees and personnel, Witte indicates that labor's role was entirely secondary. For it appears that AFL representatives were sought by the committee for participation on its advisory council. However, no one from the Federation demanded, or even actively encouraged anyone from the committee to find for any Federation people a firm place in the committee's proceedings. The manner in which Witte blandly describes the selection of labor representatives for the advisory council makes it rather clear that they passively accepted rather then sought their place on it. This contrasts very sharply with the AFL's attitude about inclusion in code-making activities under the NIRA, and even contrasts greatly with AFL behavior about government policies it regarded vital to its interests as far back as World War I:

> The labor representatives... were selected without consultation with the American Federation of Labor. To my knowledge, no one connected with the Committee talked with President Green about the work of the Committee until shortly before the National Conference on Economic Security. At that time, I outlined to him the kind of program we tentatively had in mind, and stated that we would give labor an equal number of representatives on the advisory council with employers. Mr. Green was asked whether he could serve personally, but was not asked for any other suggestions. Messrs. Harrison and Berry were selected from membership of the Executive Council of the American Federation of Labor as being the most likely to render really valuable service. Mr. Scharrenberg and Mr. Ohl were selected as representatives of the state federations of labor, and

with a view to fair territorial distribution of the council memberships.[16]

Moreover, it was noted once again by Witte, that once committee activities were under way, differences of opinion were expressed over the type of law (federal subsidy or federal-state cooperation) that should be enacted for an insurance system over the respective contributions which should be made to it by employers, employees, and government. In all of this, the labor representatives on the advisory council (which included William Green) wavered between subsidy and federal-state plans, and in any case "hardly appeared enthusiastic."[17] Nor was this lack of enthusiasm merely fleeting.

After a bill finally emerged from the efforts of the Committee on Economic Security and began a passage through Congress, and even after the bill became law, the AFL attitude remained substantially unchanged. In keeping with the president's wishes, the committee worked to prepare a "cooperative federal-state undertaking" to cover the needs of people from "the cradle to the grave." The Technical Board of the committee, headed by Arthur Altmeyer, considered three alternative plans, at least as regards the unemployment insurance provisions of the economic security legislation it was in the process of constructing. There were (1) an exclusively federal system; (2) a cooperative federal-state system on a federal subsidy plan; and (3) a cooperative federal-state system on the Wagner-Lewis federal tax-offset plan. The first of these plans would be financed and administered exclusively by the federal government. The second plan provided for the levying of a federal payroll tax of a fixed percentage while most of the proceeds from the tax would be given back to the states. The states would presumably have passed laws under which benefits would be made payable. And the small portion of the proceeds kept by the federal government would be used further "to establish a re-insurance fund, to provide benefits to migratory workers... and to finance the United States Employment Service."[18] But the third plan was the safest from the constitutional point of view because it combined the virtues of a federalist arrangement without increasing the subsidization activities of the federal government, based as it was on a tax-offset system. Moreover, it also had the advantage of appealing more strongly to businessmen who were not enthusiastic about social security legislation and whose support would be needed to make it work. Although they would have to pay a federal payroll tax of a fixed percentage, employers would be allowed credit for the contributions they would be required to pay under state unemployment insurance laws; their rates would thus turn out to be rather flexible. This twin consideration of constitutionality and employer receptiveness made the third plan under the board's consideration the one finally decided upon. Thus, the earlier Wagner-Lewis measure provided the model for the unemployment insurance provision of the Social Security Act as it was finally passed.

With respect to a security program for the aged, the committee recognized that there would have to be both assistance and provisions. Here, a straight federal system was preferred. Because of the mobility of workers, the states would not be able to estimate adequate funding necessary. The federal government could better keep a uniform system and transfer records, wage credits, and contributions of workers moving from one state to another. And so the old-age provisions of the act as finally drawn up were based on a federal plan. Because of opposition expected from the American Medical Association, however, the committee finally dropped its plans for health insurance. It concentrated instead on developing an assistance plan for children, including maternal health care and welfare services. This came from Roosevelt's request that the committee prepare a social security plan that would provide support for all major contingencies which might beset citizens temporarily or permanently disadvantaged by circumstances beyond their control. A grants-in-aid system to the states was adopted to finance this portion of the program. This was preferred so that the children's security program (Aid to Dependent Children, ADC) would not come under the authority of the Federal Emergency Relief Administration (FERA). Administration of ADC grants was vested with a Social Security Board created to carry out the terms of the act.[19]

The breadth of the program drawn up by the committee at the president's behest had the effect of reducing interest in all other bills before Congress, with the result that the Lundeen measure never did reach the floor for debate or vote. The committee proceeded to draft the program into a bill (again Thomas Eliot of the Labor Department was the major draftsman) and it was introduced in both houses of Congress several days after the president's special message. Hearings began before the House Ways and Means Committee on 21 January and before the Senate Finance Committee on 22 January.

Disagreements over the social security bill at once erupted in the House, the Senate, the press, and among various business associations. The economic basis of the act, an important area of debate, is beyond the scope of this study; but there was dispute enough on other grounds—over proper administration of the old-age, unemployment-compensation, and children's security portions of the bill; over the morality of compulsory as distinct from voluntary insurance systems; and over the miserliness or excessive generosity of the coverage provided in the bill. Amendments were proposed and constant changes were being made in the wording of the bill while it was in committee. An amendment was pressed by Senator Champ Clark which provided that exemption from the government old-age insurance system be granted to all those employers and employees participating in a private pension plan that offered "superior" or more liberal terms. This infuriated all those who felt that, laudable as the voluntary principle back of the Clark amendment was, it could and would weaken the government program severely. Senator Huey Long attempted a filibuster to defeat the bill. Finally, after the occurrence of numerous disputes, amendments, conferences, and the like, the Social Security Act was passed by both houses of Congress, sent to the president and signed by him on 14 August 1935. That which became the law of the land was not too unlike the Wagner-Lewis bill previously under consideration (about which labor had not enthused), yet was a measure more comprehensive than any other before Congress.

Throughout the debate and despite attacks leveled at the Social Security Act from congressional and business quarters, even despite the AFL's own formal endorsement of the act;

> organized labor took little part in the congressional hearings. President Green of the A.F. of L. testified as a government witness before both committees, but was quite critical of the bill. His statement before the Senate Committee was a long, carefully prepared memorandum, in which he suggested many amendments. This statement was interpreted in the newspapers as an attack upon the bill by organized labor. On the next day, before the House Committee, he talked off-hand and indicated that, while organized labor would like to see the bill amended as he had suggested to the Senate Committee, it was for the bill in any event. This accurately reflected the attitude of organized labor. *It was far less interested in social security than many other questions,* but, while *not enthusiastic* about the Administration's program, *mildly favored* this measure.[20]

Moreover, just as tepid sentiments or elusive comments on social security marked the Federation's 1934 convention, the convention of 1935 became the occasion for statements made in a similar vein. The report of the Executive Council to the convention of that year had carefully outlined all of the provisions of the Social Security Act and noted them with favor. But challenges arose from the floor and four proposals urging support and passage of the Lundeen bill were offered by various delegates. One of them, Lawrence of the Casket Makers, refused to join in a motion to accept the council's report on social security and angrily confronted Matthew Woll:

> Can we look upon the enactment of the Social Security law as a victory for labor? . . . Why was this law passed? . . .[I]t is sidetracking such legislation as . . . the Lundeen Unemployment Insurance Bill. . . such a measure has been offered as a substitute. But it cannot feed the eleven million unemployed today, and we must recognize that fact and not consider what is written on paper as a victory when it is not.[21]

To this, Woll, who obviously resented the fact that the criticism was motivated by a desire for a more radical bill, replied that no one, least of all himself, claimed perfection for the Social Security Act. Moreover, he said, the Executive Council expected to engage in close study of the act with an eye toward recommending proper amendments for it. This alone invalidated the delegate's criticism, for inadequacies of the Social Security Act would be looked into and properly improved. It was, according to Woll, all in all a splendid act, perfectible over time, flexible and open to change, and thus, little reason for complaint really existed. But other than "close study," Woll had no suggestion to make concerning a course of action that might be pursued to bring about improvement in the terms or coverage of the act. And he even ended his comments with a heavy sigh of relief that "unrealistic" social security schemes had not been instituted. Woll's statement revealed how little an interest in the social security law had to do with Federation support for it.

The statement of support for the Social Security Act of 1935, then, which was cited at the outset of this chapter, proves to have been one which hid many tense and unresolved feelings about social security, as much as it was an effort to come to some kind of harmonious terms with it. Because of this, it would be difficult indeed to insist that the AFL's position represented a full and firm departure from voluntarism.

It will be useful to briefly examine the pressures in American society during the time the social security measure was being formulated. For such an examination will reveal further and underscore the fact that the Federation's leadership took no active or enthusiastic part in bringing this legislation into being. At least until mid-1934, when the president only began to show interest in the Wagner-Lewis bill, the administration's orientation toward economic recovery was still largely based on the conviction that businessmen could be induced to reform their economic behavior toward alleviating the worst effects of economic depression. Therefore, legislation was formulated with an eye toward regulating business behavior, or at any rate, including business leaders to regulate their own activities toward the end of achieving national recovery. This "regulatory" emphasis did not involve assigning to government a direct role in the redistribution of income. Labor sentiment on social security was diffuse enough so that by itself it could not have redirected administration thinking toward "redistributive" approaches to economic difficulties. But pressure for such reorientation did arise from essentially two sources, both quite outside the labor movement, that proved powerful enough to deeply influence presidential policy. In the first place, in 1934 Roosevelt showed an increasing inclination to pay serious attention to "neo-Brandeisian" advisers with strong antitrust sentiments, like Thomas Corcoran and Benjamin Cohen, among others, who saw in taxation schemes a way to reform or curtail corporate wealth. They drafted legislative proposals for the president's attention that involved, among their other features, provisions for taxing corporations so that their size and influence could be reduced, as well as for taxation aimed at redistributing wealth through the institution of national insurance and welfare services. Many students of the New Deal are willing to attribute to the influence of the neo-Brandeisians Roosevelt's increasing concern for income redistribution, and finally, by 1935, his redistributive rather than regulatory orientation to recovery. Their influence is said to be responsible for a "Second New Deal," distinguished from the first precisely by a redistributive over a regulatory emphasis.[22] But there was also a second major consideration.

The slowness of improvement in the economic situation was causing severe discontent among all sectors of the population. Businessmen complained loudly that New Deal measures were preventing production and employment increases. Intellectuals publicly questioned in numerous articles both the administration's political acumen as well as the virtues of the capitalist system. Serious challenges to two-party politics were arising in many states from independent party movements. And, perhaps most important from the president's point of view, popular dissatisfaction was gaining in stridency and momentum all over the country, both on the right and of the left of the political spectrum. Fearfully, people began to wonder openly if the country's troubles were not, after all, so persistent because capitalism itself was sapped of vitality and its capacity for rejuvenation dwindling away. Although left-wing leaders were organizing workers' councils to fight for unemployment insurance or relief in many cities across the nation, a major movement for redistribution of wealth was taking clearer and more massive shape under the leadership of right-wing demagogues.

To appreciate Roosevelt's growing receptiveness during 1934-35 to social security programs, we should consider for a moment the proportions of this popular cry for relief and redistribution, especially as it was organized by a right-wing "populist" leadership (later scholars would attach the label "fascist" to describe some of these developments). Amid a gathering atmosphere of irritation and doubt, Father Charles E. Coughlin, a Roman Catholic priest, was building an impressive following into a movement. Though the movement was developing into an anticommunist crusade, Coughlin did not hesitate to denouce the capitalist system and make such denunciations public before sympathetic millions. Harkening back to an earlier populism for solutions to capitalist abuses, the priest called on the country to follow the way of Christianity to the remonetization of silver and nationalization of the banking system. The people wanted control over their own destinies and the surest way for them to secure it was to regain control over their money.

In 1934, the Coughlinite movement drew countless sympathizers and Father Coughlin became an established popular figure. As a noted historian describes it,

> he got more mail than anyone in America—at least 80,000 letters in a normal week and sometimes as many as a million. He received voluntary contributions of probably half a million dollars a year. The clerical staff of 150 handled his affairs. . . [and] his critics had to concede him a weekly listening audience of at least 10 mil-

lion. . . . The next fall CBS terminated the Coughlin contract. . . . But Coughlin, organizing his own independent
network, invaded CBS territory. When WCAU in Philadelphia polled its clientele on Coughlin versus classical
music, the result was 187,000 for the priest and 12,000
for the Philharmonic. . . . Father Coughlin seemed to be
rising on a mighty tide.[23]

Even more disturbing, perhaps, than Coughlin's obviously growing influence, was the popular appeal of a shrewd politician holding allied views, who could use his Senate seat to propel himself
directly into the White House. In 1934, the "kingfish," Senator
Huey P. Long, Jr. of Louisiana, decided to make a national movement of his opposition to the Roosevelt administration. As Long
reflected on American's troubles, it became increasingly obvious
to him that a maldistribution of wealth was oppressing the people
and causing them all the difficulty they were suffering. As early
as January the Kingfish launched the Share-Our-Wealth society
(S-O-W). This he managed with the assistance of fundamentalist
preacher Gerald L. K. Smith (who had once offered to set up the
first storm troops in America). Though the S-O-W movement was
formally established in 1934, Huey Long had been contemplating
its program at least since 1932. But for all the Senator's contemplation, it never acquired a complex or many-sided character:

Share-the-wealth was. . . a hillbilly's paradise—$5,000
capital endowment without work, a radio, washing
machine, and automobiles in every home. It was the
Snopes dream come true. It had almost no other quality.[24]

Whether because of or despite the vagueness of the movement's
program, by 1935 the organ of the Share-Our-Wealth organization,
The American Progress, claimed a readership of twelve million.
Long's headquarters boasted that it had on file the records of
27,431 S-O-W clubs organized in more than 8,000 cities and towns
in various parts of the country.[25]

Even if the figures were somewhat exaggerated, a movement
which no administration could ignore was clearly building. Tensions between the Roosevelt administration and Senator Long
were to be cut short, however. On 8 September 1935, the Kingfish
was felled by an assassin's bullet and his lively career came to an
end. Nevertheless, the movement did not die with its founder. For

Gerald Smith moved quickly to the center of the Share-Our-Wealth movement and planned busily ahead.

Amidst the general ·clamor, the aged population of the country, nostalgic for a more familiar ruggedly individualistic America, yet bitter at their impoverishment after a lifetime of work and effort, was moved to self-affirmation. An unemployed physician, sixty-six years old, came forth from Long Beach, California to shape a movement for the salvation of the nation's aged. In 1939 Dr. Francis Everett Townsend sent a letter to the *Long Beach Press-Telegram*. In it he argued that the solution to unemployment and economic depression was readily available and stood before the very nose of the government. The nation's economic health would be restored and flourish thereafter if old people were to be retired from their jobs and everyone over sixty given federal pensions of $150 a month. This figure was to go rapidly to $200 a month as Townsend mounted a campaign for his plan. In this way, room would be made for younger workers while the aged would be retired in appropriate dignity. The economy would be further rejuvenated by the fact that this retirement of the aged would involve their receipt of the pension on the condition that they spent the money as they got it. Money for this monthly pension plan could be raised by a national sales tax of some 2 percent, or a tax on all gross business transactions. The decline in unemployment and the increase in spending resulting from the institution of such a plan would revive the whole nation economically and be the pride of all its citizens.

Francis Townsend, with the assistance of a lawyer friend, Earl Clements, printed up a description of his pension proposal, opened headquarters in Long Beach on New Year's Day 1934, and incorporated Old Age Revolving Pensions, Ltd.:

> Townsend and Clements began sending out literature—to friends, neighbors, former clients, anyone whose name they could pick up. After five weeks, an average of one hundred replies a day were pouring into the office along with demands for the twenty-five cent leaflets they had written, 1,500 a week being purchased within two months of the incorporation. Area physicians and ministers were induced to become spokesmen for the plan, and a newspaper, *The Townsend National Weekly*, was started. Excitement began to spread across Southern California, and Townsend was forced to abandon his original headquarters and move to larger offices in Los Angeles. A staff of ninety-five was

hired to handle the mounting flow of mail and by September 1934, one year from the time the old man conceived his great idea, the letters were averaging two thousand per day.[26]

By January 1935 Townsend and Clements proudly announced that more than three thousand local units were operating with a total membership nearing five hundred thousand. Moreover, new clubs were continuously being organized and set up by congressional districts in order to minimize political pressure members hoped to bring to bear on the House of Representatives.

As each of the movements for sharing or distributing American wealth gained popular adherents, their leaders saw an opportunity to increase power and influence by merging their efforts. In 1935 Coughlin's National Union for Social Justice, Gerald L. K. Smith's Share-Our-Wealth clubs and the Townsend clubs were proclaimed a "united front" by the leaders of these movements. If each had power enough to shake the administration to anxiety by themselves, they could hardly do less together.

By 1935 the man who had been carried to the White House on a roar of public acclaim in 1932 had reason to feel a little shaky about his political future. And the *Nation* verified that there was cause for uneasiness in the Roosevelt camp:

> The uneasiness felt by Roosevelt's campaign managers over his waning popularity has been greatly relieved by the October poll taken by the American Institute of Public Opinion. The first of the polls taken in February 1934, gave the President 69 per cent of the combined Democratic and Republican votes. Then a decline set in, and from November 1934, till September of this year the curve sagged steadily downward until the President, with a majority of only 50.3 percent, appeared to be headed for defeat. But in October his stock rose to 53, an indication that if the election were held today, simply on the issue of Roosevelt, he would win by a narrow margin. Geographically, the President has lost the New England states, where he polled 51 per cent in 1932; his percentage there in October was 38 (in 1935). In the mid-Atlantic states—New York, Pennsylvania, West Virginia and Maryland—he has also lost a majority of 53 per cent and is now at 46. But in all other sections he runs ahead in the ballot, generally somewhat behind his figure in 1932, but actually ahead of it in the mountain states. The poll is instructive but it is not con-

clusive. Next year the choice will not be for or against Roosevelt but between Roosevelt and a Republican nominee. Roosevelt measured against what he might have been, cuts a far poorer figure than he will present next year in contrast with the choice of the Republican Party. We hold to our opinion that the President is not sure to win the election but that the Republicans are sure to lose it.[27]

It is clear enough from all of this that the Social Security Act, partly the result of neo-Brandeisian influence at the White House and partly the result of popular pressure, was not a response to demands brought to bear by the leaders of organized labor.

AFL thinking on the Social Security Act, however, needs to be further examined. Although the Federation revealed its ambivalence and difficulties in relation to the measure, it would yet undergo certain changes which caused it to embrace the act. And yet, as we shall see, even this embrace was to be accompanied by tenacious efforts to reaffirm voluntarist principles. In the end, the peculiar ideological cloudiness that hung over Federation thought and policy would not be dispelled.

However congenially indifferent AFL leaders hoped to remain toward social security in 1935, the matter would not rest at that point. In 1936, as we have already noted, the CIO began to constitute itself as an independent labor federation with independent ideas on legislative matters bearing on labor interests and conditions. As it forged impressively ahead with massive organizing drives among the unskilled, it developed a clear interest in promoting and supporting social security. It became prone to demand, for example, extension of benefits to classes of workers altogether excluded from coverage under the act (in nearly all early issues of the CIO News), for it is a fact that during the drafting of the act, the staff of the Committee on Economic Security recommended that taxes collected from individuals to entitle them to old-age benefits be limited to collection from industrial workers alone, excluding persons in agriculture, as well as those in domestic service, and others not in the "industrial worker" category. The committee itself opposed this limitation but finally conceded to Secretary of the Treasury Morgenthau the exclusion of these groups.[28] Hence, as the CIO sought to organize broadly, including drives among agricultural workers and joint action with farmer organizations, it developed an interest in broadening its appeal by demanding coverage for previously excluded workers.[29] Moreover, building a base among unskilled workers involved the CIO in deepening its interest in demanding amendment of the terms of the social security law. For the less-well-paid and less-skilled workmen in industry would also be subject to limits under the law by virtue of the fact that their smaller salaries would be subject to lower taxes. In the end this fact would leave them with less in the way of old-age insurance benefits due to the smaller tax percentage taken out of salaries during their income-earning years. Then, too, the less skilled were more easily discarded by employers during times of economic difficulty, leaving them more open to this hazards of frequent or prolonged unemployment. Consequently, benefits already accruing to them under the law would nevertheless have to be liberalized to support them through unusually long or frequent periods of unemployment. To gain the loyalty of the sector of the work force, the CIO publicly and regularly badgered the government for improvements in the terms of the Social Security Act.[30]

It must not be forgotten in all of this that the CIO in 1936 and 1937 had neither time nor opportunity, nor a constituency, from whom it could have extracted high dues payments for the development and stabilization of its own union benefit and service systems as did the AFL.[31] It was hence freer of ideological inhibitions about accepting government security legislation and able, as a result, to build its own appeal by demonstrating its concern for worker interest in demanding improved social security benefits from government (indeed, it may even have generated pro-social security sentiments among workers not, perhaps, otherwise inclined toward them, though there is no evidence to verify this possibility). In brief, the CIO could seize upon inadequacies in the Social Security Act to build its constituency by virtue of the fact that it was able to accept social security in principle and therefore demand that amendments in the act be made so that a vast army of unskilled workers would be better compensated than the law as passed would permit.

It is interesting, however, that in 1936 when the CIO was giving ample evidence not only of its intent to conduct organizing drives in the mass production industries for the purpose of mobilizing the unskilled, but also of its successful appeal to these millions, the AFL produced a clear and unwavering statement in favor of the Social Security Act in marked contrast to the statements, brief and bland, made in 1935:

The Social Security Act, state old-age pensions, and un-

employment compensation legislation gives legal status
to a fundamental right of labor—the right of a man in
what he helps to create. Under modern conditions of
life and collective work, investors of capital provide the
building, machines and material equipment for production while management and production staff create the
industry that serves society and supports those attached
to it. Social and economic practice as well as legal precedent recognize and provide for the rights of those who
invest capital in an industry, but only vaguely sense the
rights of those who make industry a production force.
Producing workers invest in industry their personalities, their skill, their time, their labor power—life itself.
When industry places workers on its production staff, it
assumes an obligation for their investment equal to if
not more binding than that assumed for investors of
capital. Social Security laws are an attempt to give legal
status to this obligation.[32]

This is not only whole-hearted support, but a declaration that
social security is a fundamental human right and that no justifi-
able basis exists on which it might be denied to workingmen.
Moreover, by 1937, as the CIO conducted increasingly successful
organizing drives, the AFL also felt compelled to include greater
numbers of less skilled workers among its own members than it
would previously have considered feasible or desirable. This produced a similar need for the AFL to ask for corrections of the limits of the Social Security Act. While no strong words about improving or broadening the terms of the law is particularly in
evidence at the AFL's 1936 convention, the Executive Council having mildly offered minor improving suggestions, by 1937 the AFL
is also discontentedly protesting the exclusion of agricultural
labor from coverage under the law.[33] This is but one of a number
of AFL complaints about the adequacy of the law. It is critical of
its lack of sufficient national uniformity in its terms.[34] The old
complaint about company reserves unemployment insurance systems passed by various states was also sounded, and repeatedly.
The Seamen and the Undertakers were two groups, it turns out,
which could not be classified as "industrial workers" and were
thus excluded from social security coverage. At the 1938 convention proposals were submitted for extending all social security
benefits to them. The tone of the AFL criticism grew more strident
and more demanding as increasing numbers of workers joined the
CIO. By 1938 the CIO demanded not only more liberal terms of

coverage for the whole work force, but also inclusion of new health care programs. In the same year the AFL asked for similar benefits. While further economic decline was experienced by the country during 1937 and 1938, and the AFL's membership problems undoubtedly deepened the AFL's new tendency to consider labor interests as consonant with social security. The CIO's interest in promoting social security seems to have been the initial and fundamental motivation for the change in the attitudinal tone exhibited by the AFL.

Between 1936 and 1938, then, the CIO seems to have successfully forced the AFL into total abandonment of a voluntarist position as regards social security. Criticisms of the law made by the AFL after 1936 no longer carried implications of mistrust or indifference. Rather, they exuded full support of the social security principle and legislation—demanding fuller coverage, more benefits, and scrupulously democratic application and administration. None of the earlier statements made by William Green criticizing unemployment insurance provisions, or those made by Matthew Woll concerning amendment and improvement of provisions in the Social Security Act, suggest this feeling. An editorial appearing in the *American Federationist*, reporting on discussions held at the AFL's 1939 convention, provides a clear example of this blend of criticism and full acceptance:

> The report of the Executive Council to our convention indicated that the main features of security against the emergencies that interfere with earning a livelihood have been either established or are in the course of formulation. This march of progress is a cause for real satisfaction and a stimulus to extend and perfect the provisions of a Social Security Act. . . . The convention. . . urged improvement of provisions for unemployment compensation. The low benefits now and the short duration of payment do not justify the millions spent for the administration of unemployment compensation. The convention urged that a public commission be authorized by Congress to study unemployment compensation laws and make recommendations to Congress, and further that the feasibility of a federal law be considered. The Federation further believes that provisions for workmen's compensation should be integrated with the program for social security. . . . Social Insurance is a most fundamental provision for human welfare.[35]

With AFL traditional attitudes toward economic security fully reversed under the impact of CIO growth, and with the CIO's special interest in casting aside older voluntarist policies toward governmental sponsorship of economic security, what remained of the voluntarist creed? One would expect very little indeed. But a Labor Day address delivered by William Green on 5 September 1938 indicates that such expectations would be somewhat premature. For Green proclaimed that the "American Federation of Labor was erected upon a sound and enduring foundation of voluntarism."[36] There is no implication in Green's speech that the voluntarist foundation had either crumbled or weakened. Further, it will be recalled that AFL embroilment with the Wagner Act's National Labor Relations Board over recognition of the CIO caused a resurgence of Federation suspicion of the value of legislative solutions to industrial problems, and mistrust of government agencies' capacity to comprehend, much less dabble in, the sphere of industrial relations. This mistrust was to inhibit the Federation's full acceptance of social security. Hence, while the AFL embraced the social security measure, leaders like Matthew Woll could proudly affirm labor's tradition of "anti-statism" and announce that the labor movement will prove unyielding in its promotion of the rugged "individualistic, virile spirit" that has given the nation a foremost place among the nations of the world. . . the spirit of aggression initiative and independence. . . ."[37]

To protect this "spirit," Woll cautioned that the population must not "drift" toward regulating social matters by legislation or by excessive reliance upon legislative means of redistributing income. As the CIO then pressured the AFL into confronting the less-skilled working mass, and taking up the cause of social security on its behalf, the manner in which the NLRB came to terms with the CIO provided a source for continuing voluntarist attitudes which prevented full accord with the principle of social security. It should also be noted that the AFL never did cease to warn against demanding "unrealistically" large security compensation, for all its eventual willingness to raise claims for improved benefits. Thus, even while calling for amendments to the Social Security Act to enlarge the scope of benefits, the Executive Council warned the AFL convention as late as 1939 against ill-advised plans to provide such large pensions for all which could "but...discredit the principle of Social Security."[38]

It might be added, however, that by 1938, as a result of the tensions of the previous years, AFL leaders were showing signs that they could no longer assign to voluntarism a specific and intelligible meaning, and resorted to somewhat hollow generalizations when pressed to speak concretely of voluntarism on public occasions. William Green could only define it as "democracy in the administration of [AFL] affairs, self-sacrifice, loyalty and devotion to our form of government."[39] And even when Matthew Woll denounced excessive attachment to legislation or to state regulation of any type, he would not employ the term (as Gompers frequently did) to describe or define this attitude. It cannot be known whether this loss of specificity would have occurred had the CIO not bestirred the AFL into a policy shift as regards government dispensed economic benefits (and, as we shall see, as regards other matters by 1938). But it is clear that the vagueness of years and the effects of CIO pressure left the AFL leadership at pains to recall their old identity, even when the attempt was made to affirm it most strongly.

Notes

[1] Edwin Witte, *Social Security Perspectives*, p. 11.

[2] *American Federationist* 42, no. 8 (August 1935): 916.

[3] Edwin Witte, "Organized Labor and Social Security," in *Labor and the New Deal*, ed., Milton Derber and Edwin Young, p. 272F.

[4] Ibid., p. 250. Roosevelt's preferences may also have been influenced by his experiences with unemployment relief legislation while governor of New York. See Walter J. Trattner, *From Poor Law to Welfare State*, pp. 232-34.

[5] *American Federationist* 41, no. 3 (March 1934): 173. See also comments by Thomas Kennedy of the United Mine Workers and the lieutenant governor-elect of Pennsylvania in Ibid. no. 12 (December 1934): 1295-98.

[6] *AFL Convention Proceedings*, 1934, p. 207.

[7] U.S., Congress, House, Committee On Labor, Hearings, *Unemployment Insurance Bill*, H.R. 7598, 73d Cong., 2d sess., 12-24 February 1934, pp. 16-17.

[8] Ibid., p. 285.

[9] Ibid., pp. 300-306.

[10] Ibid., pp. 298-99.

[11] Ibid., pp. 306-7.

[12] The AFL was quite voluble on all of the other legislative matters under consideration in this study. Its reaction to social security is peculiarly silent by comparison. Even if one could assume that private correspondences carried on by AFL leaders would reveal more Federation thoughts on the matter of social security, it is a striking and revealing fact that the AFL chose to say rather little about this measure in public.

[13]*AFL Convention Proceedings*, 1934, p. 603.

[14]Witte, *The Development of the Social Security Act*, pp. 250, 273n.

[15]Ibid., p. 251. For a full list of committee and advisory personnel, see Committee on Economic Security, *Report to the President* (Washington, D.C., 1935), pp. 51-53. Also, Philip Booth, *Social Security in American* pp. 6-7 gives a clear brief account.

[16]Witte, *Development of the Social Security Act*, p. 51.

[17]Ibid., p. 88n. In a lengthy footnote, Witte notes William Green's vacillating preferences for one or another types of insurance law, as well as the AFL's grievance against the President, for the latter's support of the Automobile Labor Board established under the NIRA (which reflected Johnson-Richberg thinking on the majority principle in union representation). This grievance is considered by Witte, who had little understanding of labor traditions on such matters, to have influenced AFL attitudes toward the work of the committee and rendered Green ambivalent in his participation.

[18]Altmeyer, *The Formative Years of Social Security*, p. 18.

[19]Witte, *Development of the Social Security Act*, p. 25. For compilation of materials on the Social Security Act at this time see Robert B. Stevens, ed., *Statutory History of the United States* pp. 183-289. The volume is also rich in matter covering the years prior to and following the New Deal.

[20]Ibid., pp. 87-88 (italics added).

[21]*AFL Convention Proceedings*, 1935, pp. 493-94.

[22]That the emphasis of the Roosevelt administration after 1934 fell increasingly upon redistribution rather than reformation or regulation of business behavior has been noted, not without regrets, by former presidential advisers Raymond Moley and Rexford Tugwell. Moley had rather preferred the self-regulated business commonwealth and Tugwell, a "democratic planner," had favored tripartite industrial councils to curtail business power and coordinate industrial activity toward recovery (see Moley's *After Seven Years*, p. 372; and Tugwell's *The Democratic Roosevelt*, pp. 545-46). Basil Rauch, however, makes a convincing argument that Roosevelt was influenced by business hostility toward him when he became responsive to a reform-minded electorate clamoring for economic redistribution (see *The History of the New Deal, 1933-1938* p. v). That Roosevelt increasingly defied business hostility and courted the electorate is evident in speeches he made during 1935-36 (see *The Public Papers and Addresses of Franklin D. Roosevelt*, ed. Samuel Rosenman 5:568-69; see also Marquis Childs, "They Hate Roosevelt," *Harper's*, May 1936, p. 634).

[23]Arthur Schlesinger, Jr., *The Politics of Upheaval* pp. 20-21.

[24]Ibid., p. 63.

[25]G. L. K. Smith, "How Come Huey Long?" *New Republic*, 13 February 1935, p. 15. It should be remembered that this figure does represent a boast and may not be entirely accurate.

[26]David H. Bennett, *Demagogues in the Depression*, p. 154.

[27]*Nation*, 6 November 1935, p. 1. It should be noted that the editorial ap-

pearing in *The Nation* mentions Roosevelt's improving percentages in October—two months after the Social Security Act was passed—in the West and mountain states where the Townsend movement and Coughlin's following were particularly strong, and in the South, a stronghold for Huey Long. It would appear that the Social Security Act, passed in August, is related to Roosevelt's improved standing in these states.

[28]Witte, *Development of the Social Security Act*, pp. 152-53. Exclusion had been argued for by a group in the Treasury Department on the grounds that taxation of these workers was not feasible and hence they would not be entitled to benefits.

[29]Alliances between the CIO and farm groups were assiduously cultivated by the CIO through its Non-Partisan League. Reports of conferences on joint farmer-labor action appear in the *CIO News*, 7 December 1937, 21 January 1938, 26 March 1938, and 30 April 1938. The CIO also organized the Cannery and Agricultural Workers' Union in 1936 and was engaged in supporting its strikes and protest actions.

[30]See *CIO News*, 18 June 1938, 23 July 1938, 13 August 1938. In July the CIO also demanded expanded medical and health care services.

[31]*AFL Convention Proceedings*, 1935, pp. 100-104 for a list of AFL unions having benefit funds as well as a record of benefits paid. This information is available, however, in all *AFL Convention Proceedings* on a yearly basis.

[32]*American Federationist* 43, no. 6 (June 1936): 578.

[33]*American Federationist* 44, no. 5 (May 1937): 513-14. Also Arthur Altmeyer, formerly on the Technical Advisory Council to the Committee on Economic Security, and then on the Social Security Board, notes both rising AFL and CIO criticisms of the act in 1937. See his appendix three, a memorandum for the president, 11 September 1937, in *Formative Years of Social Security*, p. 296.

[34]*American Federationist* 45, no. 8 (August 1938): 803-4.

[35]*American Federationist* 46, no. 11 (November 1939): 1183-84.

[36]William Green, "Labor Day Address, September 5, 1938," *Vital Speeches of the Day*, 15 September 1938, pp. 722-25 (italics added).

[37]Matthew Woll, "Labor's Part in American Democracy," *Vital Speeches of the Day*, 1 December 1939, p. 119.

[38]*American Federationist*, 46, no. 11 (November 1939): 1184.

[39]William Green, "Labor Day Address," p. 725.

Chapter 7
The FLSA and the Dilemmas of the AFL

To consider the Fair Labor Standards Act (FLSA) passed by Congress in 1938 from the point of view of its effects on American labor ideology, particulary the voluntarist outlook which had for so long characterized the thinking of the American Federation of Labor, is essentially to repeat themes already sounded in prior chapters of this study. It is to reveal the AFL once again in alternate states of reticence or opposition to the Roosevelt Administration's measures, of compromise and consequent ideological unclarity. Yet it is also to reveal the extent to which the CIO came to play a part in the ideological difficulties the AFL was experiencing. Thus it is useful to review the terms of the FLSA and organized labor's reaction to it at the time of its passage through Congress, not only becase it serves, as prior legislation did, to highlight the persistence of unresolved tensions in the voluntarist perspective but also because it shows the extent to which the CIO became responsible for the generation of these tensions and of changes in the terms of labor thought generally during the 1930s. In brief, consideration of organized labor's view of the FLSA provides an especially good opportunity to show that it was as much the growth of the CIO as Roosevelt's New Deal program that made AFL voluntarism diffuse, ambivalent, and even antiquated during the latter 1930s.

The purpose of the FLSA was to increase mass purchasing power by increasing, even if only minimally, labor's wages throughout the country. This was the vital intention of its minimum wage provisions. It was also intended to aid in a more equitable distribution of jobs among workingmen by establishing maximum hours of work for each and so leave more work hours available for distribution to the unemployed. In this latter respect, that of setting minimum work and maximum standards in industry, the FLSA was also expected to help strengthen mass purchasing power, and thus, to contribute to economic recovery (which seemed more distant than ever with another economic downturn in 1937). President Roosevelt had made it clear that the administration favored the continuation of a policy of increasing public purchasing capacity that had been instituted with the Social Security Act in 1935 and extending it further through the Fair Labor Standards Act. On 24 May 1937, in requesting congressional enactment of the measure, he said:

> Today you and I are pledged to take further steps to reduce the lag in the purchasing power of industrial workers and to strengthen and stabilize the markets for the farmers' products.[1]

And the report of the House Committee on Labor clearly indicated the extent to which mass purchasing notions served as a defense and support of the legislation.[2]

The Fair Labor Standards Act of 1938 required the payment of minimum wages to most workers who were engaged in the production of goods intended for interstate commerce. Agricultural workers and some few others were excluded from coverage, but basically, goods to be moved in intersate commerce was broadly construed, and the act was applicable to most workers in the nation.[3] The act required the payment of a minimum wage of twenty-five cents an hour until October 1939, with a minimum wage of thirty cents an hour from then until October 1945, and thereafter a minimum wage of forty cents an hour. (The Act has been amended a number of times since 1945 to provide for much higher wage minima.) As originally introduced in Congress, the FLSA provided for a forty cent an hour minimum wage to be made applicable immediately upon passage of the bill. But objections from businessmen extremely upset over the economic recession of 1937 on the one hand, and, as we shall see, objections from the AFL fearing the effect of the FLSA on collective bargaining on the other hand, caused a settlement on a lower wage minimum to be adopted for a seven-year transitional period. Finally, the Administrator of the Wage and Hour Division in the Department of Labor was assigned the task of setting up a board for administering the wage provisions of this law.[4]

A number of factors had entered into the choice of forty cents as a minimum wage for the nation. First, the forty cent minimum had already been negotiated into a great number of codes under the NRA when that agency was operative. It had, consequently, come to be seen as a "customary" figure and was expected to cause little opposition. Second, even the staunchest friends of the minimum wage concept, who would have preferred to establish higher wage minima than the FLSA provided for, feared that higher minima would be made applicable to labor only on a highly selective basis and would thus serve to restrict the coverage of the act. For the sake of maximizing applicability many in Congress accepted and even promoted the forty cent minimum. This is especially evident in remarks contained in the report of the Senate Committee on Education and Labor:

> The Committee feels that a minimum wage of 40 cents per hour, which will yield no more than an annual income of $800 a year to the small percentage of workers fortunate enough to find 50 weeks employment in a year, does not give a wage sufficient to maintain what we would like to regard as the minimum American standard of living. But 40 cents per hour is far more than millions of American workers are receiving today.[5]

While the FLSA provided for a forty cent an hour wage minimum to be adopted on a national scale, it also provided for a forty hour maximum work week, the forty hour maximum to be expressly stated in the law. This provision enabled workers to claim "time and a half" wages for hours worked over the maximum, while at the same time intending to make the forty hour maximum customary throughout the industrial sphere. It was to be applied, however, only on an industry by industry basis and not across the board. The agent charged with administration of the act was, therefore, to be responsible for making work week adjustments with an eye toward making the forty hour maximum general, but would not be obliged to rule in favor of it if conditions in a given industry appeared to make this standard undesirable or unfeasible.

Even a passing familiarity with AFL traditions would lead one to suppose correctly that legislation like the FLSA, which gave to a government board public authority to play a role in determining wage and hour standards, would be distasteful to the Federation. In 1914, Gompers had declared angrily and unequivocally:

> The attempts of the government to establish wages at which workmen may work, is the experience of history to be the beginning of an era, and a long era, of industrial slavery. There was a time in history where governments and courts, at court sessions, established wages, and during periods where there was a dearth of workmen to perform the work required, and the employers offered higher wages, the workmen and employers were brought into court and both punished, punished by imprisonment and physical mutilation, because the one asked, received or demanded and the other was willing to offer, or did pay higher wages.[6]

And not yet even the worst and most traumatic years of the Depression seemed to produce in the AFL a desire to reevaluate Gompers's words. In fact no indication was given, even during that terrible time, that leaders of the Federation were prepared to give more than the slightest consideration to legislation resembling the FLSA. One might study *AFL Convention Proceedings* from 1929 through 1936 with the most scrupulous care and fail to detect there the smallest suggestion that the AFL was entertaining any interest in promoting statutory wage or hour measures at the federal level. One might find some concern, and that expressed very occasionally, for the enactment of minimum wage laws for women and minors. But it was considered sufficient that such enactment occur at the state level, and at no time were even state-level enactments regarded as appropriate or relevant for male workers. Some interest was also shown, it is true, in a federal hour law for federal employees. This arose during the AFL's 1936 convention. But William Hutcheson, leader of the Carpenters Union, rose to his feet and declared adamantly that such laws might be well and good for federal employees, yet they were certainly no less than a menace to the millions of workers employed in private industry throughout the nation:

> The labor movement is going far afield . . . . Insofar as Federal Employees are concerned, I say yes to the enactment of such a law . . . When it comes to private em-

ployers, I say, establish your wages and hours by negotiation and not by law . . . What they (the government)
can give us they can take from us.[7]

The feeling was that legal statute could never be as safe, as
firm, as durable as private contracts bargained into existence by
those with the greatest stake in them and most deeply committed
to living up to their terms. And no one at the convention who lis-
tened to this statement of sentiment was willing to challenge the
burly Hutcheson, even as late as 1936, and even following upon a
developing AFL pattern of conceding to government some greater
role in industrial relations. William Green, however, did offer a
statement that might have surprised—though it probably confused—the delegates present at the 1936 convention, and it contained hints that the Federation would yet reconsider its traditional orientation toward wage-hour laws sometime in the near
future:

> I have opposed the economic doctrine that wages and
> hours of those employed in private industry should be
> regulated by law, because, as Delegate Hutcheson has
> well said, if they can give it to you they can take it away.
> Our policy, however, only is to secure the enactment of
> legislation providing for the six-hour day and the five-
> day week applicable to those employed in the produc-
> tion of goods that enter into interstate commerce. We
> are sure and certain that any other law dealing with the
> shorter workday would be declared unconstitutional.[8]

Green's peculiar remarks notwithstanding, there occurred no
dispute and appeared no dissatisfaction with Hutcheson's remarks. The Federation clearly was not disposed toward considering, demanding, or encouraging laws which would give to government boards any right whatever in the establishment of wage and
hour standards for the nation's labor force. Insofar as the AFL
approached such a consideration with any seriousness at all, it
did so very briefly in 1933 when it gave some sympathetic support
to the Black Thirty Hours bill (to institute the thirty-hour week)
then pending in Congress. The Black bill was eclipsed by the
NIRA and quickly scuttled, however, and the AFL's interest in it
waned very quickly (although traces of this sympathy must have
survived in Green's mind, influencing his otherwise unintelligible
statement cited above). For the NIRA was hailed by the public
and passed in Congress in 1933 and the shorter work week could

now be gained, it seemed, through negotiation within the NRA's industrial code-making agencies—a strategy infinitely preferable to the Black bill as far as the AFL was concerned. And, thus, all convern for statutory hours provisions died away.

Certainly the AFL had always, in the long course of its history, favored shorter hours and higher wages as a means of relieving the economic distress and high unemployment produced by depression conditions. For such reforms were considered, in addition to being instruments of union building, perfectly viable as a strategy for the economic revival of the country. But the Federation continued to insist, despite the brief attention given to the Black bill, and even in the course of evaluating it, that shorter hours and minimum wage standards could best be achieved by collective bargaining, by the "voluntary action" of labor and employers, unimpinged upon by government. The point was made repeatedly and given a special emphasis in connection with the fixing of wages. In 1933 William Green made this clear:

> The AFL feels that it would be a dangerous experiment [to fix minimum wage rates by means of a national law or use of government boards]. While it would help some, it would in our opinion tend to injure the efforts of the bulk of labor... to bring about increases in their wages.[9]

This statement simply serves to emphasize the main point, that the AFL was fundamentally hostile to legislation which violated voluntarist preferences for wage and hour fixing by means of privately negotiated contract. However, on 24 May 1937 Black in the Senate and Connery in the House introduced the FLSA, and the president sent a special message to Congress requesting passage of the act. Now the AFL would be pressed quickly to reconsider its traditional stand.

Because of its past traditions, the AFL approached the FLSA cautiously. But 1937 involved the country in new economic troubles and the president looked as if he were bent on having the FLSA. Then, too, the CIO appeared to be entirely satisfied by the Black-Connery bill. The Federation's Executive Council met four days after the measure had been presented to Congress. Age-old anxieties that federal wage and hour legislation would weaken unionism must have hovered over the May meeting, together with a feeling that its passage was probably inescapable. Thus William Green emerged from the meeting to testify at a joint hearing on the FLSA before the Senate and House Labor Committee with a formula peculiarly designed both to affirm voluntarist principles and to accept the FLSA; that is, to safeguard traditional unionism and concede to the inevitable. The result was that throughout 1937, the AFL exhibited its now habitual tendency to think in two directions simultaneously. This reduced the efficacy and clarity of voluntarist assumptions while it rendered the Federation grudging yet compromising acceptance of the FLSA.

On the one hand, Green made comments to the congressional committees which praised wage and hour legislation. It was, according to Green, no less than the very need of the hour. On the other hand, Green made it unmistakably clear that unless the proposed FLSA were amended so as to reduce the capacity of any government board to meddle in matters of wages and working hours for labor, the AFL would certainly oppose it. Hence, the legislation was entirely worthy in the estimation of the AFL, but labor's support for it was contingent on congressional adoption of amendments, proposed by Green, which would limit the power of a government wage-and-hour-fixing agency to intrude in matters best left to voluntary action or collective bargaining. With Green's formula, voluntarism came down to reducing the scope of the administration's measure, while accepting it in principle. And this was less an affirmation of the past than it was a compromise with it. Yet in spite of the compromise, many in the Federation would alternately denounce wage and hour legislation and government boards, demand the incorporation of the Green amendments, and yet confess some government wage and hour measure was probably necessitated by events. It would be most difficult to identify voluntarism in all this and just as difficult to dismiss it.

In the main Green stressed that six amendments would have to be added to the bill for Federation leaders to condone it. These amendments were stated succinctly in the report of the Executive Council to the 1937 AFL convention; it was indicated there that they were intended to

> safeguard collective bargaining and to limit the scope of government regulation to those fields wherein collective bargaining machinery is ineffective or difficult of functioning and only until collective bargaining has substantially covered the field.[10]

The amendments themselves demanded first that the FLSA be interpreted as a means of encouraging and not displacing collective bargaining between labor unions and employers; second, that Congress make it clear (and state in the act) that wage and hour standards ordered under the measure were only bare minima and were not to preclude substantial improvements attainable by collective bargaining; third, that any standards fixed by private negotiations and contract in any craft or industry constitute a guide to be followed by any government wage- or hour-fixing board, unless such a board found reason to fix higher minimum standards (in order that employers meeting standards agreed to in collective bargaining would not be penalized or that employers not obliged to meet standards fixed by contract would not escape their responsibilities to labor and take unfair advantage of employers meeting these responsibilities); fourth, that standards set by collective bargaining would prima facie be deemed fair by a government board; fifth, that when any board was created under the FLSA-conducted investigations for the purpose of determining the feasibility of standards called for in the act (and this investigation covered craft workers specifically), its investigation was to deal with employment of craft workers as a classification different from unskilled workers; and finally, sixth, that in any case where standards were set in an industry which were different from those set up by collective bargaining in that industry, these were to be set only to the extent necessary to implement the FLSA and be valid only as long as collective bargaining agreements did not cover these areas. Failure to amend the FLSA, according to Green's recommendation, "would be strenuously opposed by the AFL as . . . violating the cardinal principles of self-government in private industry."[11]

The Green strategy for rendering the FLSA an adjunct to (or at least incapable of overriding) agreements reached in collective bargaining was no merely modest attempt to curtail the power of a government board to exercise ultimate control in wage and hour fixing for industry. It was the expression of deep and unyielding mistrust of such agencies. For example, when Green was asked by Representative Wood at the joint hearings whether he would accept board intervention to prevent a union from accepting in bargaining a wage beneath the minimum allowed by the law or hours above the maximum, he said:

> No, I do not think so. I should rather preserve the principle of industrial democracy than to yield a right to the Board to interfere in the free exercise of collective bargaining. Now, I cannot conceive of very many cases

where such a condition as you describe exists. . . . [I]f there was some isolated case where some collusion occurs, it could be corrected in another way, and labor unions. . . will tend to that, rather than to vest in a Board the power and authority to come in and say, "Your collective bargaining agreement is invalid because we do not approve it".[12]

But for all that, when AFL leaders were confronted by the Fair Labor Standards Act and their traditional notions were challenged by it, they exhibited a certain hostility, but they did not adopt a stance of total opposition to it. Rather, their efforts were directed toward restructuring the act so as to reduce the possibility that government agencies would implement the legislation in ways which would have negative consequences for labor, especially for skilled craft workers. Their motivation for adopting such a strategy for dealing with the act seems to have derived from their perception that the FLSA had very good chances of getting through Congress, especially in view of the president's desire for it, and that CIO support for the measure would, in view of the CIO's growing strength and influence, improve these chances. Besides, it was very difficult to publicly deny the worth of minimum wage and maximum hour laws in the midst of the renewed economic distress of 1937. In view of this, they sought to reduce the scope of the FLSA without attacking it too severely. And so editorials in the *American Federationist* concerning the act, at least during 1937, reflected an attitude of tepid toleration of the measure: "Minimum wage laws can do much to protect workers against unfair competition in low wages and sweat shop conditions of work."[13] It is difficult to discern voluntarist vigor in such editorials despite Green's denunciation of government boards before congressional committee.

Yet if the pages of the *American Federationist* reflected the tepid Federation mood concerning the FLSA which resulted from efforts to reconcile conflicting ends, the AFL convention of 1937 revealed that old voluntarist hackles could certainly be raised on this matter of the wage and hour bill. The recorded proceedings of that event indicate that much hostility toward the Roosevelt administration's measure was clearly and loudly being voiced by Federation leaders and resolutions were raised from the convention floor which recommended firm opposition to the administration's bill. One insisted that the AFL stand unalterably opposed to giving legislators any power whatever to designate agents for the

purpose of fixing wage standards. Another urged the AFL to oppose wage fixing and to reject any government board that sought
or was assigned a role in determining wage and hour standards.
Further, it was suggested that any legislation which the AFL itself
had no hand in formulating must be regarded with suspicion if not
cold hostility, at least until the unions had engaged in painstaking
study and lengthy debate over it.[14] And it seemed that the Federation's national leadership could not agree more with the sentiments which were expressed from the floor. The Committee on
Resolutions agreed that the Black-Connery bill was certainly prepared without the advice of the AFL and reiterated that labor
feared the creation of any further government boards to deal with
labor-related matters (and the recent conflicts with the NLRB had
the effect of strengthening this feeling). The committee's clear opposition to anything that even appeared to threaten the unlimited
right to organize and to bargain collectively was declared to be
unyielding.

Still, as if in fear of carrying the implication of these statements
too far, the committee tempered its voluntaristic impulses and
recommended that the AFL do nothing about the FLSA until much
more thorough study of the measure had been done in close con-
junction with officials of the Construction Workers, Metal Trades,
Railway Employees, and Hotel Trades Department.[15] The report
of the Resolutions Committee, stating this recommendation, was
unanimously carried by the convention. The result was that voluntarist irritation with the wage and hour bill was somewhat
eased despite its persistence; and the *American Federationist*
continued to carry tepid statements concerning the FLSA.[16]

This ambivalent attitude toward the FLSA continued throughout the period the bill was pending in Congress. On the one hand,
when the House adopted the Green amendments (in the course of
hearings), the Executive Council of the Federation crowed with a
satisfaction that implied that the AFL would be able to live com-
fortably with the FLSA: "Through the adoption of these amendments the Bill is made an effective collective bargaining statute.
The fear of Fascist control over labor and capital is definitely
removed."[17] On the other hand, as one writer has noted, the Federation did not altogether give up hope that the Black-Connery
bill would be defeated: "There are well-founded reasons, supported by interviews, for asserting that the Federation was more
favorable to the Bill in public than in private and that, occasionally at least, it lobbied against the Bill surreptitiously while. . .
grudgingly supporting it."[18]

Thus AFL leaders nervously touted a formula for preserving traditional principles while adapting to distasteful contingencies. This formula was summed up by the Green amendments; they were basically an attempt to curtail indiscriminate and broad application of the FLSA, and to impose some limitations on the exercise of government board functions and to encourage discretion with respect to fixing wage and hour standards for private industry. At times, Federation leaders could reason that the restriction of the FLSA's sphere of influence would render the measure inoffensive. Indeed, such support as was expressed for the act, however cool and reserved that support was, could be given on the grounds that the FLSA was a minor piece of legislation and that, by virtue of the incorporation of the Green amendments, it would represent only a minor infringement on a more general rule to which the Federation remained steadfastly loyal. The *AFL Newsletter* proclaimed:

> President Green. . . approves as a temporary measure minimum wage regulation by the government for those earning $1,200 or less per year, but opposes the general principle of government wage fixing for men in private industry.[19]

And so, the first confrontations with the administration's wage and hour bill revealed the Federation floundering about, seeking ways to come to terms with it, now announcing that "it would be definitely injurious to the right of voluntary organization," and that its passage would mean that "the prinicple of voluntarism in the activities of free men was interfered with,"[20] and then declaring that it was but a harmless departure from customs and principles which the Federation would unyieldingly uphold and protect. The equivocation continued while the AFL consistently demanded of Congress the incorporation of Green's amendments, even demanding that Congress adopt a scheme for a slow transition toward the wage and hour standards called for in the act (so that higher minima could be established in that interim by union action). Intermittently, Green announced that the FLSA was a fine and altogether useful law.

But for all of the AFL's efforts to keep voluntarism alive in a world increasingly incongruous with it, when President Roosevelt signed the FLSA into law on 25 June 1938, the Federation capitulated completely and stepped out of the peculiar muddle in which it had dwelt up to that point. Statements appeared in the *Ameri-*

can Federationist during 1938 indicating that the AFL had experienced a change of heart, from bare toleration of the pending bill to the heartiest support for the newly instituted law, and in this, from voluntarist skepticism to an antivoluntarist stance. Federation leaders argued more and more that the severity of the economic circumstances of the time made the FLSA the most urgently required legislation. This capitulation is well illustrated by an editorial written by William Green on the occasion of the FLSA's establishment as law:

> The return of depression brings new reasons why we need fair labor standards to put a foundation under business. Otherwise the quicksand may pull the structure into it. We have reached a stage of economic and social development so that we can say human living must be on or above a prescribed level to be fixed by minimum wage and maximum hour standards. These assured minima would constitute the base on which Labor would continue its struggle for betterment.
>
> Labor is wholeheartedly supporting this basic legislation as a protection to workers during depression and as a safeguard at all times that workers shall have decent living conditions.[21]

Some of the Federation's dissatisfaction with the law, though, crept into even its new stance:

> Although the measure finally enacted by Congress does not comply with the standards recommended by the American Federation of Labor, it writes into public policy the principle that business on sweatshop levels is intolerable to modern life. . . . It is obvious that organized workers would be better able to take care of their interests under this Act than the unorganized, for unions will have the benefit of economic counsel and statistical services as well as experienced negotiations. Labor must follow the administration of this Act intelligently and thoroughly.[22]

But the AFL's firm, though new-found, commitment to the statute is clear nonetheless. Indeed, as can easily be seen, the AFL began to enthusiastically promote the FLSA as a potential weapon fortifying the hand of organized labor and enabling unions to secure highly favorable terms from employers. Such sentiments began to be expressed regularly:

The Fair Labor Standards Act is now the law of the land. Upon its administrator will depend substant'ally the administration of this law and its potentiality as a constructive measure. The administrator will as soon as practicable appoint an industry committee for every industry engaged in commerce or in the making of goods for commerce. The administrator selects the industries and designates the members of the committees. The committees shall consist of three equal groups, representing labor, the employers, and the public. From the latter group the administrator will designate the committee chairman.

These fundamentals of the administration of the Fair Labor Standards Act show the substantial advantage organized workers will have over unorganized. Organized workers will be in a position to send representatives familiar with the whole industry, experienced in joint deliberations and negotiation, and aware of crucial junctures in promoting and taking care of the interests of workers. Such negotiators will not make the mistake of conceding vital issues and will reserve less fundamental points for trading concessions. Experienced union representatives know the industry as well as employers and have work experience as their special contribution to understanding the problems of equitable distribution of returns for joint work. Unorganized workers unexperienced in negotiations will be distinctly handicapped. But organization is now much more possible for all workers. . . . Labor looks to this law for the protection and advantage that minimum standards can provide as a foundation for collective bargaining.[23]

It appears that organized unionism deepened and broadened the sophistication and social intelligence of workingmen and that thus their representatives acquired a basis for manipulating statutory requirements and provisions on behalf of the organized worker. According to the *American Federationist* the unorganized had no access to such knowledge and could not make the FLSA function on their behalf; the FLSA was seen an instrument of unionism for it virtually required that workers organize in order to deal with it properly or perhaps at all. Further, industry committees required to effectuate the terms of the act until the forty cent minimum was established would necessarily require membership from the ranks of organized labor because of the broad yet detailed knowledge of industrial conditions such worker representatives might bring regarding determination of wage and hour standards across the country. The unions saw this as both an advantage for organized labor and a stimulant to organization among the unorganized, for the unorganized worker, in desiring to avail himself of such advantages as he can secure under the terms of the act would seek labor organization in order to do so. And by propounding the idea that the FLSA required workers to organize into trade unions, the AFL abandoned its old fears that a wage and hour law would vitiate vital union functions in industrial society:

> As the Fair Labor Standards Act comes into effect, labor stipulations will be incorporated into standards of fair competition that will prevent industries from competing with each other for profits wrung out of the miseries of long hours and low wages. Competition will be forced to the plane of management and production economies to get low-cost articles or services. For Labor, minimum wage and maximum hour standards mean the necessity for taking care of its own interests. The first step is union organization.
>
> Wage and hour standards will be recommended by industry committees appointed by the Administrator of the Act. Labor will be represented on these committees. Unless Labor is organized, the Administration cannot find representatives, and individuals attempting to perform the function will not have facts on the whole industry or personal knowledge of industry-wide labor standards. Organization is necessary for the protection of wage-earners in the field of minimum fair labor standards as well as for the advancement of standards for services above the minimum through collective bargaining. Fair minimum standards build a foundation upon which collective bargaining will raise standards for those above entrance groups—for the workers with skill and experience. As higher standards are determined, the minimum can be raised. The effect of gains in either field will be reciprocal.
>
> The union will be necessary to workers for the enforcement of standards equally as much as for their determination. Workers on the job know conditions better than any inspecting force. But workers need the union channel for effective functioning in enforcement. The union can lift the issue from its personal setting and insist upon enforcement of law.

Fundamentally it devolves upon the union to wipe out artificial regional differentials. Only the insistence of workers can eliminate this element in unfair competition within an industry. Only the union can adequately advance Labor's interests which are identified with social progress for the Nation.[24]

It should be observed that in the above statement the AFL did not actually indicate that its peace with the FLSA was based on acceptance of the idea that it was proper that a government board would effectuate the terms of the law. There appears, instead, a tendency to dismiss the reality of a board and to believe rather that unions and unionism will determine the efficacy of the FLSA. In fact, one may say that on the basis of AFL statements, the FLSA became acceptable to the Federation to the extent that the AFL found some way to discuss it as a plan for the inclusion of labor in setting national wage and hour standards, rather than on the grounds that a government board might in fact play a role in wage and hour fixing. Thus, even the Federation's 1938 reversal on the matter of the FLSA does not fully represent an abandonment of voluntarism, in spite of the fact that the legislation was formerly resented precisely on voluntaristic grounds. Further, it must be remembered that the AFL succeeded in materially weakening the act. This was no small consideration in the Federation's final acceptance of the legislation. And so, in the end, the AFL showed that though its voluntaristic assumptions had been compromised by its acceptance of the FLSA, Federation leaders had nevertheless found ways by which unionism and the value of union determination of labor standards could be affirmed while a government board was rendered peripheral to the process—at least in Federation rhetoric—this after means had been discovered to effectively water down the bill while it was under congressional consideration.

The result certainly was that voluntarism as an ideology further lost coherence out of efforts to come to terms with the FLSA, for the Federation both conceded and resisted the role of government authority in the setting of wage and hour standards in private industry throughout the nation, and yet managed finally to sidestep the implications of either stand, drowning all further consideration of the matter in propaganda for unionization. In this the AFL demonstrated how habitual and continuous its ideological confusion had become, and would remain for some time.

Confusion notwithstanding, the Federation came not only to

propose that a profound harmony existed between the interests of trade unions and the provisions of the FLSA, but that the AFL itself was virtually responsible for the very existence of the law. At the 1938 AFL convention the Executive Council used the fact that the Green amendments had been incorporated into the new statute in order to promote a claim that the AFL was responsible for creating a favorable climate of opinion for the Black-Connery measure, and that the Federation's behavior in relation to it was central to getting the FLSA through Congress. From this it was reasoned that the AFL might go so far as to take credit for the wage and hour law.[25] Not even this could be said, however, without complaint about aspects of the FLSA. For example, the Executive Council did not fail to note that Section 14 of the act was objectionable and did not live up to AFL standards (on the grounds that this section provided "for a lower rate of pay" than that which the AFL felt it could secure "for learners, apprentices and handicapped workers," the first two categories applying to many in the AFL aspiring to skilled-worker status).[26] But it was nevertheless noted that the act would afford many benefits to workingmen and that it was a source of pride and satisfaction to the AFL that it could claim the responsibility for its passage.

Despite all of the above, the motivation for a reversal of AFL attitudes toward the FLSA in 1938 cannot be considered or accounted for further without regarding the role of the CIO in approving and promoting the legislation.

Generally, the CIO exhibited a much greater willingness from the outset to both accept the Fair Labor Standards Act and promote support for it among workingmen. It is true that John L. Lewis revealed himself to be somewhat skeptical about it. Testifying at the joint congressional hearings, he recommended, for example, that sections of the act giving a board power to vary minimum wages and maximum hours involved too many complications and could result in a subtle, invisible but definite drift toward excessive government intervention in wage and hour matters. He urged, therefore, that Congress specify a forty-cent-per-hour minimum wage, without exceptions, and interim periods involving lower minima, and a maximum work week of thirty-five hours, including clear limits on the power of a board to go up to forty hours or down to thirty. For Lewis feared that the bill as drafted might, if explicit provisions were not made to prevent it, lead all too easily to courtroom struggles to define complex portions of the bill allowing for board discretion in setting wage minima and hour maxima, even within specified limits and thus judges would "determine whether after all American workmen are freemen or indentured servants."[27] The history of courtroom decisions on matters of labor's rights in America did not fill John L. Lewis with confidence about labor's prospects under such circumstances. In addition, Lewis had another criticism of the bill. Section 5 of Part II of the FLSA referred to provision for a minimum wage standard and a minimum fair wage, the first referring to forty cents an hour (or approximately $800 per annum, fifty weeks of forty hours each), and the second referring to a range, subject to review by a Labor Standards Board, from forty to sixty cents an hour (or maximum yearly earnings of $1,200). Lewis held that

> the first or real minimum is based on a straightout declaration that no employer in industries engaged in interstate commerce should pay any employee less than 40 cents an hour. Expressed reversely, it means that all adult workers are guaranteed the right as against industry, to receive 40 cents per hour. Such a standard is simple, clear, and easy of application by an administrative board.
>
> The second standard set forth in this bill, or "a minimum fair wage" is defined as "a wage fairly and reasonable commensurate with the value of the service or class of service rendered." It must ... be fixed by exhaustive investigation and administrative or judicial determination and after the Board has been advised by the parties in interest. It was perhaps intended to be a step forward from the "miminum-wage standard" in order to cover semiskilled or skilled workers, but unfortunately it sets up standards that disclose it to be a wage-fixing measure.[28]

That is, Lewis made a distinction between setting labor standards and wage fixing, the latter being inappropriate business for a labor standards board.

But for all his suspicion about some elements of the FLSA, very much the result of ingraining after his many long years in the AFL, Lewis did support the bill without reservation, urged its enactment and exhibited no inclination to organize, lobby, or inveigh against it. He accepted the measure substantially as it was introduced in Congress and found no reason to discover formulas or demand amendments for rendering it "safe" for trade unions. He told the congressional committee that without equivocating or reservation the CIO wanted to give "general support to the principle of a minimum wage and maximum work week as contained in the legislation... which [the] committee [had] under consideration."[29]

In this he was supported by Sidney Hillman of the CIO's Amalgamated Clothing Workers. Indeed, Hillman went even further in his support of the bill. Hillman appeared to harbor no suspicions about the FLSA at all and even praised its "carefully drafted administrative machinery," expressing certainty that nothing to be found in the bill would either retard or hamper the practice of collective bargaining and the free growth of trade unionism. Some small differences between Lewis and Hillman concerning administration of the act arose, but both supported its objectives with vigor. And there appeared to be no dissent in the CIO from the Lewis-Hillman position. Lewis appeared to speak with confidence that the CIO concurred with him when he said:

> In its fundamental aspects and sanctions the pending bill, in my opinion, is really an extension in principle of the Wagner Act, which guarantees to labor the right to organize and bargain collectively through representatives of its own choosing.... It marks the beginning of an industrial bill of rights for workers as against industry.... The pending bill... builds up or extends the industrial bill of rights inaugurated by the Wagner Act.[30]

Consequently, the leadership of the CIO appraised the FLSA in generous terms. Moreover, it was affirmed that far from reducing or curtailing labor autonomy, it would foster labor's ability to enforce legitimate and proper wage and hour standards in industry. For the statute would promote the idea that wage minima and hour maxima were public labor rights, just as the Wagner Act fostered the idea that self-organization was a public labor right. And the time had come when the full range of labor's rights needed to be affirmed as public and not just rights to which labor was entitled on the basis of private contract. Indeed, rights established on the latter basis could be secured and made durable only if supported on the former basis. To CIO leaders, then, technicalities in administration of the act seemed less important than the fact that certain demands labor raised as a matter of public right received, with the FLSA, statutory support from the federal government. This attitude was expressed by the CIO in 1937 when the FLSA was pending before Congress and was consistently upheld by the young industrial union organization thereafter. The *CIO News,* which began to appear in 1937, urged support of the measure in spite of its deficiencies; flaws were regarded as minor, altogether reparable, and not harmful to the overall purposes of the bill. Although John L. Lewis showed some initial suspicion of government wage and hour fixing, he disclosed himself to be friendly to the FLSA and joined with other CIO leaders who were unqualified in their enthusiasm for the bill.

If the CIO's response to the FLSA is considered together with its attitude toward the National Labor Relations Board and the Social Security Act, it will be clear that a body of labor opinion had become free of voluntarist assumptions and abandoned them with neither qualms nor regrets. Further, the elements of a coherent and distinct labor ideology were emerging from the CIO, one which was distinct from the voluntarism of the past. Primary among these was a positive view of government legislation and government policies aimed at achieving economic stabilization by strengthening the government's voice in industrial affairs. To be sure, government strength must under no circumstances be extended beyond well-defined and legitimate limits, and labor representatives must sit on all councils making decisions affecting the life of trade unions. However, it had become foolish in the extreme to permit economic events to drift into chaos for want of government leadership or regulatory power to prevent it. And it often became the case that the CIO's sympathy for specific legislative reform spilled over into an avowal of the more general idea that the government of American society ought to exert its collective intelligence for the purpose of subduing powerful economic forces in the service of the whole national community and that it should do so by extending its legislative arm into the industrial sphere. Lewis himself, skeptical though he was from time to time about this trend of thought, reflected CIO inclinations in this direction when he said:

> Time was, before the depression, when the representative labor leader would have said: "Guarantee labor the right to organize and we shall do the rest." Now he knows that modern mass-production industry—not only natural resources industries but the manufacturing industries as well—are uncoordinated, uncorrelated and over-capacitated. With the guarantee of the "right to organize" such industries may be unionized, but, on the other hand, better living standards, shorter working

> hours and improved employment conditions for their members cannot be hoped for unless legislative and other provisions be made for economic planning and for price, production and profit controls.[31]

The chapter to follow will be concerned with describing the elements and implications of this turn in labor thinking. For now it is enough to note its emergence and the fact that the CIO's position on the Fair Labor Standards Act was wholly enthusiastic, even if critical at moments, and part of this ideological development.

It has already been demonstrated that when the FLSA was passed in 1938, the AFL abandoned its formerly critical and skeptical attitude toward it and hailed it as a boon to the labor movement. One important reason for this belated burst of enthusiasm appears to be the fact that the CIO claimed that passage of the law was a CIO achievement, due to CIO power and prestige as well as farsighted adjustment to economic realities. The *CIO News* boasted that "the organized power of the CIO's millions of members was shown as Senators and Congressmen, many of whom had been hostile to the wage-hour bill, voted in its favor."[32] And further:

> Enactment of the wages-hour law was a genuine triumph for labor forces which through the CIO and Labor's Non-Partisan League [essentially the CIO] had consistently campaigned on its behalf. The League and the CIO never wavered throughout the many months of congressional jockeying on this issue, though at times the fight seemed hopelessly lost.[33]

It became difficult, if not impossible, in view of any number of CIO statements of this type, for the AFL to confront the workingmen of America, at least those attracted to the CIO, without attempting to persuade them that the Federation rejoiced in their victory and in no small way was responsible for securing it. This competition with the CIO for public prestige and labor's loyalties seemed to become a major factor in the AFL's willing embrace of the law (the amendments proposed by William Green which had been incorporated into the law were probably, however, a very major consideration in producing AFL willingness). For Green, among others, felt pressed to show, that not only had the Federation singlehandedly brought the wage and hour bill into existence, but also that the CIO had proved obstructionist or impotent in the process:

As soon as the regulation of minimum labor standards was terminated with the invalidation of the NRA by the Supreme Court, I sought the advice of experts in search of new legal forms for a minimum wage and maximum hour legislation whose constitutionality would be fully sustained in the courts. ... There emerged an uncompromising fight for the adoption of a new minimum wage and maximum hour statute in which the American Federation of Labor had to counteract the opposition of reactionary employer groups as well as to seek modification of the undesirable or unworkable proposals advocated by the authors of the Administration draft. The unyielding stand taken by the American Federation of Labor was mainly responsible for the successful passage of an acceptable bill which became the Fair Labor Standards Act of 1938. Our refusal to surrender the basic standards prevented the Bill from foundering in the cross-current of deft parliamentary maneuvers by the opponents of the bill and of defeatist statements by the CIO spokesmen who were willing to compromise the most essential provisions of the legislation.[34]

While this statement issued from Green's reflections in 1939, one year after the passage of the FLSA, there is evidence even in 1938, at the Federation's convention that year, that the AFL was competing with the CIO for labor's approval (and in 1938, as we shall see, even for a following among noncraft labor), and was even then discrediting the CIO's stance on the bill. The Executive Council's report to the 1938 convention read:

A bill carrying out to a great extent the recommendations of the American Federation of Labor was reported by the House Labor Committee. Up to this time no matter how objectionable a proposed wage and hour bill might be, the C.I.O leaders favored it. They were willing from the beginning to accept the very objectionable Senate bill which provided that wages should not exceed forty cents an hour and hours not less than forty a week. This would permit a minimum wage of anywhere between one cent and forty cents an hour and the number of hours anywhere from forty hours up. Objectionable tactics by the C.I.O., inflamed the members of the Rules Committee and they refused to grant a rule. However, at the request of the American Federation of Labor on May 6 a petition was placed on the

Speaker's desk and in a little more than two hours the necessary 218 signatures were obtained. This permitted action on the bill. President Green had sent a telegram on May 3 to all members of the House urging them to sign the petition as the bill had been approved by the American Federation of Labor. On May 24, 1938, the bill was passed by a vote of 314 to 97. It was then sent to conference.[35]

Of course, the Executive Council's report failed to note the repeated obstructions that the Federation had placed in the way of passing the FLSA, not to mention the fact that the House committee had become virtually distraught as a result of the AFL's tactics.[36] But this attempt to denigrate the CIO's role in the passage of the FLSA—even to the extent where the CIO's impatience with the AFL's amendments was depicted as caprice or selfish ill temper—could not obscure the fact that it was the AFL that had come a long way in reversing its 1937 stand on the FLSA. In fact Federation representatives felt pressed to go so far as to behave amicably toward CIO representatives when both participated on the industry committees established after the FLSA was passed and by which minimum wage rates above 25 cents were set in 1939 and in 1941. This cooperation between the AFL and the CIO on the industry committees even began to be regarded as a key to the success of the wage-hour law. One who served as a public representative on three of these committees, Elizabeth Brandeis, wrote:

> Union officers on these committees handled themselves well. Their participation in setting legal minimum rates made these committees a real experiment in tripartite minimum wage fixing, very different from the wage boards under most state minimum wage laws for women of earlier years.... Both the AFL and CIO should have been pleased with the way the industry committee procedure acted under the FLSA.[37]

Consequently, the Federation's need to compete with the CIO for the loyalty of labor and to instill the belief in millions of workmen that the AFL acted to an even greater extent than the CIO as a watchdog for their interests had rendered it incapable of repeating its usual attacks on government wage and hour regulations once the FLSA was passed in 1938. This even induced the AFL to act in a highly cooperative manner in the implementation of the law.

Commentators upon the AFL's attitude toward the FLSA have generally found themselves variously but thoroughly confused by the Federations's 1938 stance. One writes that it represented the clearest evidence that the AFL had abandoned traditional voluntarism.[38] However, we have seen that this is an exaggerated claim, given that the AFL never fully recognized the legitimacy of a government board's role in wage and price fixing, and that the Federation finally managed acceptance of the FLSA more or less on the grounds that unions, not boards, would ultimately, if not exclusively, determine wage and hour standards in private industry. Another writer questioned rhetorically:

> How shall we explain the AFL attitude toward the FLSA? It probably delayed passage of the law for nearly a year and weakened it materially. In 1937 with strong AFL support a 40-cent minimum wage and a forty-hour week might have been written into the statute. In 1938 the statutory wage was set at 25 cents, with no assurance of reaching 40 cents until the end of seven years. Hours started at 44 and went down to forty only after two years. This was a big price to pay for a reduction in the power vested in a board.[39]

The writer quoted above cannot fathom voluntarist assumptions altogether and, even if they were less inscrutable, cannot imagine the Federation's motive for reversing its stance of resentment to one of support for the FLSA, given especially that the final terms of acceptance involved reduced material gains for labor. In the former case, the assumption is that the Roosevelt administration's program overwhelmed the AFL to the point of Federation acquiescence in 1938. In the latter case, the implication is there that the Federation was irrational—if not hopelessly ignorant of its own real interests—and that its 1938 stance is evidence of this fact. But the AFL was neither overwhelmed nor irrational. It neither cast voluntarism altogether to the winds nor was it oblivious to its interests, a vital one being the justification of its FLSA position before the portions of the labor public susceptible to CIO influence. The evidence shows that if the Federation drifted into states of ideological confusion or ambivalence because of the FLSA, the growth of the CIO had served, as much as the administration's legislative program might have, to aggravate its ideological crisis. The CIO, however, was to articulate an ideological orientation which was untroubled by old voluntarist suspicions of law and government.[40]

Notes

[1]Franklin D. Roosevelt, "Special Message on Fair Labor Standards," in *The Roosevelt Reader*, ed. Basil Rauch, p. 185.

[2]U.S., Congress, House, Committee on Labor, *Hearings on Fair Labor Standards Act*, 75th Cong., 1st sess., 2-22 June 1937, pp. 158-59.

[3]This was established in a number of court cases. One of the better known is *Kirschbaum Co. v. Walling*, 316 U.S. 517 (1942).

[4]The labor administrator was empowered, however, to use discretion in increasing minimum wages to 40¢ an hour (but not more) in any industry before October 1945; he could also prevent wages from falling below 30¢ an hour, and could reduce wages to the 40¢ level, under certain circumstances, after 1945.

[5]Senate, *Fair Labor Standards Act*, 75 Cong., 1st sess., 1937, S. Rpt. 884, p. 4.

[6]United States Commission on Industrial Relations of 1916, *Final Report and Testimony* (Washington, D.C.: Government Printing Office, n.d.), 2:1499.

[7]*AFL Convention Proceedings*, 1936, p. 719.

[8]Ibid., p. 722.

[9]U.S., Congress, House, Committee on Education and Labor, *Hearings on S158 and HR 4557*, 73d Cong., 1st sess., 1933, p. 66. See also pp. 3, 61-69.

[10]*AFL Convention Proceedings*, 1937, p. 165.

[11]See U.S., Congress, Joint Committee Hearings on S.2475 and H.R. 7200, *Fair Labor Standards Act*, 75th Cong., 1st sess., 1937, p. 121. See also pp. 219, 222, 271-308.

[12]Ibid., p. 226.

[13]*American Federationist* 44, no. 6 (June 1937): 590.

[14]*AFL Convention Proceedings*, 1937, pp. 500-502.

[15]Ibid., pp. 501-2.

[16]*American Federationist* 45, no. 6 (June 1938): 589-90.

[17]Joint Hearings on S2475 and HR 7200, *Fair Labor Standards Act*, 75 Cong., 1 sess., 1937, p. 226.

[18]Higgins, *Voluntarism in Organized Labor*, p. 101.

[19]AFL, *Newsletter*, 12 June 1937.

[20]*AFL Convention Proceedings*, 1937, p. 501.

[21]*American Federationist* 45, no. 6 (June 1938): 579.

[22]Ibid., no. 7 (July 1938): 689-90.

[23]Ibid., no. 8 (August 1938): 806-7.

[24]Ibid., No. 9 (September 1938): 918-19.

[25]Executive Council Report, *AFL Convention Proceedings*, 1938, p. 153.

[26]Ibid., p. 156.

[27]Congress, Joint Committee hearings on S2475 and H.R. 7200, *Fair Labor Standards Act*, 75th Cong., 1st sess., 1937, p. 286.

[28]Ibid., p. 274

[29]Ibid., p. 271.

[30]Ibid., p. 273.

[31]J. L. Lewis, "What Labor is Thinking," *Public Opinion Quarterly* 1, no. 4 (October 1937): pp. 27-28.

[32]*CIO News*, 18 June 1938.

[33]Ibid.

[34]William Green, *Labor and Democracy*, p. 142.

[35]Executive Council Report, *AFL Convention Proceedings*, 1938, p. 154.

[36]Higgins, *Voluntarism in Organized Labor*, p. 100.

[37]Elizabeth Brandeis, "Organized Labor and Protective Labor Legislation," in *Labor and the New Deal*, ed. Milton Derber and Edwin Young, pp. 233-34.

[38]Higgins, *Voluntarism in Organized Labor*, p. 88.

[39]Brandeis, "Organized Labor," p. 229.

[40]For the reader who wishes a clear account of the early FLSA and its later amendments (labor attitudes toward all of this aside) see John G. Turnbull, C. Arthur Williams, Jr., and Earl F. Cheit, *Economic and Social Security*, pp. 634-74.

Chapter 8

The CIO Reformation

Before the great crash of 1929, the American Federation of Labor had clung tenaciously to the idea that there was a fundamental incompatibility between federal legislation aimed at ameliorating industrial conflict and the interest of workingmen. For the AFL felt that, insofar as such legislation went beyond elementary recognition of trade union rights to determine and secure industrial conditions deemed just by union members, it acted to retard or defeat union efforts to elevate the standards of recompense for industrial labor. On the one hand, it tended to maintain wage and hour standards below those attainable or set by collective bargaining. And on the other, it often called for arbitration and conciliation of the parties to industrial conflict, and in this, tended to deprive the worker of his right to strike. When such legislation called for social insurance of any kind, the insurance came into conflict with the benefit features of trade unions. As if this were not enough, AFL leaders argued, such federal legislation even bred unfortunate illusions among many workers that government would act to protect their claim to such goods as a given piece of legislation entitled them.

But in fact, experience showed that the sensitivity of government to employer interests, together with the vague, universalistic language of law enabled those who sought for ways to elude or defeat worker expectations to succeed, often with the blessings of courtroom judges. "Social legislation" was hence seen as ineffectual at best and destructive at worst. Even when the nation was immobilized by economic breakdown and fatigued from economic distress, when many millions roamed jobless and hungry, and when the AFL could no longer deny or resist a trend toward legislative action aimed at ameliorating industrial conditions, the men who led the Federation were still not wholly convinced of the positive worth of legislation. They made important concessions to it and they found ways to live at peace with it; but they felt uncomfortable in the process and found themselves vacillating and often confused in the face of legislative change and the positive government initiatives toward recovery it made possible. Tradition had a strong hold on their minds. Moreover, the results of recovery legislation disappointed them. It instituted government boards with seemingly great ambitions to meddle insensitively in internal labor affairs. But since the American environment of the 1930s provided little encouragement for the Federation's customary views of the political and industrial universe, and its leaders had little to offer in the way of solutions to the bitter difficulties of the time, the AFL settled down to benign if skeptical confusion about law, government, and politics in times of crisis, and generally made the best of bad bargains, though it complained loudly from time to time.

The CIO, however, since its inception in 1936, and even when it was but an insurgent group within the AFL in 1935, clearly and consistently differed with the Federation about social legislation and about the worth of government boards instituted to administer the terms of recovery statutes. The Social Security Act of 1935 was much to the liking of CIO leaders who regarded it highly as an effective instrument of income redistribution, even though, in the years that followed, they demanded greater improvement in its terms. The National Labor Relations Board established under the Wagner Act may have been chided for inadequate methods of determining appropriate bargaining units for this was no small thing to the leaders of the CIO who, between 1936 and 1938, were furiously organizing millions in the mass-production industries and anxious to establish stable union locals. Board actions, however, were appreciated as a vital deterrent to company unionism, as a counterweight to employer resistance to unionization and, perhaps even more important, as helpful for the establishment of the CIO's public legitimacy, given that the AFL regularly denounced the young organization for illegitimate "dual unionism." The Fair Labor Standards Act of 1938 received the CIO's unqualified support on the grounds that legislative instruments were essential to the establishment of even minimal standards of industrial justice on a national scale, at least with respect to decent wages and working hours. Far from lowering the sights or crippling the efforts of unions in collective bargaining, such laws as the FLSA were regarded as important supplements to union power.

The contrast between the AFL and the CIO went rather further afield than this. Even if we discount, for the moment, the profound differences between the two organizations over the issue of craft versus industrial unionism, the differences remain extensive. For it involved the fundamental matter of what the role of government ought to be in an industrial capitalist society.

No longer, for example, would it be enough that government exhort conflicting industrial groups to seek harmony between themselves. It would not even suffice that statutory reinforcement for such exhortations be instituted. Not even government "chairmanship" over the industrial "partnership" between unions and employers, or like types of "coordination," would quite bring industrial society to peace and prosperity. CIO tenets held that the government needed to be aggressive, to regulate industry, and to send its agents forth to help individuals lost and in need. It could start in an elementary way, by providing jobs for willing workmen: "The CIO has continually taken the position that government has the responsibility to provide work for those unemployed who are willing and able to work."[1] Yet, adequate start though this might be, the CIO believed government ought to go further and plan a role for itself as a distributor of funds to citizens who may then use the money as consumers in the market exchange activity of the society. In this, government would be an "investor" in economic health:

> Only government contributions to the general consumer income can guarantee at the present time a solid movement toward economic balance. Such a contribution needs to be intelligently planned, planned as to rate, amount and type of expenditure, in order to provide a continuous forward economic trend.
>
> In making these expenditures the government assumes the role of investor. It provides investment expenditures at those times and in those places where private investment fails. Such government investment does not

replace private investment but acts as a complement to it. It is clear, however, that it would be disastrous for the Federal Government to withdraw from its responsibility to provide funds for investment, for consuming power, at the proper time.[2]

And so that the provision of jobs and economic investment in a healthy nation do not turn out to be merely occasional encounters with the problem of stabilizing industrial society, government should undertake to provide intelligent perspectives and leadership in economic affairs on a continuous basis:

> It is becoming obvious that full production in a stable economy can be created only by intelligent direction which has the power and the will to coordinate all economic controls toward that single end. Such central direction must necessarily come from government. Intelligent direction also of necessity means planning toward the future.[3]

Indeed, Philip Murray, president of the CIO's Steel Workers, and Lewis' successor as head of the CIO, accepted central governmental planning and found such economic control entirely compatible with democracy:

> A system of free enterprise and political democracy is not tantamount to a system without order. It admits of controls. It admits of centralized planning, of a sort, but of a sort which does not weaken liberty and initiative, the forces upon which we must count for the making of a better world.[4]

However, it followed from all of this that if government was to play its proper role as distributor of economic goods and guiding intelligence of economic action, it would affect the public behavior of individuals on an unprecedented scale, for good or ill. That it be staffed with leaders of sympathy and responsiveness to the individuals affected, especially labor, became a matter of the highest importance. Thus, as the CIO came to accept a theory of positive government, it simultaneously developed strong motives for exercising political influence over the shape and quality of government action. And it acquired a strong incentive for involvement in party politics. The CIO came, therefore, to reverse an AFL tradition of more than four decades standing, a tradition that had disdained a partisan and highly active role in politics for organized labor. In 1936, out of fear of a Republican victory that year, and fear that a Democratic administration might court the AFL leadership while keeping the CIO at a distance, Sidney Hillman of the CIO's Amalgamated Clothing Workers, and John L. Lewis broke with AFL custom and attempted to put their new labor organization into the presidential election campaign in a big way. Both men approached George L. Berry, head of the AFL's Printing Pressmen's Union, a union which had always had competitive relations with the Federation's more important Typographical Union. Berry had not exhibited any strong anti-CIO biases and, besides, had been on the NRA's National Labor Board, as well as involved in various ways with the Roosevelt administration. He appealed to Hillman and Lewis for these reasons, and also, because through Berry, they hoped to influence the AFL in the direction of open partisan activity on behalf of the Democratic party. The three men (though, significantly, Berry of the AFL resigned from the trio in 1937) decided to form a nationwide political association which was to be organized labor's vehicle for participation in Roosevelt's campaign for reelection. Their association is described by one historian:

> Berry, who was in high standing in the AFL and "not on either side," as Hillman said, agreed to serve as chairman, with Lewis as its director and Hillman as treasurer and fund-raiser. The name "Labor's Non-Partisan League" was chosen to indicate, as Hillman explained later, that it was "nonpartisan" only in that it sought the support of the two wings of labor, but not at all with regard to the reelection of the New Deal President.[5]

In fact the formation of Labor's Non-Partisan League (LNPL) was meant to be something more than a temporary organization to support the incumbent president. In one of Hillman's New York addresses, he left no doubt that the LNPL was meant to survive as an instrument of long-range labor political activity:

> After November 3. . . Labor's Non-Partisan League will remain a permanent political organization. In this state it is organizing under a separate emblem as a separate party, known as the American Labor Party.
>
> The interest of the country as well as of labor demands a realignment of all progressives into one party, and the

basis for that kind of realignment ought to be the organization of labor in the political field.[6]

The LNPL was to seek to mobilize and stabilize a political constituency composed of wage earners and farmers, to democratize the Democratic party, to clarify the lines of contest between the two major parties, to elect preferred candidates to government office, and possibly, to make a stab at attaining third party status if conditions warranted it. The ambitiousness, effectiveness, and departure from labor custom which the LNPL represented is well described by Philip Taft in a contemporary account:

In contrast to the policy of the Federation of endorsing the candidacy of President Roosevelt by indirection, the League conducted a vigorous campaign on behalf of the Democratic national ticket. Its local, state and national organizations expended almost one million dollars in the last [1936] campaign. Activity was, however, not limited to mere financial contributions or expenditures. The League being made up mainly of union organizations and active union men, was able to employ hundreds of active workers in the trade-union movement. . . . Its extensive efforts in the last campaign [1936] can better be grasped by summarizing its activities in the four most important states—New York, Pennsylvania, Illinois and Ohio. In Ohio the League conducted 344 rallies and had at its service a corps of 70 speakers, most of whom were active daily. In the five large cities of the state the League arranged for a daily broadcast of one-half hour daily during the last thirty days of the campaign. In New York the League operated through the American Labor Party. This organization utilized a staff of 200 paid workers and 3,500 volunteers; conducted 85 campaign offices in New York City, and 16 upstate; routed 250 speakers, who addressed 524 meetings. In Illinois the League held 109 rallies in Chicago, where its speakers visited every ward. At least one rally was also held in every county in downstate Illinois. The most intensive activity was carried on in Pennsylvania. The substantial majority given to the Democratic ticket in that state is due in large measure to the activities of the League. In the steel and mining sections and in Philadelphia, League speakers addressed nightly meetings, and parades and rallies were a frequent occurrence. A feature of the League's activities during the campaign was a daily broadcast over a network of 37 stations, stretching from Reno, Nevada to New York City, for 30 days exclusive of Sundays, 30 days prior to the election. . . . Compared to former efforts of labor in the political field, the League's activity in the last [1936] campaign can be considered as the first serious political attempt, exclusive of 1924.

The League marks a new departure in labor's political activity, and it may mean the beginning of the long-looked-for-political realignment.[7]

And so, with a shift in the viewpoint about legislation and government which the leaders of the CIO exhibited, there came a new embrace of political action and partisanship, as virtues, indeed, as obligations which workingmen needed to accept. This is not to say that the AFL did not organize its own campaign committees. In 1927 the Federation's Executive Council appointed what it called the "National Non-Partisan Political Campaign Committee." But true to AFL tradition, the purpose of this committee was kept modest and never violated the bounds within which the Federation felt political action should be contained. It merely avowed support for individuals, on a nonpartisan basis, who were aspiring to or already held congressional office and who were friendly to labor. It did not endorse any political party nor did it encourage campaigning for any candidates of the two major parties. The committee confined itself mainly to collecting information on labor records of party candidates and distributed these to AFL members for their information. After the CIO's league was formed, the AFL committee advised against affiliation with it on the grounds that it showed aspirations toward independent party status.[8] And in 1938 George Meany spoke for the AFL and its committee when, as a delegate to the AFL's national convention from the New York State Federation of Labor, he announced to approving Federation members:

I want to say now that the American Federation of Labor in that state [New York] today is non-partisan. ...[W]e are going to carry out the policies of Gompers and not bow to any political boss, no matter what party label he may bear, even if it bears the honored and scared name of labor.[9]

The reserve of the AFL about politics notwithstanding, the CIO continued to advocate legislation as an instrument of industrial reform, positive government initiatives in instituting national economic planning, and a politically partisan activism as a matter of organizational policy. Its interest in this had grown past the achievement of healthy economic balances in industrial life, but rather aimed at first-class political citizenship for labor:

> We are not only fighting for the economic emancipation of the millions of Americans who work for a living, but we are fighting also for their political emancipation, for the right to live in communities free from the corporation's domination to a point that limits and circumscribes their political action.[10]

That is to say, the CIO committed itself to securing an established place for labor in the political community rather than simply improving the capacity of workers to deal with their employers. It hoped to integrate workers as "whole people" in every public aspect of American life and in this to lift laboring men above the parochialisms of trade and craft to bring them into their society more completely.

Differences between the AFL and the CIO should not be exaggerated, however. The AFL clung to remnants of its voluntarist past, but made several important compromises with conditions of the present. While this did not lead the Federation to view law, government, and party with much enthusiasm, it did reduce the coherence and consistency of the AFL's negative view of these. The CIO's new appreciation for law, government, and politics did not contrast so starkly with the AFL's view as might have been the case at any earlier time. The leadership of both labor organizations agreed that capitalist economic relations were acceptable, consonant with liberty, and perhaps even a condition for it. They both sought to curtail the great power of big business, maximize labor's bargaining strength, and secure for labor a voice in setting industrial conditions. And they both disdained elaborate theorizing about social reform of any kind. One observer said of his interview with Sidney Hillman:

> I tried to pin him down to the espousal of some social philosophy, by repeating the charge that he leads labor into collaboration with capital to the detriment of the "social revolution." But he is a pragmatist to the core, abstract theories affect him like mist on eyeglasses, and he snaps: "Labor unions cannot function in the atmosphere of abstract theory alone. Men, women and chil-

dren cannot wait for the millenium. They want to eat, mate, and have a breath of ease *now*. Certainly I believe in collaborating with employers! That is what a union is for. I even believe in helping an employer function more productively, for then we have a claim to higher wages, shorter hours, and greater participation in the benefits of a smooth industrial machine."[11]

Hence, both AFL and CIO leaders accepted and counseled an incremental attitude toward securing the position of workers in the industrial order and felt that labor's opportunities for self-improvement through unionization within a capitalist framework were ample or, at any rate, sufficient for the attainment of justice and equity for workingmen.

It should be stressed that in all of this it was no part of the CIO's intention to surrender to government all rights to plan for industrial stability. The trade unions were not under any circumstances to be left out of government decision-making circles involved with industrial planning of any kind. Lewis made this very clear at the CIO's 1938 convention:

> The goal of full production and full employment is one to which it would be difficult to find open opposition. It is clear, however, that there are many who oppose the goal through seeking special interests. Only labor, representing the majority of the people, can guarantee a continuous movement towards full production. Labor must have a strong voice in the government and in the agencies of the government which administer a sound economic program [to see to it that they] shall not stagnate or be preverted. Heretofore, labor has too often been ignored. If the future is to be one of hope, labor must take its rightful place.[12]

The expansion of government influence in economic planning was to provide direction for the society. But it was not to lead to a government monopoly on economic decision making. Expression of a popular voice was to be institutionalized. Indeed, the best way to institutionalize the popular influence in the planning of the society's economic life was through union representation in government planning agencies.

Increasingly, Lewis and the leaders of the CIO edged toward a more systematic statement on the need of government to take the initiative in guiding industrywide planning. And also, increas-

ingly this issued into renewed justifications for both building
union strength and the inclusion of representatives of organized
labor in government planning activities on the assumption that an
increase in the numbers and power of organized labor would
guarantee the "rationality" (meaning, in this case, responsiveness
to popular needs) of government decisions concerning the fate of
the economy. Lewis was adamant about this. In fact, by 1940,
when the United States was economically already on a wartime
footing, and when a government role such as the one called for by
the CIO was also clearly in the making for purposes of national
defense and war preparation, demands arose at the CIO convention for increased labor participation in government planning and
administrative agencies concerned with matters related to labor.
For in June 1940, Roosevelt set up the National Defense Advisory
Commission (under the authority of the 1916 Defense Act); among
its other functions, it was to set up special agencies for wartime
mobilization. Among these, one agency, the Priorities Board, was
to establish two divisions, one for production and the other for industrial materials. The CIO registered its anger at labor's exclusion from these latter divisions and asserted the irrationality, not
to mention the injustice of excluding labor from such vital economic planning activity:

> There are no representatives of labor attached in any
> way to the Division dealing with Production, Industrial
> Materials, Price Stabilization, Agriculture or Con-
> sumers. . . . In effect, labor has been practically ignored
> insofar as adequate or proper representation is con-
> cerned on this important body which will adopt and
> enunciate policies that will affect the lives of millions
> of workers in the country. There are men in high places
> in the nation today who do not want labor to participate
> in the national effort. . . because they know that labor's
> voice will be raised against their efforts to pervert the
> idea of national defense to the service of private greed.
> Labor demands adequate representation and not on the
> basis that now exists of one lonely representative [Sid-
> ney Hillman] of labor to 100 millionaires.[13]

It was all the more vital that labor be well represented in government planning agencies since defense mobilization could be
used as an excuse to restore the employers' values of economic efficiency at the expense of labor's conception of justice in the industrial sphere. The toll of such a tendency, it was held, had in

fact already been taken on the CIO's Maritime Workers.[14] Philip Murray (who replaced Lewis as CIO president at the 1940 convention) went further and tried to outline positive steps to correct the injustices of labor exclusion in the national planning effort:

> In that regard President Lewis, together with the rest of us, have talked to a number of agents of the Federal government and. . . of Congress. . . suggesting that in the first instance there should be created in each important industry directly affected by national defense, joint labor, industry, consumer and government boards. That, sitting on each board, there should be an outstanding representative of the CIO labor organization having labor jurisdiction over that industry; that in the interest of public welfare the consumers should be represented and to represent the mass interests of the entire nation there should be designated to each board a substantial representative of government.[15]

A national planning scheme thus conceived, involving labor participation, would necessarily strengthen its economic rationality in the sense that labor representation would guarantee a just monetary distribution at popular levels and millions would then be appropriately "funded" for participation on the economic system. Moreover, labor representation would even reduce the possibilities for corruption of planning activity and prove morally bracing for the whole nation:

> It would tend to prevent the development or growth of racketeering...the labor representative being cognizant of the price and profit factors having to do with production in each industry, giving labor an opportunity with industry, consumers and government to furnish the necessary checks and balances against the development of possible corruption in the letting of contracts and the stealing of money from the Federal Treasury.[16]

And hence, government planning for industrial stabilization never connoted the possibility of total government control over economic affairs nor the exclusion of organized labor from decision making in the planning process.

Considered as a whole, the new CIO ideological stand came down to this. Far from weakening the self-reliance of workers, as individuals or as union men, constructive labor legislation, by reducing the evils of poverty and fear, enhances their strength and independence and makes them even more aggressive in fighting for their rights. Further, legislation which establishes certain minimum standards in industry is a good method of achieving uniformity in labor conditions on a national scale and it minimizes, at least as well as collective bargaining does, the deadly competition for jobs among workers, especially among lower-paid workers, so removing a condition which operates to the advantage of employers. And even where administrative abuses are committed under the authority of certain labor-related legislation, the legislation itself is not and should not be considered unjust, for abuses can be corrected. All in all, labor must encourage constructive legislation if it is to stand up to the many antilabor elements in society who seek to repress labor organizations. None of this, furthermore, will weaken the loyalty of already unionized workmen to their unions. On the contrary, if union leaders show union members how to take full advantage of such legislation, their prestige among the workers will be enhanced and the unorganized will seek out the unions in order to receive the benefits of such leadership. Now if legislation is a positive value, then aggressive behavior toward securing desirable legislation is warranted as an organizational policy. Indeed, labor organizations ought to organize into political associations and actively seek to place in the seats of government legislators who will formulate and institute the desirable legislation. With such individuals in office, government might be trusted to plan more aggressively and continuously for economic contingency and industrial stabilization. Labor must be included in the administration of such plans to assure their maximum efficacy as well as simple justice for the workmen. Thus, labor should demand and government should concede to it a share in the governance of industry from within administrative agencies of the government itself. In a word, labor must focus upon and seek involvement in politics on a national and not merely a local scale, and seek a place in the federal government itself, this in order to effect industrial reform and stabilization. And ultimately, pressure for constructive legislation, partisan political activity and participation in government planning activities will yield a desirable amount of industrial reform without requiring the displacement of the capitalist order.

There appeared to be no change of the old AFL image of society as a field for the competitive interaction of economic groups, each, through its "voluntary organizations" establishing some basis of accord. And certainly government was still permitted to add a benevolent influence in all this by urging intergroup harmony and giving statutory support for its attainment. But the idea that government do no more than this, that it not take a hand in the governance of industry nor institute laws to supplement the income of workers or regulate the conditions of work, was a view which the CIO discarded. And with it, the CIO discarded the AFL's admonitions against aggressive partisan political involvement. The image of the governmental relation to society, as of politics as a high priority form of activity, had been substantially changed.

First, as we have seen government had ceased to seem to CIO leaders merely a necessary evil, existing for the mere purpose of securing a citizenry against crime or foreign aggression. It could alter social conditions by the performance of "good works." It need not confine itself to occasional moral suasion as the maximum positive influence of which it was capable; for it could play an active and constructive role in shaping society. Indeed, it could and should be the brain of the body politic. Government came to be seen as a social resource and a directing intelligence, strategically located in order to oversee the whole social field, able to act to reduce the chaos of industrial life.

Second, through CIO influence government came to be seen as a living, dynamic center capable of response to all who exerted the greatest pressures on it; response could be to labor as well as business pressure, depending on the strength and persistence of either. Hence, labor could, if it willed, make it a matter of survival for government to respond to political pressure exerted by the unions. Political action acquired a new importance to the CIO for this reason. Government could fulfill its active role by passing constructive labor laws, and through economic planning be made to regard its own survival as dependent upon the inclusion of organized labor in planning activity. The results for society could be stabilization of the industrial order bolstered by a just distribution of economic goods.

Now the leaders of the CIO were no more philosophically inclined or reflective than those of the AFL. And the CIO's new views did not issue from critical contemplation of the nature of things political any more than voluntarism had emerged from the cogitations of intellectuals. Indeed, the CIO's new perspective was never even assigned a name or an "ism" to distinguish it from other perspectives, both similar and dissimilar, held by various groups or individuals in American society. It emerged almost unconsciously from pragmatic considerations and is finally intelligible only by reference to them. It was very much the outcome of mobilizing the less-skilled workers into unions as voluntarism had been deeply related to the unionization of skilled craftsmen some fifty years before. Therefore, to apprehend fully the ideological orientation of the CIO, it is necessary to consider it sociologically; that is, in relation to the constituency which rallied around it and was its raison d'etre.

One of the commonest suppositions about the results of advanced industrial growth and mechanization is that the unskilled labor population increased rapidly as the rural and skilled worker populations declined, the former finally outstripping in number the latter two in the early part of the twentieth century. This is not *strictly* speaking true. For if we consider the category of "unskilled labor" to describe tasks involving heavy arduous manual labor requiring little or no literacy at all, then industrial expansion and mechanization must be understood to have produced a sharp and dramatic *decline* in the unskilled labor force. Indeed, from Table 3, based on U.S. Census data from 1910 to 1940, we can easily see that in this thirty-year period, unskilled labor declined (especially among the male population) from 36.0 percent to 25.9 percent as a result of the rapid mechanization of industry. What really happened, instead, was the vast growth of a factory working force with less complex or intricate knowledge of "craft" than was true at any previous time in American history but with some knowledge of complex industrial instruments and some skill in handling these (even if only at the level of rapidity in their use).

Now if we adjust our use of the term "unskilled" to refer to and include a "semiskilled" work force, on the grounds that in an important sense it can apply to all who are considerably less trained in complex industrial operations than the skilled worker, we may speak of a rapid growth in the unskilled labor population with the progress of industrial mechanization. And as such we may note a trend of great consequence for the American labor movement as it stood in the early 1930s. For the AFL's continuing emphasis on unionizing mainly skilled workers (a category expanding at a much slower rate than semiskilled workers) led it increasingly to the point where it was becoming less and less representative of the work force as a whole. Moreover, the less-skilled labor force, a by-product of industrial expansion, had become concentrated in large populations across the nation, following the development of industry itself. Organization of this mass involved a policy of unionization in the mass production industries and on a national

Table 3

PERSONS 14 AND OVER IN LABOR
FORCE (EXCEPT NEW WORKERS) IN 1940;
GAINFUL WORKERS 14 AND OVER IN 1930,
1920, and 1910, CLASSIFIED BY SEX INTO
SOCIOECONOMIC GROUPS IN AMERICA

Sex and Group	Percent Distribution			
	1940	1930	1920	1910
Total:	100.0	100.0	100.0	100.0
1. Professional persons	6.5	6.1	5.0	4.4
2. Proprietors, managers, officials	17.8	19.9	22.3	23.0
2-a. Farmers (owners, tenants)	10.1	12.4	15.5	16.5
2-b. Wholesale, retail dealers	3.9	3.7	3.4	3.3
2-c. Other Proprietors, managers, officials	3.7	3.8	3.4	3.2
3. Clerks, kindred workers	17.2	16.3	13.8	10.2
4. Skilled workers, foremen	11.7	12.9	13.5	11.7
5. Semiskilled workers	21.0	16.4	16.1	14.7
5-a. Semiskilled workers in manufacturing	*	9.4	10.6	9.8
5-b. Other semiskilled workers	*	7.0	5.5	4.9
6. Unskilled workers	25.9	28.4	29.4	36.0
6-a. Farm laborers	7.1	8.6	9.4	14.5
6-b. Laborers, except farm	10.7	12.9	14.6	14.7
6-c. Factory, bldg. constr. workers	*	6.9	7.6	7.1
6-d. Other laborers	*	6.0	7.0	7.6
6-e. Servant classes	8.0	6.9	5.4	6.8
Male:	100.0	100.0	100.0	100.0

Sex and Group	Percent Distribution			
	1940	1930	1920	1910
1. Professional persons	4.7	4.0	3.2	3.1

2. Proprietors, managers, officials	22.1	24.2	26.7	27.8
2-a. Farmers (owners, tenants)	13.0	15.2	18.7	19.9
2-b. Wholesale, retail dealers	4.7	4.4	4.0	4.0
2-c. Other proprietors, managers, officials	4.4	4.6	4.0	3.9
3. Clerks and kindred workers	13.4	12.8	10.6	9.2
4. Skilled workers, foremen	15.2	16.4	16.7	14.5
5. Semiskilled workers	18.6	14.4	13.3	11.2
5-a. Semiskilled workers in manufacturing	*	7.6	8.2	6.9
5-b. Other semiskilled workers	*	6.8	5.1	4.4
6. Unskilled workers	26.1	28.3	29.4	34.2
6-a. Farm Laborers	8.5	9.5	9.6	14.0
6-b. Laborers, except farm	13.8	16.1	17.7	18.2
6-c. Factory, bldg. constr. laborers	*	8.6	9.0	8.7
6-d. Other laborers	*	7.6	8.7	9.5
6-e. Servant classes	3.8	2.7	2.1	2.0
Female:	100.1	100.0	100.0	100.0

Source: U.S. Census, 1910-1940.

*Comparable figures for 1940 not available.

basis, wherever large numbers of the less-skilled workers were gathered. The AFL, insofar as it organized the less skilled at all, gathered them at scattered local levels and put them into federal unions (granted no powers for independent action at all, unlike the craft unions), there to await eventual inclusion, after a period of training, into the craft unions. In brief, the trend to note was the changing composition of the labor force and the unchanging policies of the AFL.

As we well know, the AFL refused to embark on a policy that would have brought the less-skilled masses into its ranks, and by 1935 John L. Lewis and his associates undertook to pursue organizing policies independent of the Federation, finally establishing the CIO for this purpose in 1936. After this, both organizations were locked in competitive struggle virtually to the time of their reapprochement and merger in 1955. The AFL contended vigorously at the outset of its battle with the CIO that such mass industry workers as were unionized should be placed in the Federation's federal unions, that they should not be brought into the labor movement in great numbers in any case, and that the federal unions in which they would be placed could not constitute a base upon which to enlarge a national union movement. For the federal unions were mere halfway houses, bringing together a miscellaneous lot of workers whose interests were diverse and only for the purpose of training them slowly for entry into crafts. Until such entry could be gained, they would have little in common with workers in the rest of the country whose trade they were only training to share and thus, at best, their activities would be locally and not nationally relevant. Further, because of its diverse composition and the fact that less-skilled workers can easily be replaced by employers, the federal unions could not develop unity or financial strength enough to be counted very reliable pillars of unionism.

On the other hand, the AFL held that the autonomous craft unions properly made craftsmanship a stable basis of associative action and generated communities of workmen with common interests related to a given craft no matter where they lived or worked. Moreover, the craft worker was believed to be indispensable to an employer who cannot easily replace him; thus he remained the one best able to compel employers to come to terms with labor and was consequently in a position to set industrial standards for the rest of the work force. AFL ideology believed the less skilled were best managed by organization in modest numbers into the dependent federal unions of the AFL and left there to await the formulation of policies and programs by the craft unions and the AFL's Executive Council.

All of this the CIO strenuously denied. Lewis and others argued that the craft union was too narrow in scope, selfish in outlook, and too limited in resources to serve the needs of labor in modern industry. Besides, the autonomy of craft unions made it impossible to obtain efficient cooperation among the workers of a whole industry on any program of action. One union, prepared to make demands on an employer, was impeded from doing so effectively because other craft unions, related to the same industry refused to go along. Hence it was possible for the machinists of an industry to be blocked by the tool and die workers of the same industry from positive action. Not a little consideration in all of this was the fact that the idea of craft had little meaning for the worker in modern industry. He rather thought of himself as attached to an industry or plant rather than a craft. Finally, the CIO held that the craft principle of organization could not be applied in the mass-production industries, even with the best will and desire to do so, and even if workers in federal unions working in such industries waited indefinitely for some kind of craft status, for to expand craft membership involved *multiplying* the number of crafts practiced in modern industry. Such a feat could not be accomplished by mere union fiat. Moreover, even if it could be done, it was the mass industrial sector that was expanding; and it was there that new craft designations needed to be made or older ones extended. According to the CIO to impose craft organization in the mass industrial sector would, at best, result in the creation of dozens of craft categories, even within the same plant, and the fragmentation of the labor movement would be assured. CIO organizers felt it would be better to abandon craft unionism entirely rather than risk such disunity. Given the fact that the federal unions were constitutionally prevented from exercising influence toward a revision of AFL policy, it would be best to build them as first and provisional steps toward a broad industrial union movement in the country and then adjust Federation policy accordingly. Failing that, the CIO was to independently restructure unionism in the land, hoping always for some kind of cooperative relationship with the AFL and striving to avoid the destruction of already existent craft unions.[17]

But while AFL and CIO conflicts after 1936 remind us of the disparity between AFL policies and the composition of American labor, and it tells us much about the reasons for the emergence of the CIO, its sources of its strength and popular influence, it does not tell us why, by organizing the rising tide of semiskilled labor, the new organization needed to abandon voluntaristic attitudes toward legislation, government, and politics. It does not explain what it was about this comparatively unskilled mass which generated revised attitudes on the part of the CIO's leaders, many of whom, after all, had served long apprenticeships in the labor movement as members of the AFL. We know that the Depression was not itself a sufficient explanation for this shift, for if it were, the AFL would have been much more receptive to change. And we have seen that the AFL was, even under the Depression's impact, reluctant to really abandon voluntarist policies; indeed it often resisted doing so and might never have done so were it not for the fact that the CIO made it impossible for the AFL to avoid reconsidering and compromising its old attitudes. What then made the CIO eager to abandon older voluntaristic policies?

The leadership of the CIO was too pragmatic for the answer to this question to lie too far afield from resolutions to the problem of securing the following and loyalties of the mass industrial worker. It is, therefore, necessary to consider the problems of the less-skilled worker somewhat more fully and to come to understand that he was beset by difficulties which were more vexing than the mere fact that AFL leaders failed to bestow enthusiastic affection upon him, difficulties to which the CIO successfully responded with a revision in organized labor's policy of some five decades standing. For the semiskilled or unskilled worker in the mass-production industries—at least during the early 1930s when he lived essentially without union aid—faced the problem of interregional competition. That is, the less-skilled worker in one part of the country always faced the danger of being undercut by his counterpart in other regions of the country. This derived from the fact that with the tremendous expansion in mass production (especially during the decade of the 1920s) highly skilled labor became a less essential ingredient to include in the production process and employers felt less bound to stay in areas where skilled labor had unionized and driven up labor costs. They could locate new establishments or relocate older factory enterprises in areas where labor costs were cheap and where the absence of a pool of skilled labor was of no great concern. In some cases, they could contract with out-of-town factories to complete certain operations on their commodities (this became very much the case in the garment trade). And where the product of semiskilled labor was not "mobile," but "made" (though not used) at a given site, as in coal mining, variations in transportation costs to supply the mass industries still influenced wages on a regional basis and produced disparities between one area and another. And so the less-skilled, mass-production worker in one city or area faced a certain competition from less-skilled labor in other cities or parts of the country.

Table 4 indicates the geographical disparity in per capita income in the United States on the eve of the Great Depression, and therefore suggests why industrialists could be motivated to undercut the workers of one region by moving to and employing the workers of another region, or at least contracting out some of the work formerly performed by workers at the main site of production. The problem of "runaway shops" became very acute, for example, for the garment workers of New York City where employers, as mass production progressed, moved or contracted with out-of-state employers to finish their products at cheaper rates. These employers continued to drift in this direction until well past World War II, moving to New Jersey, Connecticut, Pennsylvania

Table 4

PER CAPITA INCOME BY STATES IN 1929

Under $400	$400-600	$600-800	$800-1,000	$1,000 & over
Alabama	Florida	Arizona	California	New York
Arkansas	Iowa	Colorado	Connecticut	
Georgia	Kansas	Idaho	Delaware	
Kentucky	Louisiana	Indiana	Illinois	
Mississippi	Minnesota	Maine	Mas- sachusetts	
North Carolina	Nebraska	Maryland	Michigan	
South Carolina	New Nexico	Missouri	New Jersey	
Tennessee	North Dako- ta	Montana	Nevada	
	Oklahoma	N. Hamp- shire	Rhode Is- land	
	South Dakota	Ohio		
	Texas	Oregon		
	Utah	Pennsyl- vania		
	Virginia	Vermont		
	West Vir- ginia	Washington		
		Wisconsin		
		Wyoming		

Source: Maurice Leven, H.G. Moulton and Clark Warburton,
America's Capacity to Consume, p. 174.

and even to the South. Workers falling into the "semiskilled" category, then, exhibited a not very surprising interest in *national* legislation that would regulate and standardize conditions of work, especially with respect to wage minima and hour maxima.

That this interest, at least during the New Deal years, derived from real interregional income disparities, can be further illustrated by reference to average hourly wage rates prevailing in several industries for a period in 1935. As Table 5 shows, such disparities were particularly wide in a variety of industries if we compare average hourly rates paid in the Middle Atlantic and New England states and those paid in the East and West South Central states.

Now it might certainly be asked if skilled workers did not, in fact, also suffer from the effects of industrial mechanization and

Table 5

AVERAGE HOURLY ENTRANCE RATES OF ADULT
MALE COMMON LABORERS IN THREE INDUSTRIES
BY GEOGRAPHICAL DIVISIONS, JULY 1935

Geographical Divison	Brick Tile, Terra Cotta		Public Utilities[1]		General Contracting[2]	
	In Cents	Per- cent- age of U.S. Avg	In Cents	Per- cent- age of U.S. Avg	In Cents	Per- cent- age of U.S. Avg
United States	38.2	100.0	42.0	100.0	48.1	100.0
New England	38.1	99.8	47.8	113.8	47.5	98.8
Middle Atlan.	40.9	107.0	46.9	111.6	50.0	104.0
E. No. Central	40.8	106.8	50.0	119.0	51.7	107.5
W. No. Central	37.8	99.0	38.4	91.4	46.5	96.7
So. Atlantic	34.8	91.1	35.4	84.3	37.7	78.4
E. So. Central	32.5	85.1	31.7	75.5	36.8	76.5
W. So. Central	24.0	62.8	29.0	69.1	35.9	74.6
Mountain	39.0	102.1	44.4	105.7	54.3	112.9
Pacific	42.9	112.3	42.2	100.5	57.1	118.7

Source: Paul H. Moncure, "Entrance Rates Paid to Common Labor, July 1935," Monthly Labor Review, March 1936, pp. 704-5.
[1]Includes street railways, gas works, electric light, power plants.
[2]Includes building, highway, public works, railroad construction.

interregional income disparity. After all, were they not being displaced by less-skilled workmen at cheaper wages and did they not show profound concern over this matter during the whole decade of the 1920s? Also, how could they escape the problems of interregional competition?

It cannot be denied that skilled workmen were beset by considerable difficulties arising from the mechanization of industry and income disparity between geographical regions in the country. They were. But while the less-skilled work force usually constitutes a larger mass than can be absorbed, even by mechanized industry, the skilled work force does not. Thus, the skilled worker is better able to find some place for himself in the industrial order than the less-skilled worker. Besides, mechanization did not make skilled labor obsolete. Indeed, it involved the design and creation of some new kinds of machinery which continued to offer promising possibilities for skilled workmen. And the census data (Table 3) do show that the number of employed skilled workers continued to grow between 1910 and 1940 (although at a slower rate than was the case for the semiskilled). So, while the fact that the skilled workman was in his way menaced by technological change is true, the fact that he was in shorter supply than unskilled or semiskilled workmen in relation to the number of jobs available in industry offset some of the pressure which accompanied mechanization (although data to support this statement more fully is extremely difficult, if not impossible, to come by). And this was bound to be especially true during the Depression decade when the less skilled swelled the ranks of the unemployed in incalculable numbers.

Even so, the skilled worker may know the degradation caused by the threat or fact of unemployment and the danger of given skills falling into obsolescence as a result of technological change. That his own plight was not as difficult or insecure as that of the less-skilled worker hardly left him disinterested in the effects of mechanization. Yet there are other factors which worked to reduce his anxiety as compared with that suffered by the less skilled, for they protected him somewhat against being undercut by workers living in different regions around the country.

These factors center around the fact that the product of skilled labor is often "static," in the sense that it is made for use in the particular locale where it was produced.[18] A building, for example, is the product of skilled construction labor of different kinds, from carpentry to bricklaying, but it is made to be used at the site of production. Thus, the product of a construction worker in one city or region is not in competition with the product of a construction worker elsewhere. At one time, even a meat cutter "produced" something that needed to be used at or near the site where animals were slaughtered (before the advent of refrigeration in transportation), and hence his product was more "static" than that of a garment worker. Such skilled workers are, therefore, more likely to be concerned about *local* rather than *interregional* competition from other workers and to show little interest in, if not strong opposition to, national legislation regulating wages and hours in the interests of standardizing them. If anything, they are much more concerned about *local* legislation in relation to industrial regulation. The building trades were well represented and highly influential in the AFL (comprising roughly one-third of the organization in 1930) and its members and leaders were always among those who resented and inveighed against national legislation aimed at standardizing wage minima and hour maxima in industry. Moreover, the long history of unionization among the skilled workers, even prior in some cases to their affiliation with the AFL in 1886, functioned to achieve a certain uniformity in wages and hours for them around the country. They were then likely to regard national laws aimed at the setting of such standards for other workers as ineffectual, setting standards well below what they themselves already achieved by collective bargaining, and therefore subverting their own efforts to aim further and realize even greater improvements. The measure of security which their skills and their unions afforded them, while hardly very great and certainly not sufficient to render them immune to concerns for national uniformity in industrial standards, nevertheless functioned to reduce the degree of anxiety they suffered over such matters as compared with less-skilled workers engaged in the manufacture of readily transportable goods intended for sale in places far from the site of production and they were less interested in federal legislative enactments as a result.

It is important, however, not to carry too far this correlation between the static product of skilled labor and the disinterest of skilled workingmen in national legislation. The printers in the AFL's Typographers Union, for example, were hardly producing a static item and yet showed such disinterest (though Charles Howard of the ITU did go with Lewis and the CIO). On the other hand, teachers in the American Federation of Teachers were so engaged and yet showed inclinations toward accepting and even promoting national legislative reform of industrial conditions. Tradition, in the case of the printing trades, and a liberal education in the case of the teachers, were no small factors in shaping attitudes. Still, the correlation is not unjustified and helps to explain the thrust of the AFL's ideological orientations.

Finally, it should be remembered that skilled workmen were substantially better paid than unskilled workers. This enabled them to do something more than build treasuries for the purpose of surviving prolonged strikes against employers. They were able to make their own "social security" provisions, establishing unemployment, sick, and death benefits as well as retirement funds. They might demand contributions to these from employers as part of a contract settlement, but they did not need or desire national legislation for this kind of support. Indeed, as has been pointed out elsewhere, the benefit features of craft unionism were considered important in the attraction of new union members, and it was feared that if national legislation made these generally available, unionism would be negatively affected. Not accidentally, the United Mine Workers, the only major semiskilled autonomous union in the AFL, made the strongest case for unemployment insurance at the AFL's 1932 convention. Less-skilled workers were unable to support such benefit funds, by virtue of their lower salaries, and were naturally attracted to legislative schemes that would institute these. When the less-skilled labor force increased in number and became a larger part of the total work force, labor developed an interest in welfare and social security legislation.

All of the above factors converged to predispose the less-skilled work force to national legislation and to political action to secure it, and to accept government as an agent which would extend the legislation's implications by rationally planning for economic stabilization. But even the strongest predispositions do not necessarily crystalize into a coherent ideological position without a catalyst that brings this about. This was produced by the organizing efforts of the CIO leaders.

Yet even the energetic leaders of the CIO might not have played their catalytic role so effectively if they had not something more than the mood of mass industry workers and their own shrewd sense of the times to guide them. A majority of the original creators of the new industrial union organization were men enriched with substantial experience in leading the less skilled, experience which they acquired during their years of service in the AFL. They could thus approach the problems of the noncraft worker with a sincerity that added much to their effectiveness as organizers. For it must be remembered that while the Federation had been slow and cautious, when not actually indifferent or hostile, about the admission of noncraft workers into its ranks, it had made a place for a certain number of them in the Federal Labor Unions. *Any number of CIO organizers could emerge from these unions*, sensitive to and informed about the special difficulties of the less skilled.[19]

In addition, the United Mine Workers was an organization of less-skilled labor which the AFL had accepted into its ranks in 1901, as a concession to pressures from within the Federation to consider the virtues of industrial unionism. Not accidentally, the spearhead for the CIO movement often came from this source and mine workers' leaders, like John L. Lewis, were especially attuned to the situation of noncraft labor. This could not help but add to their capacities to organize and sense the political needs of less-skilled workingmen throughout the country. Finally, it should be said that AFL leaders involved in the representation of the less-skilled workmen had long shown some inclinations to question the validity of at least an inflexible voluntarism, and this made it easier for them to abandon older political attitudes in favor of the newer and more serviceable ones for noncraft labor. As far back as 1913, John Mitchell, then vice-president of the UMW, called for greater flexibility in the Federation's application of voluntarist notions and suggested as a specific starting point a reconsideration of the AFL's attitude toward minimum wage laws. At the 1914 AFL convention, Mitchell sided with a number of voices (belonging largely to the socialists in the Federation) raised against unvarnished voluntarism.[20] In addition, John L. Lewis, the Miners' president, was showing distinctly antivoluntarist tendencies as early as 1930 when he said:

> If business leaders fail in the task, the people will undertake the performance on their own responsibility by exercising their voting strength in devising and enlarging the regulatory powers of their Federal and State Governments.[21]

Sidney Hillman, who brought his Amalgamated Clothing Workers Union into the AFL for a brief period before withdrawing himself and his union to join the CIO, had spent much of his life at the head of a clothing workers' organization which had been organized on a noncraft basis. This plus the fact that it was the most important independent union in America which survived outside the AFL enabled Hillman to gain a close sensitivity and sympathy for the plight of noncraft workers and a critical attitude toward the AFL's political policies. Harvey Fremming of the Oil Workers, Thomas H. Brown of the Mine, Mill and Smelter Workers, and John Brophy of the Miners were all leading lights in the formation of the CIO and all men with backgrounds in unions having sizable numbers of semiskilled workers. They were thus particularly interested in and informed about the special difficulties of noncraft labor and inclined to question voluntarist political policies.[22]

None of this means that all craft workers or all their leaders were utterly lacking in sympathy or interest in industrial unionism and the new political attitudes that went with it. For it is true that the original Committee for Industrial Organization included Max Zaritsky of the more skilled millinery workers, together with Charles Howard of the Typographers, a union of highly skilled labor (although these men associated with the CIO as individuals and never received the backing of their unions). Moreover, the American Federation of Teachers openly sympathized with the CIO, and sometimes contributed funds to CIO organizing campaigns, despite the fact that the AFT never left the AFL. Nevertheless, there was a marked tendency for local and national leaders of the AFL with a background in organizing and leading the less-skilled workers to become the nucleus of the new CIO and explore new political possibilities on the basis of their own needs and experiences. In this they were particularly sensitive and able to give effective expression to the similar needs and experiences of less-skilled workingmen all over the country.

It should be clear from all of this why new, more positive attitudes toward government, legislation, political partisanship and activism arose with the formation of the CIO as an independent force in the American labor movement. The point must also be made, however, that to the extent that the CIO articulated and promoted new views, to that extent it also promoted a labor alliance with the Democratic party and a subsequent integration of organized labor even during the 1930s into the American political system, an event which the older voluntarism of the AFL could never have brought about. This may seem ironic in view of the militance, aggressiveness and often flamboyantly angry rhetoric of the CIO during the New Deal years and the relative mildness as well as general disorientation or confusion of AFL thinking during the same period; but it is so for a number of reasons.

First, as the CIO amalgamated much of the work force industrially, it functioned to make a huge portion of it homogeneous politically; that is, the CIO organized millions in such a way that craft or occupational differences between them were submerged and simultaneously created a political organization, the Non-Partisan League, which mobilized worker sentiment around the Democratic party. Second, because the CIO had made it a virtue and an obligation for workers to participate in political campaigning and elections, especially for the purpose of placing in office candidates of the Democratic party friendly to labor, millions of workingmen acquired a new sense of political importance and became loyal to the Democrats in order to fulfill their new-found feeling of power. Third, by focusing worker attention on the national government as the important agent of social change, industrial reform and economic stabilization, labor increasingly needed to band together to affect government policy, and to elect Democratic leadership vulnerable to labor pressure to produce policies of given kinds. Fourth, in order to maximize labor's capacity to influence politics by alignment with liberal Democrats, the CIO leaders had to increasingly abandon radical rhetoric and eventually display concern for issues beyond the most immediate ones of securing material improvements in the lot of union labor (although this was not yet fully evident during the 1930s and would emerge after World War II more noticeably). This was to have the effect of urging a cooperative attitude on the part of workers toward liberals in the Democratic party and promoted a broader worker outlook on American politics.[23]

All of this reduced any significant interest that might have existed during the 1930s, at least among CIO unionists, in considering the achievement of their own security and public influence by rejection of the existing American political system.

The reasons why the AFL had been unable to make possible the marriage of organized labor and American politics during the New Deal years should be obvious enough. First, it often explicitly rejected the worth of such a union, regarding it to be full of potential dangers for organized labor. Second, even when the Federation might be said to have verged on considering such a policy, it was regarded as a temporary strategy, useful for the attainment of a specific and limited end (such as the Wagner Act) and not meant to be permanent. Third, there was little in the way of goods which AFL leaders and workers desired to gain by legislative means (although many AFL workers were enthusiastic about unemployment insurance after the Depression lasted a number of years) and hence they could hardly see the purpose of political mobilization for legislative or other change. Fourth, even when, during the

New Deal years, Federation leaders gave evidence of a change of heart, events showed that it was either slight or wavering and that they were still inhibited by traditional orientations.

But despite Federation waverings and inhibitions, the AFL began, after CIO campaigns resulted in spectacular success, to respond to the challenge presented by the CIO, both organizationally and politically. In this the AFL would lay the groundwork for a future when it would play a role on the American scene not unlike that of the CIO, even together with it in a merged AFL-CIO organization. While it would be going far afield from the purposes of this study to pursue the AFL into that period, it would be useful to consider briefly the groundwork. For whatever such consideration may do to complete our picture of the AFL, it can do no less for our understanding of the full impact of the CIO's new political outlook and policies on the American labor movement.

By 1938 CIO organizing drives in the nation's large-scale, mass-production industries had received enormous and dramatic publicity in newspapers across the nation. Throughout 1937 the leadership of the AFL was beginning to realize that unless it took quick and effective action to win the sympathy and support of American workers, the CIO would become the largest and most powerful labor organization in America. Further, CIO leaders reinforced AFL fears about the future of the CIO with pronouncements that their unions represented the shape of things to come. Even in 1937 a number of AFL unions like the Machinists, the Electricians, and the Meat Cutters began to reach out to the less-skilled worker and organize more broadly on an industrial union basis.

By 1939 the *AFL* had carried out heavy organizing campaigns, even in the mass-production industries, and Federation membership had risen by leaps and bounds. For example, the Teamsters Union rose from its 1929 membership level of 95,000 to 350,000, and in this rose from its status as the eighth largest union in the AFL to the largest. One way in which this was made possible was by including workers connected with auto production and transportation instead of confining membership to men involved in trucking. The International Association of Machinists rose from some 77,000 (1929 figure) to 190,000 by 1939, and special efforts were made to include great numbers of semiskilled and even unskilled workers from the machinery and tool manufacturing industries, as well as the developing aircraft industry.

The Hotel and Restaurant Workers ceased to include only skilled cooks and similar personnel and pressed on to organize less-skilled workers, achieving a rise in membership from 38,000—an estimated 1929 figure—to 185,000 in 1939. Impressive increases were registered among the Retail Clerks, Meat Cutters and Butcher Workmen, Building Service Employees, Bakery and Confection Workers, Pulp and Paper Mill unions, and the Pottery Workers. These, too, were accomplished largely by a revision of membership requirements which made less-skilled workers eligible. The AFL instituted new units of Cement Workers, Distillery Workers, and Pocketbook and Novelty Workers, organizing a Spinners Union and the State, County and Municipal Employees Union. Also, the Ladies' Garment Workers (ILGWU), which under Dubinsky's leadership had gone over to the CIO in 1936, returned to the AFL. The result of all this activity was that by the end of 1939, the AFL not only recovered membership losses it sustained by the withdrawal of unions going to the CIO, it added nearly a million new members, and in this attained a strength it had not been able to acquire since the World War I years.[24]

It might be added that, unfortunately, not all of the Federation's gains were derived from revision of its organizing strategies and goals. In some cases, the AFL gained because employers, alarmed by the radical appearance of the CIO and pressed at the same time to come to terms with unionism, preferred to deal with the more conservative leaders of the Federation. This was especially true in the South. There the CIO was unable to register any significant gains and had few resources to throw into a battle to organize the region extensively. For the South was still relatively rural, dotted with small business establishments and company-ruled mill towns. It is true that there were some large textile factories and mining areas and the CIO had made some inroads into these, but they were not very impressive. Also, a fear and hatred of northern labor "agitators" was common in southern states and discouraged the CIO from a major organizing commitment in the region. And so, despite the fact that the CIO resolved to pursue the unionization of the South at its 1938 convention, it had little to show for its efforts at that time, and wavered in its resolve, leaving the southern organizing field momentarily to others. The AFL stepped in and found some opportunities there, greeted in some instances by a number of political and business leaders who seemed to believe that one day the CIO would find a way to extend itself southward if the AFL were not used as a buffer.[25] In fairness, however, it should be admitted that the AFL did not gain too greatly from its southern ventures, and it did not register its *primary* gains because of employer fears of the CIO. Its main membership increases derived from its changed organizing policies and the intensification of its organizing efforts.

The outcome of the AFL's response to the growing power of the CIO had been to build its membership substantially by a shift in its policies and approach to the semiskilled worker of the mass-production industries. In fact, this constructive drive of the AFL managed to place it ahead of the CIO in sheer membership gains in a short time, for the AFL was richer than the CIO and could commit greater resources to unionization drivés and full-time organizers. By the end of 1939 the CIO was less than one-third the size of the AFL. And the AFL maintained this lead—though it was later narrowed somewhat—for many years. It was, however, aided in this by the fact that a number of political crises in the CIO caused some of its largest unions to withdraw (like the United Mine Workers who became independent in 1940), or to be expelled (in the later 1940s for harboring Communists). At any rate, Table 6 indicates that the AFl's response to the CIO was far from unsuccessful.

Table 6

ESTIMATED MEMBERSHIP IN AFL, CIO, AND INDEPENDENT
UNIONS, 1936-1941 (in thousands)

Year	AFL	CIO	INDEPEN- DENT	TOTAL
1936	3,422	800	742	4,164
1937	2,861	1,580	639	5,080
1938	3,623	1,717	604	5,944
1939	4,006	1,700	974	6,680
1940	4,247	1,350	1,072	6,669
1941	4,569	2,850	920	8,339

Source: Walter Galenson, The CIO Challenge to the AFL, p. 587.

With this great influx of mass industry's semiskilled workers into Federation ranks, it might be reasoned that AFL leaders would soon give way ideologically to accommodate their needs in much the same way that CIO leaders had by revising their political outlook. This, according to all accounts, is what happened to the Federation by the early 1950s. In fact, while the CIO strove to accommodate a rapprochement between the two organizations (which would become a fact with their merger in 1955), the changes in the AFL politically and organizationally at that time went far toward making this possible. But during the latter years of the New Deal, and quite despite its organizational expansion, the Federation was not yet quite ready for such departures.

The CIO had embarrassed the leaders of the AFL into support for the Fair Labor Standards Act as it pressed the Federation to confront America's semiskilled labor force. This managed to prevent great damage to the AFL's prestige among the less-skilled workers. Although they found great difficulty in rejecting social security as well, despite a marked lack of enthusiasm for it, the fact that they did not openly inveigh against it, and even made significant gestures of support for it in 1936, kept the AFL from alienating itself from less-skilled labor. It did not oppose the Democratic party (though it stiffly posed as nonpartisan and some of members, like the Carpenters' Hutcheson, supported Republicans after 1939). This also prevented the gap between themselves and the less skilled from growing wider (it should be noted that Lewis opposed Roosevelt in 1940 and supported Republican Wendell Wilkie and in this became isolated, even rejected, by UMW members). It helped the AFL that some, like Daniel Tobin of the Teamsters, aligned themselves openly with the Democrats—Tobin even served as head of the Labor Committee of the Democratic party in 1940. All of this managed to make it easier to secure a following among the noncraft workers after 1937, despite the fact that AFL leaders still had one foot in the past and could not really come to terms with positive government, legislative remedies for industrial problems, or political action and partisanship. Warnings about government boards and about the CIO's Non-Partisan League issued from them regularly (the LNPL split in the 1940 election campaign, however, and dissolved soon thereafter. In 1943, however, a "Political Action Committee" was formed in its stead under Hillman's and Murray's leadership). But for all that, the foundation for change had been laid. Although AFL leaders strove through the whole of the Depression decade in two directions at once, muddling slowly through toward survival formulas, they would one day acknowledge that voluntarist antipolitics belonged to an irretrievable past. One scholar, James Morris, cites George Meany, president of the AFL-CIO, as saying in 1956:

The great departure of the organizations from the AFL

to form the CIO did one thing. . . . I can assure you it woke up some people in the AFL—and that's a matter of record, not just talk. From that point of view, it was good.[26]

And Morris himself cannot refrain from noting:

Perhaps it was the CIO, after as well as before 1938, which was more important than anything else in awakening the conservative leaders of the labor movement to a full sense of their duties and to a genuine appreciation of the urgent need for revising traditional principles.[27]

Notes

[1]*CIO Convention Proceedings*, 1938, p. 49.

[2]Ibid., p. 57. See also Report of Committee on Resolutions, *CIO Convention Proceedings*, 1938, pp. 118-19.

[3]*CIO Convention Proceedings*, 1938, p. 59.

[4]Philip Murray and Morris Cooke, *Organized Labor and Production*, pp. 244-45.

[5]Matthew Josephson, *Sidney Hillman: Statesman of American Labor*, p. 395.

[6]As cited in ibid., p. 400.

[7]Philip Taft, "Labor's Changing Political Line," *Journal of Political Economy* 45, no. 5 (October 1937): 641-42. It should also be noted that the league was instrumental in defeating Republican Dewey for governor in the state of New York and made the difference in the election of Democrat Herbert Lehman.

[8]The AFL's committee was eventually disbanded. After the passage of the hated Taft-Hartley Act in 1947, the AFL formed Labor's League for Political Education (LLPE). The LLPE was in some of its cautious ways like its committee predecessor which had been formed twenty years before. But by 1948, it gave evidence of a somewhat more aggressive political tendency and even cooperation with some of the CIO's political activities. A variety of conflicts and disintegrating influences also beset the CIO's Non-Partisan League after its first few years of existence. Lewis would not support Roosevelt for his bid for a third term in 1940, whereas Hillman staunchly supported the president. The Non-Partisan League had also attracted numbers of left-wing workers, including Communists. This opened it to harsh public criticism. By 1943, to campaign for Roosevelt, then seeking a fourth term in office, Hillman and others began to form the Political Action Committee (PAC) to replace the old league. And a policy of partisan political action, directed especially at influencing the

federal government was firmly instituted as a feature of the CIO organization. After the AFL-CIO merger in 1955, however, the Committee on Political Education (COPE) became successor to the PAC and the LLPE.

[9]*AFL Convention Proceedings*, 1938, p. 405.

[10]As quoted in Max Kampelman, "Labor in Politics," in *Interpreting the Labor Movement*, Industrial Relations Association, p. 186.

[11]Cited in Matthew Josephson, *Sidney Hillman*, p. 439.

[12]*CIO Convention Proceedings*, 1936, p. 59.

[13]*CIO Convention Proceedings*, 1940, pp. 48-49.

[14]Ibid., p. 104

[15]Ibid., p. 132.

[16]Ibid.

[17]I have not repeated here the entire conflict between craft and industrial unionists since the facts are well known and several detailed accounts exist that make them clear. For two of the better accounts, see James O. Morris, *Conflict within the AFL*; and Edwin Young, "The Split in the Labor Movement," in *Labor and the New Deal*, ed. Milton Derber and Edwin Young.

[18]Higgins, in *Voluntarism and Organized Labor*, briefly raises this point, but leaves it undeveloped.

[19]The *AFL Convention Proceedings* between 1934 and 1936 show demands for industrial unionism, in the form of resolutions, being raised from the leaders of these unions, their willingness to commit themselves to large organizing campaigns and their sympathy for the emerging CIO.

[20]*AFL Convention Proceedings*, 1914, pp. 423-43.

[21]As quoted in Cecil Carnes, *John L. Lewis: Leader of Labor*, p. 236. It should also be noted that even William Green, formerly of the Miners before his rise to presidency of the AFL, could never be numbered among more extreme voluntarists of the AFL like Frey, Woll, and Hutcheson.

[22]It might also be noted that in 1933, when AFL organizing was picked up, unionization proceeded most successfully in areas where unions long had a foothold. Dramatic success occurred in bituminous coal regions (West Virginia, Pennsylvania, Ohio, Indiana, Illinois) and large garment-producing centers (New York). Such successes probably stimulated the aggressiveness of the miners and clothing workers in their increasing desire to depart from AFL policies (see Milton Derber, "Growth and Expansion," *Labor and the New Deal*, pp. 8-9.)

[23]On this matter of the outcome of the CIO's activity in national politics involving the relative integration of labor into the political system, see J. David Greenstone's *Labor in American Politics*, especially pp. 67-80. While it will be seen that Greenstone does not touch on all the factors noted here, and that he is mainly interested in labor in post-World War II politics, he does stress that a positive view of government and legislation, produced by the special needs of CIO labor, and the reduction of the political alienation of labor, were preconditions for a workable Democrat-labor alliance and a certain integration resulting from it. To further support this, he cites a highly insightful study by Walter D. Burnham, "The

Changing Shape of the American Political Universe," *American Political Science Review*, 59, no. 3 (March 1965): 7-28. The study indicates, among other things, that despite the formal enfranchisement of the population, the results of the 1896 elections in the United States had the effect of reducing voter participation in the electoral system and causing political alienation which increased over time. After 1938, this trend was partially reversed, the New Deal having brought about at least a modest upsurge in popular voting participation. Greenstone shows that the CIO's politicization of labor contributed to this upsurge and, he argues, in so doing produced a greater identification of labor with the American political system because workers could now participate on terms of political equality in the national community. This made socialism as a goal unnecessary. The assumption here is that socialist goals emerged from a need to affirm *public*, rather than merely economic, equality. When the latter was seen as unavoidably necessary to produce the former, workers veered toward socialism. When public equality could be seen as attainable without institutionalizing a system of economic equality, worker interest in socialism drifted off to insignificance.

[24]Membership figures cited above were taken from Milton Derber, "Growth and Expansion," in *Labor and the New Deal*, ed. Milton Derber and Edwin Young, pp. 15-16.

[25]Walter Galenson, *The CIO Challenge to the AFL*, pp. 594-95.

[26]As quoted in James O. Morris, *Conflict within the AFL*, p. 289

[27]Ibid.

Conclusion

From 1886 to 1932 the American Federation of Labor, then the dominant labor organization in America, was guided by an outlook it referred to as voluntarism. Voluntarism had two outstanding characteristics: it involved a negative stance toward legislative solutions to industrial conflict and toward government intervention in the industrial sphere; and it affirmed the idea that the self-organization of labor and the engagement of its unions in battle and negotiations with employers was the primary and ultimate source of justice for the workmen of industrial society. Voluntarism counseled, therefore, that collective bargaining entered into by labor unions and employer groups, the voluntary organizations of industry, was a sufficient means of improving the conditions of life for the working class of an industrial nation. Labor had no need of united political action, partisan political alignments, legislative enactments, or positive government actions to aid its cause. Indeed, these would actually impede the institution of justice for the laboring millions since they go on in ignorance of industrial conditions, labor's traditions, problems, and interests.

This "pure and simple unionism" developed less out of a triumph of AFL "practicality" over crude labor utopianisms than it did from the roots which the Federation established among America's better-off working class elements, its skilled craftsmen, machinists, typographers, and building trades workers, among others. For in the late nineteenth and early twentieth centuries, numbers of these workers had often come to the labor market and to the AFL with former experience in management or from ownership of small business enterprises. They were, therefore, prone to retain nineteenth century laissez-faire images of the world hostile to positive government, legislative regulation of industrial activity, and united political action. Forms of group action aimed at economic improvement, as well as retention of complete union autonomy from external agencies, appealed to them most and when they became the dominant force in the labor movement, they popularized these values. The AFL, in organizing such workmen, sought to represent their attitudes and interests. What it finally called voluntarism was very much the result of this effort.

Voluntarism remained profoundly important within the AFL for many years and for various reasons. First, the American ethos was congenial to its antilegislative and economistic orientation. Thus, it helped Federation members to appear loyal to American traditions and to pacify suspicious or hostile public attitudes toward their union-building actions. Second, the failure of politically-minded labor organizations, like those led by the Knights of Labor, socialists or Communists, worked to strengthen Federation influence among American workers and to validate its approach to labor problems. Third, as long as federal courts and federal policy remained hostile or indifferent to labor's cause, voluntaristic claims about the worth and effect of government actions appeared to be borne out; thus voluntarism could survive as a creed despite criticism leveled against it, the difficulties it encountered, and some departures from its leading assumptions that the AFL's Executive Council was willing to make from time to time.

It should be borne in mind that there was a certain flexibility to voluntarist antipolitics, at the level of practice if not always in theory. For its followers did involve themselves in disseminating information about candidates put forward for public office by the major political parties in order to gain at least some influence over national government policy. They also sought a certain influence over municipal governments. This was so largely because the latter were responsible for licensing and apprenticeship laws relevant to the work lives of skilled craftsmen. Then too, Federation members may have wanted to minimize the antilabor ferocity of local police forces. Furthermore, some kinds of federal government action and legislation were found to be potentially useful means of facilitating industrial equity; they were thus declared more or less desirable and worth the exertion of some political pressure to secure. For example government statements or laws which recognized the legitimacy of trade unions and which removed the burdens imposed on workers by court injunctions were considered especially promising and the AFL actively sought these by aggressive political action. Finally the AFL was inclined to adapt voluntarism to an era of positive government by stressing the useful coordinative function the latter could serve, providing this did not extend to actual regulation or arbitration of industrial activities and conflicts.

For all these reasons the voluntarist creed never reached the point of total or wholesale negation of government, legislation, and political action. Nevertheless, it remained marked by diffidence to the whole sphere of politics, its agencies, agents, and effectuating instruments. And it was almost dogmatically committed to the notion that union building and voluntary labor-employer negotiation held the key to justice and goodness in the age of industrialism.

By contrast with the AFL, the CIO promoted more positive views toward law, government, and politics. While it did not formulate or popularize a distinctive name for such views, it nevertheless framed a coherent and identifiable perspective which departed radically from the AFL's traditional voluntarism. For example the CIO regarded federal labor and economic security legislation to be constructive aids to unionism and it even thought law more generally to be an effective instrument of justice for the workmen of modern industry. It considered government and its agencies capable of intelligent, socially useful industrial planning and of carrying out a positive regulatory role in the industrial sphere, particularly as regards the outbreak of employer-employee conflict there. It promoted the idea, moreover, that simple union building would be insufficient to secure for workers the protections to which they were entitled under modern circumstances. Thus, the CIO valued aggressive and united political action on the part of labor unions to gain them. It even set up its own internal mechanisms to facilitate this and to forge a working alliance between organized labor and the Democratic party. In sum the CIO's views of law, government, and politics were much more broad and positive than those of the AFL and it advocated the extensive participation of organized labor in all of these spheres.

The CIO's outlook was not merely the contrivance of forward-looking or innovative persons in the labor movement anxious to revise or discard long-held AFL views about policy appropriate to modern industrial society. Rather, it was very much a product of the new federation's attempt to meet the needs and conditions of the semiskilled and unskilled workers it was gathering into industrial unions during the Great Depression years. Since these workers competed for jobs and wages with their fellows in various parts of the country, not just with others in their immediate locale, they were interested in federal legislation which would standardize conditions of employment across the country. Furthermore, since their salaries were insufficient to help support comfortable union-controlled economic security schemes (like unemployment insurance and retirement benefits), they were interested in national legislation which would provide these from government resources. In the light of all this, they could not also fail to be open to aggressive political action and coalitions with political parties, in this case the Democratic party, to secure their goals. Thus, the CIO, in the process of seeking out the less-skilled working class, developed a perspective very much with the latter's needs and circumstances in mind.

We must remind ourselves that the CIO's understanding retained much in common with that of the AFL. The CIO and the AFL agreed, for example, that any planning, regulative, or other action government took in relation to industry had to be taken with labor's approval and participation. Government per se was never to be permitted an utterly controlling hand over industrial affairs. Moreover, both the CIO and the AFL favored incremental solutions to labor's problems within the prevailing capitalist framework. Revolutionaries, whether of the socialist type or some other, who promised the workingman his salvation, liberation, or merely complete command over the industrial apparatus through the destruction of capitalism, were mistrusted as insincere, incompetent, or misguided visionaries. For both the CIO and the AFL the capitalist order was associated with efficiencies, liberties, and instruments for the control of unbridled power which it was vital to preserve. Furthermore, capitalism was seen as open and flexible enough to permit substantial and continuous improvement in the workingman's lot. Thus, despite the ideological antagonisms between the two great organizations, they were some considerable distance from total disagreement with one another.

Despite the fact that the AFL harbored its views adamantly and for many years, it would give way to the CIO and the more "political" outlook it advocated. This was so for a number of reasons. First, as early as 1932, the AFL began to dilute the terms of its traditional viewpoint. This was partly due to the fact that Congress had passed the Norris-LaGuardia Anti-Injunction Bill, a measure which prompted the AFL to reduce the antistatist tenor of its voluntarism (since it allowed government to play the one role considered proper for it by the Federation). And it was partly due to the fact that the Federation was forced, by dissidents from within, to accept, however grudgingly and confusedly, the long-abhorred idea of unemployment insurance legislation. Second, this dilution progressed further between 1933 and 1935 by virtue of the effects of the National Industrial Recovery Act (and the National Recovery Administration set up under its terms) upon the AFL's understanding and policy. Third, though the Federation's voluntarism would survive the Wagner Act (because of alleged sympathies for the CIO shown by the National Labor Relations Board established under its provisions), it was hard pressed to avoid its further weakening because of an increasing reliance the AFL was exhibiting upon the government arbitration for which the act called. Fourth, the dilution of AFL voluntarism was paralleled by its growing need to compete for a following with the CIO and to do so by giving at least modest support for measures it would traditionally have opposed, like the Social Security Act and the Fair Labor Standards Act. This had the effect of so compromising its voluntarist premises as to almost obliterate them. The result of all this was to increasingly clear space in the ranks of organized labor for the CIO's new and vigorous antivoluntarism.

The last mentioned factor in the dissolution of AFL voluntarism should be given some special emphasis. For commentators have usually drawn attention to the distress casued by the Depression as the primary factor in changing the orientation of the AFL. But occasional departures from a narrow voluntarism had been periodically made by the AFL, even in its infancy, under the impact of economic distress. Yet these had never proved anything more than temporary strategies, often pursued with the express intent of saving voluntarism from decline. It was only when the AFL was forced to come to terms with the CIO and the mass-production workers that organization brought into the labor movement, and forced to recognize that voluntarism could not encompass their needs, that AFL leaders became especially prone to "flexibility." Needless to say, the 1929 crash and the policies of the New Deal administration figured importantly in inducing change in the AFL's attitudes. But nevertheless economics and politics could not strike so close to the heart as a powerful rival for labor's loyalty.

It is possible that ultimately departures from the voluntarist tradition had their greatest significance in the fact that they helped to enlarge labor's constituency. For this helped to create an umbrella under which the diverse crafts, semiskilled, and unskilled elements in the labor force could gather with a sense of quality. And this allowed organized labor to become one of the largest, most unified, and influential "publics" in American life. Further, ideological revisions had allowed organized labor to build an enduring alliance with the Democratic party, and this gave labor unprecendented access to power and influence in the American polity, far beyond anything which the AFL's older nonpartisan policy made possible. If citizenship in an industrial society was to include more for labor than enfranchisement alone, and as T.H. Marshall and Reinhard Bendix have pointed out, include also the right to influence public policy by the exertion of pressure on and direct representation in government, then the alliance between organized labor and the Democrats, made possible by the CIO's new view of politics, helped to extend labor's political citizenship rights in American life.

It is possible that the significance of labor's ideological transition during the 1930s lies chiefly in the fact that it allowed for the mobilization of the largest and most united labor constituency America had ever seen and made possible the exercise of citizenship rights for workingmen to an extent which they had never previously experienced. None of this could have resulted merely from some purely self-interested and rational calculation of economic gain anticipated from a revision of ideological terms. Rather, it emerged from painful difficulties in perceiving through layers of tradition that a new era of enlarging industry, enlarging government, and an enlarging population of unprotected workingmen was developing, and that the liberties of workers could now be safeguarded only by active extension and politization of the union movement.

Bibliography

PRIMARY SOURCES
Addresses and Editorials
DeLeon, Daniel.*Speeches and Editorials*, vols. 1 and 2. New York: New York Labor News Co, n.d.
Editorial. *The Nation*, 6 November 1935, p. 521.
Green, William. "Labor Day Address, September 5, 1938. *Vital Speeches of the Day*, 15 September 1938, pp. 722-25.
_____. "Address to Economic Club of Chicago, December 15, 1938." *Vital Speeches of the Day*, 15 January 1939, pp. 208-10.
_____. "Amend the National Labor Relations Act, Address to the Saturday Discussions Committee of the National Republican Club in New York." *Vital Speeches of the Day*, 1 March 1940, pp. 311-14.
Lewis, John L. "The Future of Labor, Labor Day Radio Address, September 7, 1936." *Vital Speeches of the Day*, 15 October 1936, pp. 22-23.
_____. "Guests at Labor's Table, Radio Address, September 3, 1937." *Vital Speeches of the Day*, 15 September 1937, pp. 731-33.
Woll, Matthew. "Address Before the New York Herald-Tribune Forum, October 26, 1939." *Vital Speeches of the Day*, 1 December 1939, pp. 118-20.

Articles
"A.F. of L. About Face: Traditional Philosophy of Voluntarism Buried by Delegates at New Orleans." *Business Week*, 7 December 1940, pp. 22-24.
Lewis, John L. "What Labor is Thinking." *Public Opinion Quarterly* 1, no.

4 (October 1937): 23-28.

Murray Philip. "Labor's Political Aims." *American Magazine*, February 1944: pp. 28-29, 98.

Smith, Gerald L. K. *The New Republic*, 13 February 1935, pp. 14-15.

Books

Altmeyer, Arthur J. *The Formative Years of Social Security*. Madison: University of Wisconsin Press, 1966.

Gompers, Samuel. *Seventy Years of Life and Labor*. 2 vols. New York: E.P. Dutton Co.' 1925.

_____. *Labor and the Common Welfare*. 2 vols. Edited by H. Robbins. New York: E.P. Dutton Co., 1919.

_____. *The American Labor Movement: Its Makeup, Achievements, Aspirations*. AFL Pamphlet, 1914.

Green, William. *Labor and Democracy*. Princeton: Princetion University Press, 1939.

Moley, Raymond. *After Seven Years*. Lincoln: University of Nebraska Press, 1971.

Murray, Philip and Cooke, Morris *Organized Labor and Production*. Harper's Publishing, 1940.

Perkins, Frances. *The Roosevelt I Knew*. New York: Viking Press, 1949.

Roosevelt, Franklin D. Jr. *The Public Papers and Addresses of Franklin D. Roosevelt*. Edited by Samuel Rosenman. New York: Random House, 1938.

Witte, Edwin E. *The Development of the Social Security Act*. Madison: University of Wisconsin Press, 1963.

_____. *Social Security Perspectives*. Edited by Robert Lampman. Madison: University of Wisconsin Press, 1962.

Woll, Matthew. *Labor, Industry and Government*. New York: D. Appleton-Century, 1935.

Union Serials

AFL Convention Proceedings, 1900-42.

American Federationist (Monthly Journal of the AFL). 1890-1942.

CIO Convention Proceedings, 1938-42.

CIO News (Weekly newspaper of the CIO), 1937-41.

Government Documents

Chamber of Commerce of the United States. *Federal Regulation of Labor Relations*. Washington, D.C., 1937.

U.S. Congress. Senate. *Fair Labor Standcrds Act*. 75th Cong. 1st sess. 1937. S. Rept. 884.

U.S. Congress. *Senate Reports*. 74th Cong. 1st sess. 3 January-26 August 1935. Volumes 1-4.

United States Industrial Commission of 1899. *Report on the Relations of Capital and Labor*. Washington, D.C., n.d.

U.S. Bureau of the Cenus. *Population: Comparative Occupation Statistics for the United States, 1870 to 1940.* Washington, D.C.: Government Printing Office, n.d.

U.S. Bureau of the Census. *A Social-Economic Grouping of the Gainful Workers of the United States.* Washington, D.C.: Government Printing Office, 1938.

United States Commission on Industrial Relations of 1912. *Final Report and Testimony,* vol. 2. Washington, D.C., n.d.

United States Commission on Industrial Relations of 1916. *Final Report and Testimony,* vol. 2. Washington, D.C., n.d.

U.S. Executive Office. Committee on Economic Security. *Report to the President.* Washington, D.C., 1935.

_____. *Social Security in America.* Social Security Board, Washington, D.C., 1937.

U.S. Congress. House. Committee on Education and Labor. *Hearings on S. 158 and H.R. 4557.* 73d Cong. 1st sess. 25 April — 5 May 1933.

U.S. Congress. House. Committee on Labor. *Hearings on Unemployment Insurance Bill, H.R. 7598.* 73d Cong. 2d sess. 12 & 21 February 1934.

U.S. Congress. House. Subcommittee on Labor. *Hearings on Unemployment, Old Age and Social Insurance, H.R. 10, H.R. 185, H.R. 2857, H.R. 2859.* 74th Cong. 1st sess. 4-15 February 1935.

U.S. Congress. House. Joint Committee Hearings on S. 2475 and H.R. 7200. *The Fair Labor Standards Act.* 75th Cong. 1st sess. pt. 1-3, 2-22 June 1937.

U.S. Congress. *House Documents.* 74th Cong. 1st sess. 3 January — 26 August 1935.

U.S. Congress. *House. Report 1928, Minority Report on Proposed Amendments to the National Labor Relations Act.* 76th Cong. 2d sess. 12 April 1940.

U.S. Congress. *House Reports.* 74th Cong. 1st sess. 3 January — 26 August 1935, vols. 1-4.

U.S. Congress. Senate. Committee on Education and Labor. *Hearings on the National Labor Relations Board.* 74th Cong. 1st sess. pts. 1 and 2, 11-15, 18-19 March 1935; pt. 3, 21 March — 2 April 1935.

U.S. Congress. Senate. Committee on Finances. *Hearings on S. 1130.* 74th Cong. 1st sess. 22 January — 20 February 1935.

SECONDARY SOURCES
Articles

Cooper, Lyle. "American Labor Movement in Prosperity and Depressing." *American Economic Review* 22 (1932): 641-59.

Childs, Marquis. "They Hate Roosevelt." *Harper's* May 1936, pp. 634-42.

Fitch, J.A. "A.F. of L. and the New Deal." *Survey* 69 (1933): 374-75.

Greenbaum, Fred. "The Social Ideas of Samuel Gompers." *Labor History* 7 (1966): 35-61.

Handman, Max. "Conflicting Ideologies in the American Labor Movement." *American Journal of Sociology* 43 (1938): 525-38.

Hardman, J. B. S. "The Federation Faces the Facts." *Nation*, 21 December 1932, pp. 615-16.

Harris, Herbert. "Dr. Townsend's Marching Soldiers." *Current History* 43 (1936): 455-62.

Kleiler, F. M. "Governmental Determination of Units for Industrial Representation." *Political Science Quarterly* 54 (1939): 343-63.

Kutler, Stanley I. "Labor, the Clayton Act, and the Supreme Court." *Labor History* 3 (1962): 19-38.

Magruder, Calbert. "Half Century of Legal Influence Upon the Development of Collective Bargaining." *Harvard Law Review* 50 (1937): 1071-1117.

Moncure, Paul H. "Entrance Rates Paid to Common Labor, July 1935." *Monthly Labor Review*, March 1936, pp. 698-706.

Rogin, Michael. "Voluntarism: The Political Functions of an Antipolitical Doctrine," in *Labor and American Politics*, Edited by C.M. Rehnus and D.B. McLaughlin. Ann Arbor: University of Michigan Press, 1967.

Saposs, David. "The American Labor Movement Since the War." *Quarterly Journal of Economics* 49 (1935): 236-54.

Soffer, Benson. "Theory of Trade Union Development: The Role of the Autonomous Workman." *Labor History* 1 (1960): 141-63.

Taft, Philip. "Labor's Changing Political Line." *Journal of Political Economy* 45 (1937): 634-50.

Books

Aaron, Benjamin, ed. *The Employment Relation and the Law*. Boston: Little, Brown, 1957.

Abbot, Edith. *Public Assistance: American Principles and Policies*. New York: Russell and Russell, 1966.

Aiken, Charles, ed. *National Labor Relations Board Cases*. New York: John Wiley and Sons, 1939.

Alinsky, Saul. *John L. Lewis: An Unauthorized Biography*. New York: G.P. Putnam's Sons, 1949.

Auerbach, Jerald, ed. *American Labor: The Twentieth Century*. New York and Indianapolis: Bobbs-Merrill, 1969.

Bellush, Bernard. *The Failure of the NRA*. New York: W. W. Norton, 1975.

Bennett, David H. *Demagogues in the Depression*. New Brunswick, N.J.: Rutgers University Press, 1969.

Bernstein, Irving. *The Turbulent Years*. Boston: Houghton Mifflin, 1970.

_____. *The Lean Years*. Boston: Houghton Mifflin, 1960.

_____. *The New Deal Collective Bargaining Policy*. Berkeley: University of California Press, 1950.

Black, Forest R. *Should Trade Unions and Employers Associations Be made Legally Responsible?* National Industrial Conference Board special report no. 10. New York, 1920.

Bok, Dered and Dunlop, John T. *Labor and the American Community*. New York: Simon Schuster, 1970.

Booth, Philip. *Social Security in America*. Ann Arbor: University of Michigan, Institute of Labor Relations, 1973.

Bowman, Dean O. *Public Control of Labor Relations: A study of the National Labor Relations Board*. New York: Macmillan, 1942.

Brody, David. *Steelworkers in America: The Nonunion Era*. Cambridge: Harvard University Press, 1964.

Broehl, Wayne. *The Molly Maguires*. Cambridge: Harvard University Press, 1964.

Brooks, Robert. *As Steel Goes . . . Unionism in a Basic Industry*. New Haven: Yale University Press, 1940.

Carnes, Cecil. *John L. Lewis: Leader of Labor*. New York: Robert Speller, 1936.

Commons, John R. and associates. *History of Labor in the United States*. 4 vols. New York: Macmillan, 1918-1935.

Cronon, E. David, ed. *Labor and the New Deal*. Chicago: Rand McNally, 1963.

Daugherty, Carroll. *Labor Under the NRA*. New York: Houghton Mifflin, 1934.

Derber, Milton and Young, Edwin eds. *Labor and the New Deal*. Madison: University of Wisconsin Press, 1957.

Dunn, Robert W. *The Americanization. of Labor*. New York: International Publishers, 1927.

Ely, Richard T. *The Labor Movement in America*. New York: Macmillan, 1905.

Executive Council of International Typographical Union. *A Study of the History of the International Union, 1852-1963*. Colorado Springs, 1964.

Falcone, Nicholas S. *Labor Law*. New York: John Wiley and Sons, 1962.

Farber, Milton. *Changing Attitudes of the A.F.L. Toward Business and Government, 1929-1933*. Ph. D. dissertation, Ohio State University, 1959.

Fine, Nathan. *Labor and Farmer Parties in the United States, 1828-1928*.

Fleming, R. W. *The Arbitration Process*. Urbana: University of Illinois Press, 1965.

Galenson, Walter. *The CIO Challenge to the AFL*. Cambridge: Harvard University Press, 1960.

Galenson, Walter and Lipset, Seymour M. *Labor and Trade Unionism: An Interdisciplinary Reader*. New York:John Wiley and Sons, 1960.

Green, Marguerite. *The National Civic Federation and the American Labor Movement, 1900-1905*. Washington, D.C.: Catholic University of America Press, 1956.

Greenstone, J. David. *Labor in American Politics*. New York: Adolph A. Knopf, 1969.

Grob, Gerald. *Workers and Utopia*. Chicago: Quadrangle Books, 1969.

Haber, William, ed. *Labor in a Changing America*. New York: Basic Books, 1966.

Harris, Herbert. *American Labor*. New Haven: Yale University Press, 1938.

Hawley, Ellis W. *The New Deal and the Problem of Monopoly*. Princeton: Princeton University Press, 1966.

Higgins, George G. *Voluntarism in Organized Labor in the United States, 1930-1940*. Catholic University Studies in Economics, vol. 13. Washington, D.C.: Catholic University of America Press, 1944.

Hutchinson, John. *The Imperfect Union: A History of Corruption in American Trade Unions*. New York: E. P. Dutton, 1970.

Interpreting the Labor Movement. Madison:Industrial Relations Research Association, University of Wisconsin, 1952.

Josephson, Matthew. *Sidney Hillman: Statesman of American Labor*. Garden City, N.Y.: Doubleday, 1952.

Larson, Simeon. *Labor and Foreign Policy: Gompers, the AFL, and the First World War, 1914-1918*. Rutherford, N.J.: Fairleigh Dickinson University Press, 1972.

Laslett, John. *Labor and the Left*. New York: Basic Books, 1970.

Leuchtenberg, William E. *Franklin D. Roosevelt and the New Deal: 1932-1940*. New York: Harper and Row, 1963.

Leven, Maurice, Moulton, Harold G., and Warburton, Clark. *America's Capacity to Consume*. Washington, D.C.: Brookings Institution, 1934.

Litwak, Leon, ed. *The American Labor Movement*. Englewood Cliffs, N.J.: Prentice-Hall, 1962.

Lorwin, Lewis. *The American Federation of Labor*. Washington, D.C.: Brookings Institution, 1935.

Lorwin, Lewis and Hinrichs, A. Ford. *National Economic and Social Planning*. Washington, D.C.: Brookings Institution, 1935.

Lorwin, Val R. *The French Labor Movement*. Cambridge: Harvard University Press, 1954.

Lyon, Leverett, Watkins, M. and Abramson, Victor. *Government and Economic Life*. 2 vols. Washington, D.C.: Brookings Institution, 1939-1940.

Lyon, Leverett, Horman, Paul T., Terbough, George, Lorwin, Lewis, Dearing, Charles L. and Marchall, Leon C. *The National Industrial Recovery Administration: An Analysis and an Appraisal*. Washington, D.C.: Brookings Institution, 1935.

Mandel, Bernard. *Samuel Gompers: A Biography*. Yellow Springs, Ohio: Antioch Press, 1963.

Meriam, Lewis. *Relief and Social Security*. Washington, D.C.: Brookings Institution, 1946.

Meriam, Lewis and Schlotterback, Karl. *The Cost and Financing Of Social Security*. Washington, D.C.: Brookings Institution, 1950.

Metz, Harold. *Labor Policy of the Federal Government*. Washington, D.C.: Brookings Institution, 1945.

Miller, Glen W. *American Labor and the Government*. Englewood Cliffs, N.J.: Prentice-Hall, 1948.

Millis, Harry A. and Brown, Emily C. *From the Wagner Act to Taft-Hartley*. Chicago: University of Chicago Press, 1950.

Morris, James O. *Conflict within the A.F.L.* Ithaca, N.Y. : School of Industrial and Labor Relations at Cornell University, 1958.

Mueller, Stephen J. and Myers, Howard A. *Labor, Law and Legislation.* 3d ed. Cincinnati: Smith-Western, 1962.

National Industrial Conference Board. *Collective Bargaining Through Employee Representation.* New York, 1933.

_____. *Employee Representation and Collective Bargaining: A Report to the Business Advisory and Planning Council for the Department of Commerce.* New York, 1934.

_____. *Individual and Collective Bargaining in May, 1934.* New York, 1934.

_____. *Individual and Collective Bargaining Under the N.I.R.A.* New York, 1933.

_____. *A Statistical Survey of Public Opinion Regarding Current Economic and Social Problems.* New York, 1936.

_____. *The Townsend Scheme.* New York, 1936.

Patterson, James T. *The New Deal and the States.* Princeton: Princeton University Press, 1969.

Rauch, Basil. *The History of the New Deal, 1933-1938.* New York: Creative Age Press, 1944.

Reed, Louis. *The Labor Philosophy of Samuel Gompers.* New York: Columbia University Press, 1930.

Reeve, Carl. *The Life and Times of Daniel DeLeon.* New York: Humanities Press, 1972.

Robinson, Dwight E. *Collective Bargaining and Market Control in the New York Coat and Suit Industry.* New York: Columbia University Press, 1949.

Roos, Charles F. *NRA Economic Planning.* Bloomington, Ind.: Principia Press, 1937.

Rosenfarb, Joeseph. *The National Labor Policy and How It Works.* New York: Harper and Brothers, 1940.

Ross, Philip. *The Government as a Source of Union Power.* Providence: Brown University Press, 1965.

Schaffner, Margaret A. *The Labor Contract From Individual to Collective Bargaining.* Madison: University of Wisconsin Press, 1907.

Schlesinger, Arthur M., Jr. *The Coming of the New Deal.* Boston: Houghton Mifflin, 1959.

_____. *The Politics of Upheaval.* Boston: Houghton Mifflin, 1960.

Shister, Joseph, ed. *Readings in Labor Economics and Industrial Relations.* Philadelphia and New York: J. B. Lippincott, 1951.

Shotwell, James T. *The Origin of the International Labor Organization.* New York: Columbia University Press, 1934.

Silverberg, Louis G., ed. *The Wagner Act: After Ten Years.* Washington, D.C.: Bureau of National Affairs, 1945.

Stevens, Robert B., ed. *Statutory History of the United States: Income Security.* New York: Chelsea House, 1970.

Taft, Philip. *The A.F. of L. from the Death of Gompers to the Merger.* New York: Harper and Brothers, 1959.

Taggart, Herbert F. *Minimum Prices Under the NRA.* Ann Arbor: University of Michigan Press, 1936.

Thorne, Florence C. *Samuel Gompers: American Statesman.* New York: Philosophical Library, 1959.

Trattner, Walter I. *From Poor Law to Welfare State: A History of Social Welfare in America.* New York: Free Press, 1974.

Troy, Leo. *Trade Union Membership, 1897-1962.* New York: National Bureau of Economic Research, 1965.

_____. *Distribution of Union Membership Among the States, 1939 and 1953.* New York: National Bureau of Economic Research, 1957.

Tugwell, Rexford. *The Democratic Roosevelt.* New York: Doubleday, 1957.

Turnbull, John G., Williams, Arthur C. Jr., and Cheit, Earl F., *Economic and Social Security.* 4th ed. New York: Ronald Press, 1973.

Twentieth Century Fund. *Labor and the Government.* New York: McGraw-Hill, 1935.

Ware, Norman. *The Industrial Worker, 1840-1860.* Gloucester, Mass.: Peter Smith, 1959.

_____. *Labor in Modern Industrial Society.* New York: D.C. Heath, 1935.

_____. *The Labor Movement in the United States, 1860-1895.* New York: D. Appleton, 1929.

Wolman, Leo. *Ebb and Flow in Trade Unionism.* New York: National Bureau of Economic Research, 1936.

_____. *The Growth of American Trade Unions, 1880-1923.* New York: National Bureau of Economic Research, 1924.

Wyatt, Birchard E. and Wandel, William H. *The Social Security Act in Operation.* Washington, D.C.: Graphic Arts Press, 1937.

Name and Subject Index

NAME INDEX

SUBJECT INDEX